The Managerial Grid Illuminated

LEADERSHIP DILEMMAS— GRID SOLUTIONS®

Blake & McCanse

Gulf Publishing Company
Houston, Texas

Gulf Publishing Company
Book Division
P.O. Box 2608 ☐ Houston, Texas 77252-2608

10   9   8   7   6

Library of Congress Cataloging-in-Publication Data

Blake, Robert Rogers, 1918–
    Leadership dilemmas—Grid solutions / Robert R.
Blake, Anne Adams McCanse.
        p.   cm.   — (The Blake/Mouton Grid management and organization development series)
    Includes bibliographical references and index.
    ISBN 0-87201-488-6
    1. Leadership.   I. McCanse, Anne Adams.   II.
Title. III. Series.
HD 57.7.B55 1991
658.4′09--dc20   90-38432
                                                                    CIP

Dedication

This book is dedicated to the memory of Jane Srygley Mouton and to her signal contribution to the Grid formulation, as well as her many other contributions to the field of human effectiveness.

Contents

Preface

As a result of positive developments in four significant areas of investigation, this book represents a milestone in the development of the Grid® approach for promoting human effectiveness.

First, the Grid has been the topic of intensive research into the validity of the theory framework itself. This research is evaluated elsewhere, but it has been relied on in strengthening the formulation and refinement of the concepts presented here. The styles also have been written in a broadened and more comprehensive manner with the addition of two leadership styles, previously only alluded to, but now presented in full. These are Paternalism (Chapter 5) and Opportunism (Chapter 8).

As of this time, significant demonstrations of the Grid's utility in understanding how to strengthen the exercise of leadership have resulted in specific studies involving chief executives[1], managers[2], supervi-sors[3] and employees[4], teamwork in the jetliner cockpit[5], doctor-patient relations[6], nurse leadership in ward management[7], sales effectiveness[8,9], leadership of our higher education institutions [10], and others too numerous to mention.

A third extension has shown its value in understanding leadership as exercised in more than 37 countries—the USSR and Korea among the most recent. These represent cultures that are different in dominant religions, political systems, and other dimensions such as development stage, i.e., whether third world or post-industrial. Its value in understanding leadership has been shown to be consistent across these important dimensions of contrast, suggesting that strong leadership creates effective human relationships that are culture-free and essentially independent of these differences.

In a fourth area, literature now is available to aid in comprehending how physical and other diseases may correlate with various kinds of stresses resulting from personal barriers to the exercise of effective leadership[11]. Based on these and other developments, it is our vision that by now the Grid has been tested, retested, revised, broadened, and expanded to the point where it can be regarded as a general and comprehensive theory of leadership. It is capable of accounting for and predicting not only the conditions that result in effectiveness but also the conditions that render behavior ineffective.

Continuing research into the further refinement and widened application of the Grid for solving leadership dilemmas in other areas of application are natural extensions of what has come before. For example, it is now practical to develop and validate comprehensive psychometric Grid instruments and measures, furthering its utility in grappling with problems in marriage, parent-child relations, and teaching as well as in revealing new and pertinent insights into management and supervision.

We would like to express our appreciation for the critique and feedback from members of the Austin headquarters staff, as well as from our worldwide network of associates. Special thanks go to Antonio de los Reyes in the Philippines who stimulated our thinking regarding the motivational dimensions of Grid. Additionally, we would like to express our appreciation to Claudette Knause for supervising this project to its completion, and to Walter Barclay for his editorial contribution and assistance in preparing the index.

We trust you will find this portrayal of the Grid instructive and refreshing, producing new insights into why people operate in the workplace as they do. To achieve organization excellence, or even to survive amidst competition, requires a sound theory of human behavior to guide us into the future.

Robert R. Blake
Anne Adams McCanse
Austin, Texas

Introduction

If you are new to this book, you may be asking yourself: "What exactly is the Grid?" Though described in more detail in Chapter 2, it makes it easier to explain what we mean by Grid concepts and Grid Organization Development if we first provide a brief introduction to the theory itself.

The Grid is a framework for making sense out of how people accomplish results in working with each other. Different leadership approaches can be plotted against the criteria of concern for performance (getting the job done) and concern for people (those with whom you work). It is a conceptual tool that provides a common language by which we can understand how people operate in seeking to achieve organization purpose. Once people within the same organization can speak the same language, they have set in place a foundation for communicating as to how each can be more effective. Without a common theory and language for examining our leadership behavior, we are operating in the dark; we are coming at a problem from different perspectives with no sound methodology for meshing effort. Change of any magnitude is unlikely to occur.

While the Grid has undergone significant changes in this book, the underlying principles of earlier editions remain intact. This new book expands and completes the Grid formulation, now encompassing in a comprehensive way all major approaches, or Grid styles, for managing work and people in organizations. Heavy emphasis is placed on how people deal with conflict, because this is a key factor in approaching any situation. A second major emphasis is placed on critique, because it provides a significant opportunity for change in many of today's organizational settings. The potential for learning how to be more effective through the sound use of feedback and critique is critical to moving organizations into a competitive future.

This book includes some major changes in presenting the Grid. First of all, we have taken a new approach for presenting the theory through a story about a group of people in a company called Celarmco. It's a story about a team that lives on the edge, a team that has, so far, been able to get it together but only when faced with crises. One member, however, senses the need for improved team interaction and pushes for better use of resources to achieve sounder results. Each of the characters in the story portrays an approach to working with and through others. Thus, the Grid styles come to life and you can see them in action with each character being highlighted in the respective Grid style chapter.

By virtue of the story provided to illustrate effective and ineffective action in work settings, the theory has become sufficiently concrete for ready understanding that it can now be used in high school and college courses. Study of it can aid students who are about to enter the work force to understand how they may increase their own effectiveness, not only as employees who are being led but as potential leaders who may be asked to assume the responsibility for leading others.

Additionally, we have concentrated upon the motivational under-pinnings of each of the Grid styles. Here we address the issue of, "What makes a person tick?" The plus and minus dimensions of each Grid style provide significant insight into why people do what they do, what they strive to achieve on the plus end and what they seek to avoid on the minus end of this dimension. Once these underlying motivations are brought to our attention, it becomes possible to change ineffective ways of operating into sounder approaches for working with others.

Another major change is the inclusion of consequences created among others who experience supervision under any Grid style. This also serves to complete the loop, showing both sides of the equation—the person initiating action as well as the reactions of the recipient of that action. Relationships between people are two-sided; interaction occurs between people of different rank and people of same rank. This new approach allows us to look at Grid style from both perspectives and helps answer the question of why people act and react as they do. Often we hear the question, "If my boss (or colleague, or subordinate) operates in this manner, how do I go about relating to him or her in a more effective way?" The Grid provides solutions as a means for strengthening our behavior in any context.

The final three chapters are concerned with bringing about change: individual, team, and organization. Here we examine steps for personal change, concentrating on those things an individual does have control over and can change to increase personal effectiveness. Then we study how a group of people can improve their teamwork, emphasizing the dimensions of team interaction. Finally, we examine the big picture, where change of great impact occurs within an entire system. This is Grid Organization Development, a step-by-step process of moving an organization from its current level of achievement toward what it can optimally become. This is change by design[12] rather than relying on evolution or revolution as a means for change.

With Grid concepts consistently illustrated in use by the story that develops along with the text, the style of writing of this revision represents a unique departure from past efforts.

One additional word of explanation completes our transition to this new Grid book. This book contains the essence of Jane Mouton and her work. We have included her name in the title line: The Blake/Mouton Grid Management and Organization Development Series.

Chapter 1

Leadership Dynamics: How to Transform Resources into Results

We often hear the question, "Are leaders made or is leadership something only a select few are born with?" If the latter is true, it leaves most of us in a hopeless situation. The evidence is in our favor, however, because it indicates that leadership can indeed be learned. The trick lies in the learning. How do we develop and sharpen the skills that can enable us to lead our organizations in a truly excellent manner?

The new pursuit is visionary leadership at the top as organizations find themselves in the midst of accelerating change, suddenly thrust on a global scene with new financial markets, rapidly advancing technology, and a multitude of other factors that demand attention. With such a rapid fire chain of events, we may pause and reflect, "How can my organization keep up with competition, much less hope to get ahead?" It all comes back to leadership. Effective leadership is the key to success for the future.

This book offers a sound theory-based approach that permits you to determine what effective leadership is by contrasting it with what it is not. The operational framework presented allows

1

you to identify actions that limit effectiveness and actions that enhance it. The concepts demonstrate how you can make a greater contribution to organization success while at the same time strengthening your own leadership capabilities.

What Is Leadership?

Leadership can be depicted in many ways—inspirational, prescriptive, etc.—depending on what the leader thinks will work. A sound way of exercising leadership is through the use of what we call the "three R's of leadership"—Resources (R_1), Relationships (R_2), and Results (R_3) (See Figure 1-1). How a person operates in this context can make the difference between organization success and failure.

R_1—*Resources* are what people as individuals have to contribute; they are the human resources, i.e., the knowledge, abilities, skills, and motivations people have available in using technical, financial, and other non-human or indirect resources.

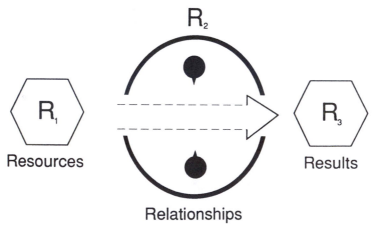

Figure 1-1. The three R's of leadership. *

---

*The figures that appear in this book are the property of Scientific Methods, Inc. and are reproduced by permission.

R_2—*Relationships* are the interactions between people. They are symbolized in Figure 1-1 by two black heads facing one another. Of course, in a team situation we may be talking about more than two people. R_2 characterizes the degree of individual and team commitment to teamwork in all face-to-face groups, whether among co-workers or different departments and in relations with customers, clients, or whomever one deals with in day-to-day interactions. This is the domain of organization culture—it defines "how we do things."

R_3—*Results* are realized from team interaction and problem solving. These are measurable as evidenced in productivity, profit, creativity and innovation, sales, and service, i.e., they measure the degree to which organizational purpose is met.

We focus on the domain of R_2. This is where an excellent organization succeeds over a mediocre one because how well an organization uses the resources available to it is directly related to the results achieved. An excellent leader enables the team to use the resources brought to the table to achieve maximum results. The area in which a manager has the greatest impact, therefore, lies in R_2, although the stronger and more complete the R_1's that people have to contribute, the better.

We should pause a moment to clarify what we mean by resources because we're not talking about money, technology, raw materials, etc. Resources are what *people* have to contribute; what they bring to bear on solving a problem. The other resources, what we might call "indirect resources," are vital, of course, but they are useless unless the people in an organization know how to think about them, use them, and apply them. That's why the spotlight is on people and what they currently possess in terms of ability, talent, knowledge, and motivation to work together in solving problems, whether the problems being solved involve finance, technology, raw materials, or whatever.

Too often we rationalize a situation where we have been beaten by a competitor, saying, "They just got lucky," "Their financial resources are better," or "They've got the latest technology; we were at a disadvantage." We excuse failure with self-justification instead of looking at what we can influence, which is how we interact together as a group of people to accomplish the work that needs to be done. When R_2 is operating in a sound manner, R_1 flows into R_3, showing up in concrete results. But if R_2 lacks strength and soundness, R_3 is bound to suffer. More often than not, the true problem lies in R_2. People's resources get "lost" in the arena of relationships and move sluggishly, if at all, into tangible results. It's a leadership dilemma in that the resources for solving a problem are ineffectively used and either get blocked or diverted.

This book focuses on how people use or fail to use the resources available to them in doing their jobs. So we are concentrating on the area of R_2. Relationship problems abound in organizations today. Trust and respect among those who must work together is often low. Disagreement and conflict may impede productive effort. Creativity and innovation are stifled or nonexistent. Morale suffers. Nobody wants to work here anymore. People have an attitude of, "What's in it for me?" No one cares about the organization. Each of these is a significant R_2 factor that must be remedied if we expect our organizations to be competitive in the global marketplace. Interdependence of effort is critical.

The Effective R_2 Leader

Leaders don't operate in isolation. The very nature of the role implies interaction. They must—and do—work with other people in accomplishing any task. The effective leader is one who can convert resources (R_1) into results (R_3) in working with and through others by establishing and maintaining sound relationships (R_2).

Sometimes we observe very talented people who don't produce the results we expect. Frequently, the reason for this is faulty relationships (R_2). Such is the case of a person who appears to have great resources at his or her disposal but is repeatedly unable to establish constructive relationships with those who must help produce the results. Often the solution lies in recognizing the adverse consequences of one's leadership—those things a person does that negatively impact others or those things a person fails to do that, if done, could prove to be beneficial.

The key to greater productivity lies in recognizing these adverse consequences of leadership. Once people have an objective view of how they operate, change towards more effective behavior becomes an option. In other words, as long as we continue to do things—of which we often are unaware—that adversely affect teamwork and organization productivity, little or no change can occur. We must be able to see and diagnose our weaknesses in order to move toward a sounder way of operating. We also must be able to see our strengths so we can reinforce them.

This book's goal is to help you identify areas where improvement is possible, to measure the importance, validity, and impact of change in these areas, and to offer suggestions for removing the obstacles to corporate excellence. Several of the key areas we examine include the dimensions of teamwork encompassed by R_2. We find that many aspects of relationships within the team inhibit individuals from contributing resources or effectively tapping the resources of others.

When a leader optimizes interaction in the arena of R_2, resources can be fully mobilized and even expanded. Something greater is achieved than what each person contributes individually on a task. This is *synergy*. Instead of $1+1+1 = 3$, we may get an outcome of 5 or 6 or 7; maybe even 8 or 9. We're not limited to adding together each of our unique individual efforts, the sum of which constitutes our output; rather our effort can be multiplied several times over to create truly sound results.

This is the very purpose of organization, to allow us to do more together than we could do alone. It is cooperation to produce better results, which in turn permit the organization to win the competitive game in the marketplace. It is a leader's job to manage this process in a way that produces sound outcomes. The kind of leadership a person exercises is a function of how he or she integrates R_1, R_2, and R_3. The results achieved depend on the effectiveness of the approach used.

Let's pause a moment and take a look at how one team operates in its daily affairs. The following illustration demonstrates several Grid ® leadership styles in action. (The Grid styles themselves are discussed in Chapter 2.) We will look at different members of this team as we explore the various styles throughout the book. The setting is R_2, the domain of relationships. The characters in the story are talking about R_3, the results they achieved in a recent triumph over competition. Each member had significant R_1 resources to offer; *how* these resources were used is detailed in their conversation.

□ □ □

How Al Jennings' Team Snatched Victory from the Jaws of Defeat*

Al Jennings, vice-president of a key division at Celarmco, a large multinational firm, stood proudly at the head of the long conference table. Al had convened this meeting of his key players after the culmination of a successful proposal that meant big dollars for the company. The bidding had been close but they had beaten their toughest competitor out of the deal. The news had just been relayed to Al that they had emerged victorious, and this meeting was to announce a plan to celebrate the occasion.

The bid itself had called for getting agreement from all team members on a shared strategy. Al provided direction on which way to proceed and eventually everyone joined in. In the weeks that followed, an endless amount of detail and cross-checking was required to submit a proposal. The initial momentum associated with this project had been strong but seemed to taper off midway. The team sank into complacency and effort began to drag despite the fact that no apparent obstacles were encountered. Part of this was due to poor coordination, with each team member doing his or her job in isolation from the others—the right hand didn't know what the left hand was doing. This was typical of the manner in which Al's team normally functioned. Finally, at the point of breakdown, the team snapped out of its complacency when, by sheer coincidence, a message came via the corporate grapevine that they were way off track. Instead of the relaxed two-week period they thought remained, only 48 hours was left until the deadline. Quite simply, there had been a failure to communicate at some point along the chain. Through this fortuitous happenstance, the team stepped up its efforts and moved into action. They cut a few corners and came in with the winning bid.

As Al surveyed the contingent gathered around the table, he felt a deep sense of reward for the loyalty and dedication so apparent on their faces. He appreciated the long hours and lost weekends they had devoted to making his plan a success. He felt he had demanded perfection and they had delivered. On the other hand, the pure dollar profit Celarmco stood to enjoy hadn't missed his attention either. Though the success was inherently motivating, he couldn't deny

---

The entire story entitled "How Al Jennings' Team Snatched Victory from the Jaws of Defeat" is copyrighted by Robert R. Blake and Anne Adams McCanse. It is quoted here with permission and is not to be reproduced.

himself the secret pleasure of anticipating the acclaim he'd receive once the full implication of this achievement was measured by his superiors. Headquarters would be elated and he would get credit for this accomplishment.

To Al's left was Dan Smith, head of human resources for the division and a loyal supporter throughout the years. Dan was a good member of the team, his primary function being to keep people together and maintain friendly attitudes. Dan could find something positive in any situation; he was seldom without something nice to say. Al knew he could count on Dan to lavish the group with praise and affection and keep morale from flagging.

Next around the table was Elizabeth Parker, resident marketing manager, and a fairly new recruit. Everyone called her Liz. She had been sent from headquarters with sterling recommendations. There was no doubt about her credentials—she had a doctorate in physics from MIT and an MBA from Harvard. Although she generally let others know about her background, she didn't flaunt it. She was a team player in every way. She knew enough to back down in an argument when there were forces at work larger than herself. Her role was to help the team smooth out its differences, enabling it to reach an accommodation, a reasonable middle ground when disagreements arose. Liz's assistance was critical in helping the team maintain a steady pace.

At the end of the table was another young man recently promoted to this division to head up operations. Benjamin Thomas—or Ben—was known as a real up-and-comer, having only been with the company five years and having climbed quickly through the ranks. Ben had established a reputation for himself as a leader; he seemed to have discovered the secret for working with others in a way that led to sound results. Ben didn't shy away from conflict; he openly confronted situations with which he disagreed, sometimes offering suggestions that, in Al's opinion, might best be kept to himself. Though Ben never tried to railroad his opinion through, he was reluctant to give in on a point as long as he believed it the right way to go, even if he stood alone in its support. "In a few years," Al thought, "he's bound to straighten up. He just hasn't learned our ways yet."

To Ben's left sat Ed Jackson, head of production. Ed was good at his job—the best—but he had considerable difficulty getting along with others. He had a sharp tongue and a sarcastic humor and was rarely reluctant to interject his point of view. He tended to bully and belittle those who dared to contradict his way of thinking. Ed was a strong leader and he enjoyed giving orders. Al felt a certain reluctance to confront him on issues because he could "blow up." Instead Al preferred a solicitous approach in an effort to win Ed's favor. In a lot of ways, Ed and Al agreed on many things. They were both strong believers in getting results. Furthermore, because Ed enjoyed ironing out problems, this served to relieve Al of many unpleasant tasks. Nevertheless, in Al's opinion, Ed had a long way to go in terms of being a good manager; he'd be halfway there if he simply learned to treat his people better.

Moving to the next person, Al found himself looking at his fair-haired boy, Frank Jameson. Frank's area of expertise was product innovation and design. He was an alert team member, seldom absent from team meetings. The only time other activities took precedence was when unscheduled meetings at headquarters were called and Frank, as the informally designated representative of Al's unit, was sometimes required to be present. As often as not, however, Frank's attendance at the functions was optional. Only Frank didn't see it that way. Frank would report to the team that headquarters needed him, making profuse apologies for his unexpected absences. But the team knew where his loyalties were placed. Frank wouldn't miss an appointment at headquarters for the world; he saw it as his ticket to the top. This tended to irritate Al, but Frank had a knack for saying just the right thing to regain Al's favor. In fact, for the most part, Frank got along well with everyone. He was more solicitous with those of higher stature than with colleagues, where his dealings were more along the lines of give and take. Frank's distinguishing feature was that he sought a trade-off in every relationship. He seldom exerted effort if, now or somewhere down the road, there wasn't something in it for him. Frank wasn't out to hurt other people, but he certainly placed priority on furthering his own cause.

Finally, Al's gaze settled on Gil Phillips, another loyal supporter and head of engineering. Gil could be counted on to be there; he seldom missed a regular working day, although he managed to take whatever vacation days and sick leave due him as defined by company policy. Gil rarely had anything to say, but he seemed to get the work done. He wasn't the best manager by any stretch of the imagination, but he got the word through to subordinates. Al wished Gil could be more self-initiating rather than taking such a reactive stance, waiting for an order or request before he would respond. "Someday he'll get his act together . . ." hoped Al.

Al brought his focus back to the group as a whole, paused a moment to clear his throat, and then began, "This is a special occasion for us and I want to celebrate our victory. It was nothing short of miraculous in that during this last 48 hours we all performed superbly. I'm proud to be in charge of this team!"

"It was a spectacular feat!" exclaimed Frank. "But it wasn't without a lot of blood, sweat, and tears as well. We should all be proud of ourselves."

"You're both right," stated Liz. "It's a miracle we came through and that's exciting; at the same time, I agree, it was hard work. But somehow we put our individual efforts together and hit on the right combination for teamwork. Al, you led the way, and I think I can speak for all of us when I say we do appreciate it. The competition almost caught us on this one and you saved us from disaster." Liz sighed, as if a load had been lifted. But she still waited for Al to acknowledge her praise.

"Thanks, Liz. I appreciate your vote of confidence." Al looked at her approvingly.

"Well, it seems to me that we're right back at the beginning," Ed said sarcastically. "Nothing has changed, not really. We got lucky on this one just like we have every time before. Somehow we manage to pull together in an emergency to get the job done. Then as soon as it's over, we fall apart again. Tell me, why are we sitting around and patting each other on the back? We should be hard at work on the next project."

"I think we deserve a little relaxation," said Dan. "After all, we just finished a difficult assignment—successfully."

Ed looked at Dan with some disdain.

"Ed," Liz chimed in. "Tell me what you mean by 'lucky.' I don't understand."

"Then you're not with it," Ed retorted. "You should get up to date on the latest news."

Liz turned red from embarrassment and shifted uneasily in her chair.

Al broke into the conversation. "That's enough. I think we can drop the subject."

"Wait a minute," said Ben. "I think I know what Ed is referring to, but if others on this team aren't familiar with the entire background of this project, I think it's important to take the time to discuss it."

"This already sounds like bad news," said Dan. "Can't we just let bygones be bygones?"

"Is that what you think we pay you for?" sneered Ed. "To be the team 'happy face?'"

Dan hung his head. Frank took the initiative to relieve the mounting tension. "Ed, you're talking about that little misunderstanding over the deadline, right?" Without letting Ed respond, Frank proceeded, looking in Al's direction for his reaction. "It was an oversight on our part but not irresolvable by any means. We thought the deadline was several weeks off, but in a meeting with the headquarters group I discovered we were off track. Of course, I kept my mouth shut. No point in letting them know about our mistake."

"Well, it could have been disastrous," said Ed. "That's why I say we got lucky."

"I had no idea," said Liz. "I thought I was the only one operating in the dark. I felt so humiliated!"

"Frank," remarked Ben, "I heard a slightly different story. Tell me, who exactly caught the error?"

Before Frank could respond, Ed interjected, "I did! I spotted the mistake. Frank was reviewing the headquarters meeting with me and said he was baffled by the deadline they had mentioned."

"It was strange," said Frank. "It's like they knew we were headed for a fall. In that meeting one of the headquarters' people, Joe Thompson, deliberately turned to me and said, 'We're counting on you and Al and the rest of the team on this bid. We'll know in two days, *won't we*?' And he winked at me and smiled. I didn't know what he was talking about, but I kept my mouth shut anyway."

"But I was the one who put two and two together," said Ed, "and then we went to Al. We discovered the real facts. It was an odd mistake. Somewhere along the line we just got off track. I think that sums it up. Can you add anything, Al?"

"That's about the way I recall the chain of events," replied Al. He was eager to set this subject aside. He felt like it made him look bad in the eyes of the team. After all, he was supposed to be the expert and to know all the facts. He was disturbed by being caught short on this one. "Look, it all worked out okay so let's just move on. Success is success no matter how you get there."

"But it's important to understand how we succeeded so we can capitalize on the talents of team members in other situations. It's also important to understand our failures, and our 'almost-failures,' so we don't repeat those actions." Ben paused. "Can't anyone see that?"

"I do," responded Ed. "I think you're right. When people make mistakes they have to be willing to take the blame for them. I think we need to tighten up control around here. We've been pretty lax lately and it's catching up with us."

"All that's well and good but this is supposed to be a celebration. You don't want to rain on *my* parade, do you?" It was apparent that Al did not like the direction this conversation was taking.

"Hold on a minute, Al," said Ben. "This is a valid point. We need to examine how we've been operating. We rarely stop to see and evaluate the quality of our teamwork unless some event comes along and forces us to."

"Here it comes," said Ed. "Ben's going into one of his long-winded dissertations on participation and that's not what I had in mind. As you know, I have no great love for these meetings. For the most part, I think they're a waste of time. It's a much better use of resources to communicate on a need-to-know basis. Those in charge should have the guts to make the decisions and live with the consequences; those not in charge are paid to carry them out. It's as simple as that."

"You and I aren't as far off as you think, Ed," responded Ben. "I think we're shooting for the same goal; we just have a different perspective on how to get there. You say 'Tell people what to do to move toward the bottom line.' I say you get better results working with and through subordinates by gaining their understanding, giving them background and rationale, and soliciting their ideas, involvement, and commitment in thinking through the outcome. It's a difference between telling people how to do something and getting them to understand how, what, who, and why. It's going a step further to ask for their input, finding out if they agree or disagree. You know, they just might have a better solution. Remember the saying, 'Two heads are better than one?'"

"Please, spare me," groaned Ed.

"Don't you see?" pleaded Ben. "You're only using a fraction of your resources. I'm suggesting you use all your resources in order to get the best thinking on the solution to any given problem."

"I've already got the best resources," Ed retorted. "Right here in my head."

Gil chuckled. "They're at it again, aren't they?"

Liz decided to take another shot at putting an end to this argument. "Look, I know you two could go on all day, but in the interest of time how about just agreeing to disagree?"

Ben and Ed both cast a sharp glance in her direction.

Al nodded approvingly at Liz. "Liz, if you ever leave this company, you'll make a fine politician." Then voicing his implied unhappiness with the haranguing occurring over the Ben/Ed polarity, "You're very adept at bypassing needless disagreement."

"Why, thank you," Liz replied.

Ben was not to be deterred from his topic. "Ed, what I was saying about resources . . ."

Ed didn't let him finish. "Ben, Ben, Ben. Everything you say is very nice, but it just doesn't work in practice. If you give people an inch, they'll take a mile. A boss who doesn't keep things in tight control soon loses control altogether. Get the point? People need strong direction. That's what they understand. It's the only way to get results."

Dan shifted uncomfortably in his chair. He disliked conflict, and he knew from personal experience that it was impossible to change Ed's mind. He spoke up meekly, redirecting the conversation to Al. "This doesn't seem to be getting us anywhere. Al, why don't you bring us back to the subject of a celebration?"

"Give me a break, Dan," Ed boomed. "I'll let you know when what we're talking about is important or unimportant!"

Dan cowered and cast his eyes to the ground. Gil took the lull that followed as an opportunity to raise a concern of his own. "Did anyone get the football score last night? My wife invited dinner guests and I missed the whole thing, including the news report."

"What does that have to do with anything?" Ed snapped. "Sometimes, Gil, you're hopeless!"

Everyone grew quiet. Al thought to himself, "What a bunch of children!" Then he broke the silence.

"We seem to have gotten off track. Since we've been talking about taking control, that's exactly what I'm going to do. Now, I would like to celebrate our victory on getting this bid and I don't want to do it by myself! Reservations have been made at Mario's, and that's got to be the finest restaurant in town. I want everyone to be there Thursday evening. Spouses are invited; be sure to bring them. We all need a little bit of downtime, some relaxing and socializing. That builds team spirit. Now that that's settled, I have no more business to attend to. OK?"

People looked at one another. This decision was like many others that occurred on this team. Al always seemed well intentioned enough, but his decisions came through as ultimatums. He had his mind made up in advance. Team members knew they could try to argue, but the easier, softer, and safe way was to go along with what Al wanted.

Liz said, "You know, this is why I have real mixed emotions about these meetings. It's much easier to sell an idea when you work with others one on one. These public debates are nerve wracking."

"Yeah," said Gil, "I'd rather be off doing my own thing. It's Al's job to coordinate the work."

Ed chimed in, "That's probably the only area on which you and I agree!"

"Wait a minute," Ben said. "What we're touting is mediocre teamwork. It may be okay when we're able to join forces in the face of a real or suspected crisis; but it's disastrous otherwise. All we do is settle for good enough. We lose so much ground by not taking full advantage of our potential."

Al seemed irritated. Before Ben had joined the team, he hadn't had any problem controlling his people. "Ben, what are you trying to say?"

"Okay, let me get back to the present situation," said Ben. "Despite our most recent success, I think we're still in the dark about 'how' we operate—like Liz said. Can anyone explain how we were caught off guard on this deal? It's important to know so it doesn't happen again."

"Maybe we need to appoint someone to stay on top of things," suggested Liz.

"I wish it were that easy," Ben smiled.

"What about this last triumph?" asked Dan. "We must be doing something right. Even you can't deny that!"

Ben replied, "Look, I'll go back to Ed's remark that 'We got lucky'. That's not operating as a team. We could just as easily have fallen flat on our faces. Is that a reason to party? Personally, I don't want to celebrate the illusion of success. I want us to look at how we operate. We don't mesh effort. Each of us just operates in our own little sphere of influence and we hope the work gets done. Usually we're working toward the same goal but sometimes we're not. We could do so much better than what we're doing right now!"

Liz replied thoughtfully, "I guess you're right. We really don't operate in an interdependent way, except maybe when we're in a crisis. Then we seem to pitch in, letting go of our vested interests long enough to take the larger view and do what is needed to succeed. Normally, though, we just rock along and try to stay out of one another's way."

No one spoke. They knew what Liz had said was true.

"Gil, we haven't heard your opinion," said Liz. "What do you think about all of this?"

Gil shifted awkwardly in his chair. "I think we probably should study this situation a little more before we jump to conclusions. There are a lot of different ways to look at this thing."

"What exactly are you saying?" barked Ed.

Gil stammered, "Only that we don't have all the data. There are so many points of view and people have gotten so emotional. It's hard to tell fact from fiction."

"You'd have us perpetually in committee studying problems. Just once I'd like to hear your clear opinion on an issue!" Ed clenched his fists.

"Now, now," said Al, "we're getting overwrought. I want to end this discussion . . ."

"Do you agree to revisit this topic? I've got some ideas for how we can move forward," said Ben.

"Unfortunately, I have no doubt you will raise the matter again," muttered Al. He disapproved of Ben's initiative, but he was reluctant to suppress it because he knew Ben had the support of others on the team and was not alone in his opinions; furthermore, it was rumored that key people at headquarters had an eye on Ben. "But back to the party. Do each of you promise to show up Thursday evening and to have a good time?"

Frank, aware of Al's mounting anxiety, sought to alleviate it by drawing the meeting to a close through summary remarks. First, speaking to Al, he ventured, "I think you can count on each and every one of us to be there." Turning to Liz, he commented, "You said it for me when you pointed to Al as the pivotal point in drawing our resources together." Addressing the group as a whole, he concluded, "I think Ben might have a point in the potential gain to be had by examining our teamwork process at a deeper level. We should explore that possibility further. But, that's not to discount Ed's position, because I can certainly understand that. I'm sure there's not one of us here that doesn't believe in the final result achieved—the payoff from all our hard work. Of course, that's what we're here for. We do believe that, don't we?"

Ben's head was whirling by the time he interrupted this soliloquy. "Frank, you're talking out of both sides of your mouth. Just yesterday we had a conversation about how Ed deals with his people and you gave me a completely different version of the story. I thought we saw eye to eye on this."

This exchange naturally brought Ed to the edge of his chair. "What do you mean by that remark?"

Before Ben could reply, Ed turned to Frank and let him have it. "What's all this about? You told me over lunch earlier this week that Ben kept stirring things up in order to get Al's attention. I thought you agreed with me. Now I'm hearing something different. Which is it? Who do you agree with?''

Frank twisted nervously in his chair. ''There seems to be a little misunderstanding here.''

''I'll say,'' snapped Ed. ''I want to add one more thing, Frank. If you've appointed yourself as the team expert on how I treat my subordinates, let me comment on what I've observed you doing. You are a shifty character. Most of the time you parade around here with your nose up in the air because of your contacts at headquarters. But if there's something you need from any one of us, you bend over backwards to treat us nice. If there's something in it for you, you're the first one in line.''

''Are you any different?'' Frank responded defensively, looking hurt by Ed's caustic remarks.

''You know what I mean,'' said Ed. ''I come right out and say what I want. You, on the other hand, are sneaky. I never know exactly where you're coming from.''

''Let's just hold it right there, people,'' said Al. ''We've had enough for one day. We're all tired and edgy from the hard work of getting this successful bid into shape. With a victory under our belts, it's certainly no time to bicker. A little relief from the pressure we've been under will do us all a world of good. A celebration dinner will not only symbolize our success on this latest venture but a new beginning as well. What do you say?''

The room was silent, with people still recovering from Ed's outburst.

Al moved right along, ''Wonderful. I'll take that as unanimous agreement. Let's quit.''

The meeting came to an abrupt halt. People got up and started to disperse. Frank took care to engage Al in conversation and walk out the door in the safety of his presence. He had no desire to renew his conversation with either Ed or Ben, not while tensions were still high.

□ □ □

What was really going on in Al's team? Look at it from an R_1-R_2-R_3 point of view. They have sufficient R_1 resources to achieve their objectives. R_3 meant getting a good bid for the company and beating the competition in doing it. The real issue, however, is that Al's team succeeded only by a fortuitous circumstance. Someone slipped them a piece of information that enabled the team to take action and prevent major calamity.

As Liz said and Ben reiterated, they had been operating in the dark. There's a teamwork problem here, but no one, save Ben, is ready to get to the bottom of it. Ben proposes they really dig in and study how the team operates in order to get answers and solutions for how to boost R_3 effectiveness.

The solution is centered in the area of R_2 relationships among team members, because each person constitutes a part of the problem. It's not just Al's problem, or Gil's problem, or Ed's. A problem that impacts team effectiveness is one that the whole team owns. They can't hope to operate more effectively until each member participates openly and fully in an objective self-examination of personal strengths and weaknesses. Such objectivity can only be gained by getting feedback from others with whom one works. For example, if Al were serious about becoming a better leader, he might try to find out what he does that blocks the resources Ben has to offer. At the moment, Al has no intention of changing. In the story we see him complaining—albeit indirectly—about all the problems this team has had since Ben came on board. Al's not particularly concerned about the flow of resources into results. Ben, on the other hand, thinks it's critical that the team become aware of the actions they take that limit their effectiveness. Without a shared understanding of these barriers, there is little possibility of increasing the team's productivity.

This book provides a behavioral model of leadership that can make the difference between this team's long-term success or failure. It applies to the behavior of every member, not just Al's. Under Al's supervision, each member is seeking to influence outcomes, and in this sense every member exercises leadership within this team as they seek to solve the problem of team effectiveness. Beyond that, each member has leadership responsibility over his or her own team of subordinates.

With this in mind, let's refocus the leadership issue and break it down into components that we can study and contrast.

Elements of Leadership

Leadership is a complex process, but it can be broken down into key elements that make it easier to examine and understand. Though we may isolate an element for deeper analysis, it is important to remember that each is a facet of the whole and that all operate in concert with one another. In other words, each element can be likened to one facet of a brilliant gem; we can examine each facet individually, but it cannot be realistically separated from the other five. There is an implied interdependency and no one element stands alone. Furthermore, as a result of this close linking between them, some degree of overlap may appear as we examine the various elements within a particular approach to working with and through other people.

The elements of leadership are *conflict solving, initiative, inquiry, advocacy, decision making*, and *critique*. All six are vital to the exercise of effective leadership and teamwork. They are briefly described in the following sections.

Seven statements that depict different leadership approaches appear under the description of each element. The statements provide benchmarks for describing leadership as a process involving people who have resources to contribute as they work together to achieve organization objectives. As you read these statements, ask yourself, "Do I know someone—a boss, colleague, or subordinate—who manages in this way?" Try to identify the members in Al's team for how they fit these various elements. Next rank the statements for how they apply to you. 7 represents the sentence within each element that most typifies how you operate; 6 represents your next most typical approach; and finally down to 1, which denotes the approach least typical of the way you do things. Do this for each of the six elements. React to the statement in its entirety rather than evaluating isolated segments. Put your self-ranking in the blanks to the left of each statement. These rankings are referred to later in the book.

Conflict Solving

When people have different points of view and express them, disagreement and conflict are inevitable. Conflict can be either disruptive and destructive of results or creative and constructive, depending on how it is handled. A person who can face conflict with others and resolve it to a mutual understanding evokes respect.

The inability to cope with conflict constructively or the tendency to avoid it and keep it covered up leads to disrespect and even increased hostility and antagonism.

6   A __ When conflict arises, I acknowledge it but reemphasize the importance of what I propose to bring others around to my point of view. LIZ

1   B __ I maintain a neutral stance or try to stay out of conflict altogether. GIL

2   C __ When conflict arises, I shift and turn in an effort to get around it; I avoid getting caught head on. FRANK

5   D __ When conflict arises, I try to find a reasonable position that everyone can live with. DAN

7   E __ When conflict arises, I seek out reasons for it in order to resolve underlying causes of tensions. BEN

4   F __ When conflict arises, I try to cut it off or win my position. ED

3   G __ I avoid generating conflict, but when it appears I try to soothe feelings to keep people together. AL

Initiative

Initiative is exercised whenever effort is concentrated on a specific activity, to start something that was not happening, to stop something that was happening, or to shift the direction and character of effort. A leader may take initiative or avoid taking initiative even when others expect action. Initiative, then, is the character and intensity of effort, or drive, supporting the actions taken.

5   A __ I exert vigorous effort and others enthusiastically join in. LIZ

4   B __ I drive myself and others. ED

7   C __ I initiate whatever actions might help and support the efforts of others. DAN

6   D __ I expect others to follow my lead and extend positive appreciation to those who support my efforts. BEN

1   E __ I put out enough to get by, generally in response to requests from others. GIL

2   F __ I seek to maintain a steady pace and confine my effort to the tried and true. AL

3 G __ I initiate actions that are in my own best interest by seeking a trade-off with others. I help them get something that they want if they'll help me get something I want. *Frank*

Inquiry

Inquiry permits us to gain access to facts and data from those with whom we work as well as other information sources. The quality of inquiry often depends on thoroughness. A person who is not thorough may ignore the need for inquiry. Alternatively, an individual operating by standards of excellence may be very thorough, demonstrating a keen interest in learning as much as possible about work activities. Inquiry is asking the relevant questions rather than taking matters for granted.

4 A __ I dig out areas of vital private concern to me in an inquisitive but nonthreatening way. *FRANK*

5 B __ I expect others to keep me informed and I show appreciation when they do; I look with disfavor upon those who fail to keep me up to date. *AL*

7 C __ I search for and seek to verify information; I invite and listen for ideas and attitudes different than my own; I continuously test the soundness of my own thinking by comparing it with the thinking of others. *BEN*

3 D __ I stay on top of information to be sure that I am in control and doublecheck everything I hear to be sure that others are not making mistakes. *ED*

2 E __ I search for information that suggests all is well. For the sake of harmony, I am not inclined to challenge what others say. *DAN*

6 F __ I solicit information in order to see where others stand on an issue; this lets me know whether my own thinking is on track. *LIZ*

1 G __ I rarely ask questions. Usually I just go along in a more or less tongue-in-cheek way with whatever others tell me. *GIL*

Advocacy

To advocate is to take a position; to express one's opinions, attitudes, ideas, and convictions. A person may have strong convictions but think it risky to take a stand. Alternatively, an individual may not advocate his or her point of view because of low or nonexistent convictions. Another person may embrace a point of view simply to oppose someone else or to win. Therefore, ==the strength of the convictions a person holds are one thing to look for; how this individual advocates what he or she believes in is another== and ==indicative of that person's leadership style for dealing with people.==

2   A __ I keep my own counsel but respond to questions when asked. I rarely reveal my convictions because then I don't have to stand behind them.   GIL

1   B __ I tell others what they want or expect to hear.   FRANK

3   C __ I express my convictions in a tentative way and try to meet others halfway.   DAN

7   D __ I feel it is important to express my concerns and convictions in order that others can know what I am thinking. I respond to ideas sounder than my own by changing my mind.   LIZ

4   E __ I stand up for my convictions because I know I'm right. If others oppose me, I try to prove that they are wrong.   ED

6   F __ I embrace the ideas of others even though I may have private reservations. I feel it's better to be supportive than right.   AL

5   G __ Although I seldom back off my own convictions, I do permit others to express their ideas so I can understand where they are coming from and help them see the error of their thinking.   BEN

Decision Making

It is ==through decision making that resources are applied to performance.== It may involve solo decision making, in which the leader alone is the ultimate decision maker; delegation of responsibilities to one or more individuals; or teamwork, in which all available resources are brought to bear on making and implementing decisions.

4   A __ I search for decisions that maintain good relations and encourage others to make the decisions for me when possible.   LIZ

6   B __ Although I seek the final say in decisions, I still listen to what others have to say. In this way they get the benefit of my thinking but I maintain their loyalty.   AL

C __ I let others make decisions or else leave it to fate. *GIL*

D __ I lobby my point of view to others in order to "sell" my position; I may use persuasion or indirect threat to ensure that my wishes are carried out. *ED*

E __ I search for workable decisions that others find acceptable. *DAN*

F __ I place high value on arriving at sound decisions; I seek input from others and work for understanding and agreement. *B FN*

G __ I place high value on making my own decisions and am rarely influenced by what others have to say. *FRANK*

Critique

There are several ways to evaluate how team members solve operational problems as they seek to accomplish goals. Critique is key to this process. It means stepping away from or interrupting an activity long enough to study it, to see alternative possibilities for improving performance, and to anticipate and avoid any actions that may have adverse consequences. Without taking advantage of the learning available through the process of feedback and critique, future work activities are unlikely to change. Relying on critique to learn from experience, on the other hand, provides a sound foundation for working more effectively with and through other people in order to accomplish a task. When critique is done effectively, a path has been cleared for moving resources into measurable results. Without critique, people are operating blindly; with critique, they have insight into what they are doing and how they might be doing it more effectively.

A __ I pinpoint weaknesses or failure to measure up; in the event of a mistake, I assess blame. *E D*

B __ I give encouragement and offer praise when something positive happens but avoid saying anything negative. *A L*

C __ When I give others feedback, I expect them to appreciate it because it is for their own good. *LIZ*

D __ I avoid giving feedback and rarely critique the work of others or myself. *GIL*

5

E __ I use critique to motivate and inspire others to further action that is in my best interest; I tend to discount negative aspects of performance as this lowers the level of enthusiasm. FRANK

6

F __ I give informal or indirect feedback to keep others moving forward at an acceptable pace; if I have to say something negative, I make sure I have something positive to say as well. DAN

7

G __ I encourage two-way feedback to strengthen operations. I place high value on critique and it is evidenced in everything I do. BEN

Each of the statements under the elements represents one approach to leadership. They rest on certain distinctive *assumptions* each of us holds about achieving results with and through others. The next area we focus on is how assumptions guide behavior.

Assumptions Underlie Leadership Behavior

Leadership is no exception when it comes to underlying assumptions. Whenever people approach a situation, they act on the basis of their subjective appraisal of it, which may or may not resemble objective reality. This appraisal includes assumptions about what is true or reliable. The objective reality and the subjective appraisal of it can be close together or far apart. Al's assumptions about the significance of a celebration dinner are not shared by the others, but their attitude is "better to show team spirit" than to go against Al's will. Ben sees the team using its resources in one way, Ed in another, and Dan from still a different point of view. Because the members of this team are viewing exactly the same situation from his or her unique perspective (how Al's team "works"), it is clear that the different assumptions each derives from the situation become visible in their different approaches to working with and through other people. Assumptions guide behavior, and this behavior is clearly evidenced in the various approaches to leadership.

Because assumptions organize our relationships and our ways of conducting our affairs, it is important to understand them because usually they are silent. As a result, their central role in controlling behavior is likely to be unseen. To go a step further, when an assumption we make is embraced by those around us, it becomes an "absolute," not subject to question. Other possibilities are then ignored. The "absolute" nature eliminates courses of action and blinds us to options that might produce sounder results.

People seldom verbalize their assumptions, but they do act on them. Because some assumptions lead to good results and others lead to poor ones, not all assumptions are equally sound as a basis for exercising effective leadership. The idea that various sets of assumptions are "equal but different" has appeal because it permits people to avoid making a choice. The choice of assumptions, however, becomes an important issue for people to consider because some assumptions produce negative R_3's and others produce positive ones.

A comprehensive theory of leadership is possible because only a limited number of assumptions about how to achieve performance with and through others are available. Understanding our assumptions about leadership can help us to see the impact of our behavior on the production efforts of those with whom we work and on whose resources we depend.

Assumptions Can Be Changed

We return now to the question with which we started, "Are leaders made or are they born?" People can and do change by changing the underlying assumptions that guide their behavior. A first step is to become aware of the less-than-effective assumptions we hold. Sometimes we explain an action by saying, "I assumed that this would work, but obviously I was wrong." Far more often we are completely unaware or we provide ourselves an easy but incorrect rationalization of what accounted for our conduct. Sometimes we are as baffled about why we do things as others are in trying to explain our actions. Without new experiences to challenge our assumptions and a theory-based framework for understanding, it may even be difficult to identify them. With every new experience we have the opportunity to reflect on what we did and why and to get feedback from others regarding our actions—the principal ingredient for examining R_2. Only then can the assumptions on which our behavior is based be reexamined. This is the critical step that permits change to become a realistic possibility.

This book provides various ways to identify and examine assumptions about how we operate. Once we become aware of the depth and character of our assumptions, we can analyze them and identify the positive and negative *consequences* of actions based on them. We can consider alternative assumptions that may provide a sounder basis for our actions and practice applying them until they come to characterize a sounder approach to working with others.

Summary

The Grid presented in Chapter 2 is useful for identifying the assumptions we hold as we work to get results with and through others. By using theories to identify our unique assumptions, we come to see ourselves and others more objectively; we learn to communicate more clearly and to understand the source of our disagreements; we discover how to change ourselves and to help others have more productive and rewarding experiences at the same time. The more skilled a leader is in using sound theory, the more capable that person becomes in reducing frustration, resentment, and other negative emotions. The shift away from these feelings toward enthusiasm and dedication promotes a sense of contribution, reward, and personal fulfillment.

In the final analysis, how a person exercises leadership in the arena of R_2 is everything. The best technical or financial resources in the world—the latest equipment, the most advanced product design, the finest facilities, and the most highly qualified people— count for little or nothing if leadership is ineffectively exercised in taking advantage of these potentials. It is important to note that even with minimal resources, good leadership can accomplish stronger results. Leadership is what converts the R_1 available to an organization into effective R_3.

Next we turn to the Grid as a way of examining leadership style.

Chapter 2

The Grid: A Framework for Understanding Leadership Style

Chapter 1 began exploring leadership by studying its impact on the resources people use to solve problems. How leaders use these resources to manage the process of people working together (R_2) significantly affects productivity. The Grid portrays the seven different ways in which power and authority are exercised in the R_2 arena. It is a useful framework that provides a common "language" by which we can begin to understand how people go about achieving organization purpose.

As we examine the seven leadership styles, it is immediately apparent that some are more effective than others. When resources are wasted by mismanagement in R_2 and as a result not fully converted into R_3, an organization has failed to maximize its potential.

By studying the seven leadership theories of the Grid, you can learn to identify what you are doing that is effective and what you are doing that is not. Then you are in a position to take steps to increase your effectiveness.

The Grid is built on three dimensions. The horizontal axis represents *Concern for Production*, or results (Figure 2-1). The vertical dimension is *Concern for People*, that is, how you feel about and treat those with whom you work to get results (Figure 2-2). "Concern for" indicates the character and intensity of the assumptions that lie beneath any leadership style. It is not a mechanical number that tells how much you produced or that depicts some quantifiable amount of concern expressed toward people.

When these two axes intersect, a third dimension is formed relating to motivations. This dimension answers the question, "Why do I do what I do?" Unlike the first two dimensions, which range from a little to a lot, this one is bipolar. It has a plus (+) or positive end, represented by what we are drawn to achieve, and a minus or negative (-) end, representing those things we seek to avoid.

Concern for Production

Production represents any outcome or result. Obviously, concern for production is not present in all people to the same degree. Similarly, it is subject to fluctuation and change in the same individual at different points in time. Therefore, it is necessary to have a systematic way of expressing the meaning of degree of concern.

Think of concern for production as a scale of degrees. This can range from *1*, a very low concern, to *9*, a very high amount of concern, as illustrated in Figure 2-1.

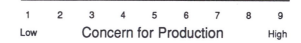

1	2	3	4	5	6	7	8	9
Low			Concern for Production					High

Figure 2-1. Concern for production is the horizontal axis of the Grid.

In the business sector, concern for production is spoken of in different ways. These include results, bottom line, performance, profits, or accomplishment of mission. It is present when a key executive finds new directions for organization growth through acquisitions or launches a program of innovative research and development. Covering both quantity and quality, concern for production is apparent in the scope and soundness of decisions made, the number of creative ideas converted into salable items, the accounts processed in a collection period, or quality and thoroughness of services provided to other organization members or to the customer.

When work is physical, concern for production may take the form of efficiency measurements, number of units produced, time required to complete a certain production run, sales volume, or reaching a measurable level of quality. In a hospital, it may be patient load, number of diagnostic tests completed, or length of hospital stay. In a government agency, productivity may be delivery time, number of forms correctly processed, or number of union-management conflicts successfully resolved. Results may be measured in a university setting by the number of students graduated, students per faculty member, teaching load, research papers published, or graduates in any given year who complete advanced degrees at a later time. Production, in other words, reflects purpose and is seen in whatever an organization employs people to accomplish.

Concern for People

The second dimension is the vertical axis, Concern for People. These are the people in our lives—bosses, subordinates, colleagues, customers—with whom we interact day in and day out. Concern for people also extends through a number of degrees, ranging from 1, a very low concern for people, to 9, a very high degree of concern. This 9-point scale is shown in Figure 2-2.

Because leadership is exercised with and through others, our assumptions about people are important in determining effectiveness, whether they are basically selfish or altruistic, destructive or well intentioned, manipulative or straightforward, closed and hidden or open and transparent. People are people regardless of the context in which the work occurs—industry, government, educational and medical institutions, or the home.

Concern for people is revealed in many different ways. Some leaders show great concern to get subordinates to like them. Other bosses are more concerned with getting the work done and making people comply rigidly with the instructions provided. Still others try to balance the two. No matter how a boss goes about getting work done—by forced compliance, friendly gestures, "guilt trip-

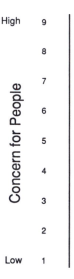

Figure 2-2. Concern for people is the vertical axis of the Grid.

ping,'' neutral message passing, accommodation and compromise, bargaining and trade-offs, or gaining the commitment and understanding of others—all are variations on the concern for people theme. Specific variations include working conditions, salary structure, fringe benefits, and job security, to name a few. However this concern is expressed, it elicits reactions, i.e., others may respond with enthusiasm or resentment, involvement or apathy, creativity or dull thinking, commitment or indifference, a willingness to take risks or a resistance to change.

How Concerns for Production/People Affect Leadership Style

The concern-for-production and the concern-for-people axes combine in various ways, with each way expressing how an individual thinks about achieving production through people. For example, when a high production concern coexists with a low people concern, the leader is interested only in getting the job done. Opposite to that, when a high concern for people is joined with a low concern for production, the individual seeks to promote harmonious relationships to make others happy. There are numerous other ways in which these two concerns can combine, but seven major theories are crucial for understanding individual differences in how people exercise leadership. Each of these theories or orientations defines a Grid style and represents a unique set of assumptions for using power and authority to link people to production. Figure 2-3 portrays five of these Grid styles.

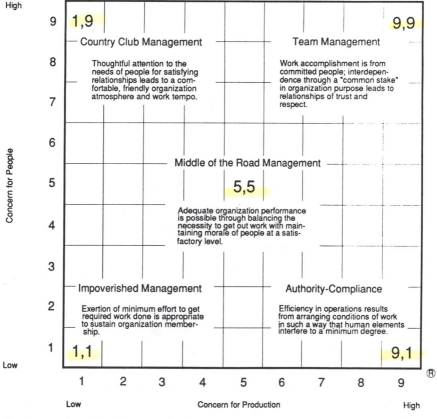

Figure 2-3. The Leadership Grid®. (The Grid® designation is the property of Grid® International, Inc. and is used here with permission.)

Two additional leadership styles are combinations of the first five styles. *Paternalism* (Figure 2-4) is a linking of the production "9" of the 9,1 Grid style and the people "9" of the 1,9 Grid style. An alternative name for paternalism is 9+9 to denote that it is an additive style, combining aspects of two other Grid styles. This is in contrast to the 9,9 Grid style, which is an integration or fusion of the two 9's and quite different from the 9+9 Grid style. The distinction becomes clearer as we explore these two styles in more depth in later chapters.

9+9: Paternalistic Management

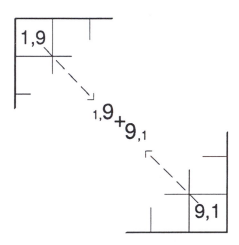

Figure 2-4. In 9+9 paternalistic management, reward and approval are granted to people in return for loyalty and obedience; failure to comply leads to punishment.

The other combination Grid style is *Opportunism* (Figure 2-5), which incorporates several or all of the other Grid styles, including paternalism.

Grid style is a pattern of thinking about or analyzing a situation. Any Grid style is subject to change to another orientation as a result of increased understanding and practice. Thus, an orientation is not a personality characteristic or a fixed trait. The important

Opportunistic Management

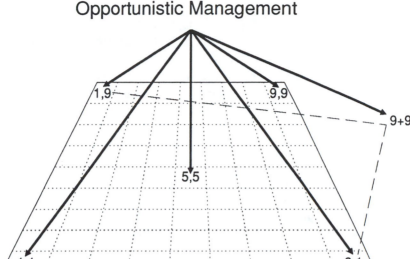

Figure 2-5. In opportunistic management organization performance occurs according to a system of exchanges, whereby effort is given only for an equivalent measure of the same. People adapt to the situation to gain maximum advantage from it.

point is that to increase productivity a leader must be aware of alternative modes of operating, select the soundest approach, and apply the requisite skills to behave in more effective ways in real work situations.

Before we summarize the seven major styles, let's take a closer look at the third dimension, or the motivations underlying Grid styles.

The Motivational Dimension

Grid styles provide guidelines for recognizing the assumptions that guide our behavior. They are a sound basis for self-analysis and for permitting us to see others in more objective terms, permitting us to identify our assumptions and those made by others for how we go about achieving results.

A significant part of our thoughts and feelings about production and people involves the question, "How am I (and others) motivated in life and work?" Up to now, we have had no valid way of sorting these out and of comparing one set of motivations with another. Personal motivations have never been well understood. Thus, it has been difficult to determine how to get people to be more productive. Only when we have a means for understanding what motivates people can we expect to appreciate how leaders, others, and ourselves included, work with one another to get results. By employing sound motivations to lead people we can expect to strengthen production, stimulate creativity, build morale, and make ourselves healthier in mental and physical terms.[13]

The three-dimensional Grid framework provides a basis for understanding personal motivations. With it we can answer the question, "What are the personal motivations of people who operate according to each of the Grid styles?"

This third dimension provides insight into *why* we act as we do by showing us the motivations that exist beneath any Grid style. From this we learn why a person who is oriented in a particular way behaves as he or she does: what the person seeks as a *desirable* situation to promote (the plus motivation) and what he or she *fears* as threatening (the minus motivation). The midpoint of this bipolar axis, the point at which it intersects the Grid, is designated as the neutral or comfort zone where neither a positive nor negative motivation is currently operative. This is where an individual may take his or her behavior for granted; it is almost second nature.

The (+) end of the motivational axis tells us something of what a person feels when the going is smooth and favorable to realizing his or her objectives—the proactive, outgoing, forward-looking point of view. The (−) end tells us what the person is likely to feel when the going is rough, when he or she encounters obstacles that are experienced as threatening. They tend to be defensive behaviors, indicating action that is reactive. The (+) behaviors are unlikely to be observed as characteristic of a person who is in trouble or difficulty and the (−) terms are unlikely to be seen when the going is smooth, positive, or favorable. The situation, in other words, determines that aspect of a Grid style that is prominent at any given time.

The situation, whether favorable or unfavorable, does not determine the basic or primary Grid style. Grid style is what a person brings into whatever situation he or she enters.

9+9: Know-It-All Subordinate

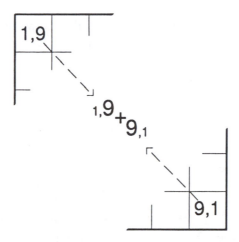

Figure 2-10. The paternalistic subordinate is the simultaneous joining of the 1,9 and 9,1 subordinate Grid styles. It is characterized by the attitude that "I can command the boss's favor by being a confidant and informal advisor. This is helpful because I ensure I know all there is to know about everything and everybody. I am the boss's right hand and lieutenant."

Opportunism: The "Me-First" Subordinate

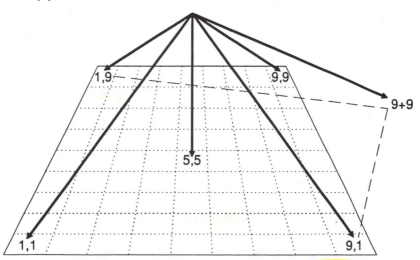

Figure 2-11. The opportunistic subordinate uses all six of the other Grid styles to get ahead. This person's attitude is "I sell myself up and down the line to gain support for getting to the top. I build credit by doing favors that I can call due at a later time. I tailor what I say depending on the person with whom I am dealing."

The 9,1-Oriented Subordinate

The main concern of a 9,1-oriented subordinate is accomplishing the task as he or she defines it. Concern for you, the boss, is minimal.

What are the assumptions of a 9,1-oriented subordinate when interacting with his or her boss? There is a strong desire to tell the boss how a job should be done. Opposition is immediately resisted. If others pose counterarguments, the 9,1-oriented individual is unlikely even to hear them because he or she is busy preparing a counterpoint. The subordinate plays down the points lodged by others and builds up his or her own presentation of the facts. This has a tendency to turn the discussion to a win-lose situation. As a 9,1-oriented subordinate, you are right and "they" are wrong. Period. You are out to prove yourself and nothing else counts. The burden is placed on the other party to present evidence that they have a stronger position but all the while you are discounting whatever they say. When things get hot, talking to you is like talking to a brick wall. You already have your mind made up.

From the story in Chapter 1 we see that for a 9,1-oriented person like Ed, his view towards Al is one of impatient tolerance and is expressed as, "Al's going to try to get me to do it his way but I'll convince him I'm right. I'll tell him that the success of this project is contingent on my being in control. If he wants my full support, he'll back off." The attitude of a 9,1-oriented subordinate in general is, "I'm not going to let *anyone* walk on me!"

The 1,9-Oriented Subordinate

This subordinate has low concern for getting the job done, but still seeks to curry favor with a tough-minded boss because of a desire to please. With a less production-oriented leader, the combination of boss and subordinate is likely to reveal itself in low productivity. Both parties maintain their primary focus on non-work-related activity. Because Dan was a member of a team that operated with a relatively strong production mentality, he tended to stay focused on his share of the work. However, his main preoccupation was maintaining a friendly atmosphere. This is because a 1,9-oriented person considers good working relationships prerequisite to productive effort. Dan's avoidance of conflict and efforts to cover it up impede the team by keeping them from tackling real issues and solving problems that block progress.

Dan's soft qualities of 1,9 show themselves in his interaction with Al. He may not approve of everything Al does, especially when it impacts people adversely, but rarely does he admit it. Dan values togetherness and harmonious relationships. He cowers when Ed enters the room because he is particularly sensitive to the sarcastic and abrasive comments that Ed takes special glee in directing his way. When it comes to situations of disagreement or conflict, the 1,9-oriented subordinate backs down; he or she fears rejection. The objective that this person pursues is to discover what *you* want and then to do it.

The Paternalistic (9 + 9-Oriented) Subordinate

Paternalists have difficulty when cast in a subordinate role because they seek to control rather than be controlled. Because of their subordinate position, however, they cannot dole out reward and punishment to a level above. Patting the boss on the head and saying, "Good boy or girl," is not permissible.

As a result, the basic approach can play itself out in one of two ways. As a paternalistic subordinate, you may embrace and endorse what the boss says. This is likely to win you the role of assistant leader or lieutenant, which enables you to control your colleagues because you have become the boss's right hand. In this capacity you may lead other team members to comply with what the boss wants and thereby demonstrate the extent of your loyalty and dedication. The hidden aspect of this is that you increase the boss's dependence on you, making you an indispensable aspect of his or her leadership. This further heightens your control.

The option to embracing the boss's point of view is to procrastinate and seek delay. This is often what happens when you disagree with the boss's position. Rather than openly contradict and fight with another person, you try to buy time to develop a strategy for bringing the other party over to your way of thinking. To do otherwise might provoke a win-lose contest, and you'd rather not risk being the loser.

Al Jennings is a paternalistic boss. In later chapters we have an opportunity to see him operate in a subordinate position when he interacts with people at headquarters.

The 1,1-Oriented Subordinate

With a low concern for the job (other than to try and keep it) and low concern for the boss, the 1,1 subordinate relies on others to do the work. When interaction is required, it is perfunctory because compliance is easier than resisting.

This individual's major motivation is to find the path of least resistance while at the same time staying out of trouble. To avoid conflict with a boss, this subordinate follows instructions exactly as outlined with a minimum of translation. If things do not work out as planned, it's not the subordinate's responsibility because he or she only did what the boss said to do.

Gil reveals these attitudes from his back seat position on Al's team. He engages in little inquiry as it might relate to team tasks; seldom does he advocate his position on an issue. His main preoccupation is staying out of the line of fire, such as in the argument between Ed and Ben. His tendency in general is to hide in the shadows and in this way to be present but not seen.

The 5,5-Oriented Subordinate

This subordinate expects to be treated in a polite, give-and-take way. Such an individual normally operates on the basis of precedent and protocol, so when the boss outlines how something is to be done, it is assumed that the boss, a person of higher rank, is right. If questions are asked, they tend to be superficial or concerned only with the logistics of implementation. This subordinate feels comfortable with conventional thinking and finds great security in the tried-and-true. If you, as a boss, ask such an individual to launch out in a new direction, the reaction is likely to be one of fear, stemming from the possible embarrassment of taking a wrong step. This person is "lost" when there is no experience by which to gauge effort. Without experience or exposure to others with experience, there is no model to follow. Then, the 5,5-oriented subordinate must depend on the boss for step-by-step instruction. This person is a linear thinker who has no problem with the fact that "do" is followed by "re" is followed by "mi" in a musical scale—but don't try to describe a dynamic process by which the notes come together to form a melody. The subordinate will be dumbfounded as he or she has not yet learned to think in such dynamic terms.

Because desires are rooted in conformity to the norms and values of social groups to which this subordinate belongs—in terms of "what other people think"—it may sometimes be unclear to a boss what this individual is seeking to achieve. Primarily the subordinate wants to be liked, to be popular, while staying within the boundaries of acceptability in order to avoid being different. In looking at the boss, this subordinate seeks to avoid criticism as this can lead to the experience of shame and humiliation.

Liz is a 5,5-oriented subordinate and she relates to Al and her team members in typical 5,5 ways. She values being seen in the "right" places with the "right" people at the "right" times as these enhance her prestige. She seeks to be a balancing influence within the group and to draw others toward a middle-of-the-road way of thinking, but she knows when situations have become polarized and when to back off from forces that she perceives as bigger than herself.

Liz is motivated to avoid extremes and to find a middle ground with which everyone can live. She takes her lead from what others have done in the past as this is seen as the "safe" approach. She is more production-oriented than Dan, but her fear of taking a risk keeps her locked in the status quo.

The Opportunistic Subordinate

Subordinates operating under opportunistic assumptions want to get ahead but without posing a threat to the boss or others.

There is a desire to avoid friction with levels above or to become the target of antagonism from peers. Boss ingratiation is the most common subordinate reaction from an opportunist who sees the boss as a stepping stone to the top. It is not seen as taking unfair advantage of one's colleagues by selling your own best interests to the boss because it is justified on the basis of equal opportunity. However, opportunistic behavior tends to be unethical because such overtures to the boss are made "in private," behind closed doors and on a one-to-one basis. Self-interests are placed at the front of the conversation while the interests of others are seldom represented, and sometimes even misrepresented. The rationalization for doing so is "competitive advantage" based on the assumption that we all look out for ourselves. While this is true to some extent, there is an element of fair play in how what we do impacts others and whether what we do is being done in a straightforward and honest way that presents the full story rather than a vested interest, one-sided rendition of it.

The underlying motivation of an opportunistic subordinate is to gain a personal advantage, but this is rarely made explicit. When it comes to the game of "truth or consequences," the opportunist plays the consequences angle that is most favorable to him- or herself. The subordinate's upward focus doesn't stop with the immediate boss; it continues on up. This is particularly true when the subordinate perceives that his or her boss can no longer serve a useful purpose for getting to the top; then the boss is bypassed altogether in favor of higher levels. We see this more concretely in Frank's behavior in his interactions with headquarters in later chapters.

The 9,9-Oriented Subordinate

A subordinate with a high concern for completing the task in a productive manner coupled with a high concern for those with whom he or she works is accustomed to thinking and acting in an open and honest way. If the boss is not on the same wavelength, the 9,9-oriented subordinate is prepared to exercise leadership to bring the discussion to a problem-solving level. For example, Ben continues to refocus the team problem of poor use of resources despite Al's attempts to distract him and Ed's efforts to negate his words. Ben has a clear sense that Al's team is not able to mobilize the individual talents of its membership to achieve the most productive results. He persists in making the point, particularly to Ed who seems the most blinded to the need for teamwork. Al is reluctant to address the issue and anxious to end the discussion, but Ben does not buckle under. He seeks a commitment that the team will readdress the topic at a later occasion.

The 9,9-oriented subordinate is unwilling to accept limitations as given without a thorough exploration of the facts. Although in a subordinate role, he or she won't condone ineffective boss behavior. Though it is necessary to work to some degree within the confines of protocol (you can't fire your boss!), the 9,9-oriented subordinate persists in establishing a problem-solving atmosphere characterized by open inquiry and critique, confrontation of conflict, active advocacy based on sound convictions, the pursuit of shared goals and objectives, and decision making aimed at finding the soundest solutions to problems. Other people tend to be drawn toward the kind of leadership that characterizes a 9,9-oriented individual and, although the personal Grid styles of others may not shift, the quality of interaction is likely to be 9,9.

You can think of the Subordinate Grid as the other half of the equation. Some combinations of Grid styles—whether between boss and subordinate, or between two colleagues—are compatible in that they are not abrasive to one another. Study the relationship of Dan and Liz in direct contrast to that between Dan and Ed. In the latter case where Grid styles are dissimilar, the result may be that when face-to-face dealings are necessary, one or both of the parties moves to a backup style.

Dominant and Backup Grid Styles

People at work can be characterized by one of these seven major Grid styles, but this doesn't mean we act the same way all of the time. Not at all. A backup style reveals itself in situations where the dominant style cannot be applied or in situations where an individual feels uncertain about operating in the dominant mode. For example, a person may revert to a backup when under pressure, tension, or in situations of conflict that cannot be readily resolved. Alternatively, an individual's dominant style may be present when the stakes are high, but a backup style reveals itself when concern for the outcome is low, under extreme fatigue, when stress is negligible, or when stress is extreme. Sometimes a backup style is a reaction to the Grid style of another person, such as a boss.

Why a particular person reverts to a backup style is unique to that individual. The distinction is that dominant style defines the underlying consistencies in a person's behavior over time. Backup style characterizes the next most consistent behavior, and so on through whatever number of backup styles characterize any given individual.

The following illustrates the connection between dominant and backup styles as a supervisor seeks to deal with a recalcitrant worker. The typical approach of this supervisor may be 9,1 and, in a crisis situation, pressure is applied as the preferred R_2 way of getting results. This particular subordinate resists. No longer able to apply the dominant style in a way that produces results, the supervisor may switch to a backup style, 1,9, making friendly gestures and offering encouragement in the hope that this brings the subordinate around. If the subordinate continues to resist, a third set of assumptions may come into play. The supervisor continues to be friendly, now offering rewards for compliance but also threatening punishment for failure to comply. If the subordinate still persists in opposing the boss, the supervisor may resort to a fourth style, 1,1, withdrawing completely and saying, "What's the use? I'll do it myself." In this example a dominant Grid style and three backup Grid styles were used to deal with a situation. The dominant Grid style characterizes actions most frequently employed, the first backup the next most, and so on.

It is important to remember that the style or styles employed by people at work can be complex. In the preceding example, the first style employed was the dominant style but this is not always the case. Additionally, there is no particular rule for which style may back up any other style. A 1,9-oriented person, for example, may prefer to yield and defer but, when the pressure becomes too great, become stubborn and demanding in a 9,1 way. Alternatively, a leader who seeks domination and control may continue to meet resistance and, as a result, shift to a 9,9 teamwork basis of cooperative problem solving. A dominant-to-backup shift is also observed when an individual works with others in a 9,9 way in routine situations, but then switches to some other style in a time of crisis. This person may shift to a 9,1 backup when uncertain of how to use resources in the most effective way when time is at a premium. The great array of dominant-backup combinations is what makes each individual so unique.

Factors that Influence Dominant Grid Style

Organization Culture. Actually, organization culture is composed of many cultures, encompassing all the relationships of its members. Culture impacts leadership behavior by cultivating or inhibiting the assumptions a person holds. For example, some organizations have strict rules and regulations that suppress an individual's style, perhaps forcing the individual to shift or adapt, or even to leave. In this case the person's Grid style may reflect less of his or her preferred assumptions about how to lead and more about organization beliefs regarding ''the way we do things.''

Values. A person's assumptions are consistent with his or her values, beliefs, or ideals regarding the way to treat people or the way to achieve results. Every Grid style has corresponding values attached to it. For example, the 9,1 Grid style values results. The 9,9 Grid style values results through motivated and fulfilled people. What a person values influences dominant Grid style.

Personal History. A person's dominant Grid style may, to an important degree, result from deep-rooted personal history. An individual may be predisposed to one approach over another as a result of early training. In other words, because of life experiences, a particular Grid style may be employed repeatedly until it becomes the dominant style.

No Awareness of Options. Usually our behavior is guided by assumptions that we adopted earlier in our lives without considering the consequences that such behavior might bring. Indeed, our belief systems at that time told us this was the right choice. In the present context they may be anything but sound, yet until we discover new sets of assumptions by which to act, our dominant behavior continues to be governed by antiquated rules.

The Grid permits us to describe attitudes and behavior. It is not a psychological assessment or evaluative mechanism; nor is it intended to categorize individuals or to place them in "slots." No individual consistently adheres to a single Grid style. Rather, people adopt different approaches or display different levels of concern at various times, and the dominant/backup formulation provides meaning to the range of assumptions a person may hold.

Another question frequently asked is whether there exists a relationship between an individual's intelligence (IQ) and the dominant Grid style. No clear correlation exists. A 1,9-oriented or a 1,1-oriented individual is not necessarily less intelligent than a person oriented in a 9,1 or 9,9 way. Suffice it to say that the Grid is a set of theories about how people *use* their intelligence and skills in working with and through others to achieve results. The significance of this issue, however, is that Grid styles truly extend our ability to see ourselves and others in terms no less important than formulations such as IQ.

The Grid gives meaning to what we do day in and day out. Once we can gain insight into our own dominant and backup Grid styles, the first step has been taken for introducing whatever changes are needed to strengthen personal effectiveness on the job.

The Benefits of Putting the Grid to Work

Numerous benefits are to be derived from using the Grid framework as a conceptual foundation on which to build leadership excellence:

Comprehensive. The Grid framework identifies all significant approaches for working with and through others in an organization.

Comparative. Grid theories permit comparison of similarities and differences of each approach to working with people. We can contrast how effective our current approach is with alternative ways of dealing with people. If more effective ways to operate are found to exist, we may be motivated to change.

Consequences. The Grid permits evaluation of the consequences of our actions in terms of productivity, creativity, career success, our own satisfaction and the satisfaction of those with whom we work, and health. We can then ask ourselves if these are the consequences we want or if alternative approaches offer sounder consequences.

Subjective Appraisal. The Grid is a self-convincing approach that permits you to draw personal conclusions for yourself as to what constitutes effective leadership. It is not our intent to prescribe to you how you should operate. On the basis of insight into the alternative ways in which people operate and an examination of each of these behaviors you can select the soundest approach for working with and through other people.

Objective Evidence. Fifty years of research on leadership style and operational consequences provide a basis of empirical assessment of the validity of the 9,9 orientation in comparison with others[14,15], thus providing an independent source of confirmation. Numerous examples of independent research in this area abound. This is elaborated in a recent study by van de Vliert[16].

Shared Concepts and Language. Because the Grid provides a standard language for thinking about and discussing leadership, it promotes discussion among organization members about how leadership should most effectively be exercised.

Organization Development. The Grid provides a basic model for developing an organization into a system characterized by effective leadership that stimulates sound participation-based teamwork throughout its membership. It permits us to examine the R_1-R_2-R_3 connections and enables us to improve what we are doing in the arena of relationships in order to maximize the use of our resources to achieve the best results possible.

Useful for Selection, Development, and Performance Appraisal. Once understood, the Grid can be used not only for the exercise of leadership but as the basis for selecting, developing, and evaluating people. It provides a comprehensive framework for an integrated system of human resource utilization.

Wide Applicability. A Grid framework is applicable to any situation for achieving results with and through people. Several examples include:

- ☐ Pertinence wherever work occurs in business, industry, government, education, or human service organizations.
- ☐ Constructive use by persons of any technical background, at any organization level, at any level of experience. It is equally pertinent in high tech as in low tech business environments.
- ☐ Applicability to organizations of any size because sound leadership is the same whether exercised in a small, medium, or large organization.
- ☐ The "culture-free" quality of the Grid and its utility for strengthening problem-solving leadership across companies that operate around the globe.
- ☐ Pertinence for understanding personal relationships such as those that occur in family life, child rearing, and other community settings; that is, wherever problems arise that need resolution with and through others.

Are there limitations in using the Grid? Our answer would be, "Only in terms of people's preconceived notions." Some people think that self-learning or trying to teach and coach others to be an effective leader or resource is an impossible task; others subscribe to the school that says you either have "it" (leadership ability) or you don't. Still others profess that you just can't teach an old dog new tricks. All of these beliefs rest on false assumptions about human learning.

People can and do change. The significant aspect about the Grid is its comparative approach, allowing those who learn it to envision both effective and ineffective ways of working. It is this contrast—or the "gap" created between an actual situation and what can, with theory, be seen as an ideal situation—that creates the motivation for change. Once people gain an objective awareness of how they are using their R_1 resources to get R_3 results, they can focus on what needs to happen to improve how they operate in the realm of R_2.

Summary

The Grid helps us identify the assumptions underlying our behavior as we work with others to achieve organization purpose. By using theories to identify our unique assumptions, we come to see ourselves and others more objectively; we learn to communicate more clearly and to understand where our disagreements come from; we discover how to change ourselves and to help others have more productive and rewarding experiences at the same time. The more skilled a leader is in using sound theory, the more capable that person becomes in reducing frustration, resentment, and other negative emotions. The shift away from these feelings toward enthusiasm and dedication promotes a sense of contribution, reward, and feelings of personal fulfillment.

The Subordinate Grid provides the full picture, completing the relationship by adding the Grid style of the other person with whom we are interacting. Additionally, dominant and backup Grid styles add depth and serve to explain the range of assumptions that make every individual distinctive.

Now we turn to a closer examination of each of the individual Grid styles. As you read through the chapters that follow and consider the different characters in our story, you may have difficulty distinguishing between similar instances of behavior.

Ask yourself, "What motivational scale best fits the whole person?" The apparently similar behavior sorts itself out because you begin to recognize the key distinction: *why* the person is doing what he or she is doing. Motivation analysis allows you to get beneath the surface and see through similarities for what the behavior really means.

We'll start by taking another look at Ed Jackson, the 9,1-oriented member of Al's team.

Chapter 3

9,1: "Nice Guys Finish Last!"

The team meeting had just drawn to a close. Several of the members stayed to chat while others gathered their belongings and headed in different directions.

Ben closed his notebook and started to walk toward the door. Liz, who had been talking with Gil, moved to Dan's side and started a conversation. They laughed as they reminisced over the last company barbecue. Initiating these monthly off-hour employee gatherings had been a pet project of Al's and was administered in large part by Dan. Al loved the camaraderie and fellowship. Ben's reaction was that such sociality may have contributed to improved employee morale but did little by way of solving deeper organization problems. Ben's dilemma with the gatherings was his feeling that they tended to keep people from seeing the big picture, leaving Al as the sole person to mastermind a solution. Ed thought the whole thing a waste of time and had yet to attend one of these parties; in his opinion, company outings were just an excuse for taking people's minds off their work. Privately, Frank felt the same way, but publicly, he embraced Al's initiative.

Ben had started down the hall when Ed called out, "Wait up a minute!"

Ben turned and smiled. "I was just about to grab a bite of lunch, Ed. Why don't you join me?"

Ed looked at his watch. "I've got quite a bit of work to do. These meetings certainly take a lot of time. I don't understand why Al feels compelled to meet so much. No wonder we have problems with productivity! How are we ever supposed to get real work done!"

"You still have to eat," laughed Ben. "Come on down and get a sandwich. By the way, what were you and Liz saying to Gil?"

"Oh, nothing," Ed grumbled. "That guy is really asleep at the switch!"

Ben didn't react and Ed wasn't interested in expending any more time on the subject of Gil. Ben continued, "Well, what's on your mind then?"

"It's what I said in the meeting," stated Ed. "You're part of the movement, too."

"What movement?" asked Ben.

"All this participation nonsense means one thing to me," replied Ed, "a lot of talk, talk, talk that goes nowhere. You're pretty sharp and it strikes me that you've got an eye for results. But, I have a hard time figuring you out. You leave the rest of the gang behind when it comes to brains and talent. So why waste your time hashing out the issues, I mean, when you already know the best way to go?"

"Only because I'm smart enough to know that I'm not that smart," laughed Ben.

"Come on, don't be so modest," chided Ed. "You might as well take credit when it's due."

"That's not it," replied Ben. "It's just that I've learned a lot by being open to the thinking of others. Getting alternative points of view permits me to test and evaluate the soundness of my own thinking. More than once I've been made aware of some factors I was failing to consider. Know what I mean?" Ed looked blank and Ben continued. "At any rate I feel more confident that I'm moving in the right direction when I hear how others think about the issues. Furthermore, I gain their support to the final decision."

"Come off it! It's a waste of time. I'll grant that you may win people over to your point of view, but is it really worth the effort? Cost and benefits, Ben!" Ed continued, "Deep down, what people really want is to be given the word, to be told what to do. It's much simpler for everyone. After all, it's a clear-cut separation of roles. I say; they do."

Ben smiled and shook his head. "Ed, I think you and I are operating according to two different outlooks. You see some inherent contradiction between the needs of production and the needs of people. I don't. In fact, I believe the soundest results come from working *with* people, and in doing so, getting their creative thinking, involvement, and commitment in achieving the results for which we're all responsible."

"I'll tell you what's wrong with your argument," Ed said frankly. "First of all, I can't trust people with that kind of responsibility. You know, I'm accountable for the final results. It's my neck that's on the line. If you think I'm going to leave it up to a bunch of new kids, you've got another thing coming. It's imperative that I stay in control of my operation. That's the only way I can be sure things are going to come out right.''

''Maybe right, maybe not,'' chuckled Ben. ''When you *are* right, that approach may work okay, at least in terms of the decision being sound. But how dedicated are your people to doing what you tell them? They may do it because you're the boss, but with what amount of commitment? You see, you keep tight control of the solution and, as a result, they feel no ownership. Rarely do you listen to what they have to say. That brings me to the second possibility. What happens when you're wrong? What happens when you *don't* have all the facts?''

Ed's face turned white. Then he said, ''What do you mean?''

''Look,'' said Ben. ''Let me describe my own situation. There are times when, no matter how hard I try, I simply don't know everything I need to know to make the best possible decision. I *have to* rely on the resources of others. It's more than that. I want to be aware of others' thinking, including their doubts and reservations, to make sure that I'm not exercising poor judgment.''

''Ben, Ben, Ben!'' exclaimed Ed. ''Who's the boss here, you or the people you manage? It sounds like you've relinquished all authority. Now, I ask you, what kind of leadership is that?''

''I'm not giving up authority,'' replied Ben. ''I'm still the head of my team and responsible for results. What it is, though, is leadership based on using all the resources that are available so that the best decisions possible can be made. That's not saying I won't make the final decision. I do. And there aren't any guarantees that I don't make mistakes. I do make mistakes, but the odds are in my favor that I'll come out ahead. Furthermore, if I choose to go in a different direction, my people know that I listened to what they had to say before I took that action. In other words, they know I didn't walk into a situation blind. Finally, there's always critique to keep us on target or get us back on track when things go wrong or seem less than sound.''

''Oh, no,'' groaned Ed. ''There's that word again. 'Critique.' That's a waste of time if I ever heard of one.''

''I disagree with you on that,'' Ben said sternly. ''In my opinion critique is about the *only* learning tool we have after we leave college and the textbooks. How do you figure out what's going on if you only listen to yourself or, worse yet, if you only hear your own rationalizations? How can you learn from experience if you shut out feedback?"

"If I took the time to listen to all the nonsense that other people have to say, I wouldn't get anything done," Ed replied coolly. "It's more important to be decisive, to take action, and to get the job done. I'll know if I was wrong if I get bad results, which, by the way, I don't plan on doing. Being decisive is what they pay me for, you know."

"You didn't answer my question," said Ben. "What happens when you're wrong? What happens when you do get bad results and those bad results spell disaster?"

Ed looked somber. He took a deep breath and answered slowly. "I haven't been wrong yet, have I? And like I said I don't plan to be."

"What about that last transfer shipment?" Ben couldn't restrain himself any longer.

"That wasn't my fault! You go check with Engineering. They're to blame and I got Gil to admit it!"

"Okay, settle down," said Ben.

"Don't worry about me! I'm fine. But I meant what I said. Mistakes aren't a part of my game plan. That's why it's important to stay on top of things. The last thing I want to do is get caught short. You see, I make sure I have *all* the information. Then I don't need to depend on others for critical data. Other people implement my decisions. That's what *they* get paid for. I keep a close eye on everything that's happening—you can be sure of that!"

Ben shrugged his shoulders. "Have it your way. You'll have to be convinced that there's a better way to work with people before you'll be willing to change."

"That'll be the day," chuckled Ed.

They arrived at the cafeteria. Ben turned to Ed and said, "Are you going to join me?"

"No, thanks," replied Ed. "I need to get back to my office. I've got a few heads to crack before the day's over."

"What do you mean?" asked Ben.

"Oh, nothing," said Ed. "Just a few problems but nothing I can't handle. It's like I said. You just can't turn your back on subordinates. Give a little and they'll take a lot. Pretty soon the whole operation is out of control."

"Does this have to do with our last project?" queried Ben.

"Well, to some extent," responded Ed. "Actually it has to do with my remark about us getting lucky. There were a few, . . . hmmm, minor problems in my department involved in that deal. Even though everything turned out all right this time, I want to make sure they don't happen again. There's one fellow who's on the top of my list and he's going to get it. Besides, that's the way to get other people to notice. They'll snap into line. Just mark my words!''

Ben studied Ed's expression closely. He sadly shook his head. Ed still didn't have the problem of productivity in focus because he just didn't know how to work *with and through* people; all he knew how to do was *push.*

"Well," said Ben, "I've enjoyed our conversation, impasses and all. You're not exactly in my corner but at least you make yourself clear. See you later."

"Yeah, later," said Ed as he strolled off down the hall.

□ □ □

Ed is a 9,1-oriented manager—high concern for production and little concern for people. You can see this Grid style illustrated in the lower right-hand corner of the Grid, as shown in Figure 3-1.

The 9,1 leadership style rests on the assumption that there is an inherent contradiction between the organization's need for results and the needs of people. Therefore, the latter is sacrificed in order to achieve the former. The other belief is that production objectives can only be met when people are controlled and directed in a way that compels them to complete the necessary tasks. A 9,1-oriented manager like Ed is an exacting taskmaster who already knows how to get the job done. There is one single-minded and short-term purpose and that lies in achieving results. The tendency is toward an R_3 tunnel vision.

Work is arranged in such a way as to eliminate the need for subordinates to think. Close supervision prevents these "human elements" from interfering with complete and efficient accomplishment of the task. When people do as they are told, results can be

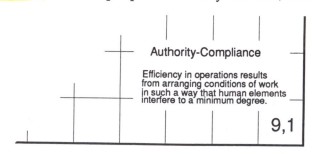

Figure 3-1. The 9,1 Grid style is located in the lower right corner of the Grid.

achieved without wasting time to solve conflicts and disagreements. The 9,1 motto can be summed up as "produce or perish."

A person with a 9,1 managerial orientation is likely to be committed to the task to the exclusion of people considerations. Such an individual drives him- or herself and others in the interest of results. Subordinates are employed to carry out the boss's dictates.

Examine the 9,1-oriented manager from a different angle. Think of every organization member as having 100% of the resources needed to contribute to the effort. Unfortunately, many people only deliver a limited amount of this potential power. How can we explain this, especially in the case of a person who is driven to succeed?

One limitation on full delivery of R_1 resources into R_3 results lies in how other people respond to our behavior, or Grid style. A Grid style like 9,1 is unlikely to elicit the cooperation, involvement, or commitment of those who are expected to complete the task. This is why Grid style is so important. Basic assumptions about *how* to deliver the resources you have to corporate interests may not be what is needed to solve existing problems. When problems arise in a boss-subordinate relationship, R_2, the boss's Grid style may prevent delivery of results even though the resources are there.

Motivations

Why does a 9,1-oriented manager exercise leadership this way? The 9,1 motivational scale provides an answer. As seen in Figure 3-2, this bipolar scale runs through the Grid perpendicularly at the 9,1 corner. The point on the motivational scale that intersects the Grid is the neutral zone where neither positive nor negative motivation is evident.

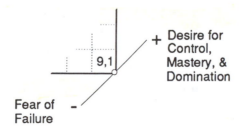

Figure 3-2. The plus and minus motivations of the 9,1 Grid style.

The plus end of the motivational scale—what a 9,1-oriented person strives for in work—is ''desire for control, mastery, and domination.'' Individuals motivated in this way seek to exercise direct control over the people and situations for which they are responsible. Remember Ed's comment: ''We really need to tighten up the ranks.'' He doesn't want to leave anything to chance, and leaving things up to other people is, in Ed's mind, doing just this.

A strong ''desire'' means that the person directed in a 9,1 way has the urge to tell others not only how everything is to be done, but also when, where, and by whom, sometimes down to the last detail. When this condition is satisfied, the 9,1$^+$-oriented person feels proud of a job well done because nothing has been left up to someone else's discretion, someone who might mess things up. Seldom does such an individual bother to provide background reasoning or rationale to subordinates because concern for people is low. There is no justification for wasting time talking to ''the doers.'' Giving them the necessary orders is enough. ''Why explain details that are not an essential part of the task itself? Who cares if they understand? That's not their job!''

A 9,1$^+$-oriented leader's sense of strength comes from feeling powerful, submitting to nothing and no one, gaining unquestioned compliance from subordinates. Control is key. Recall how Ed talked about subordinates. He likes to feel in complete control. He remarked to Ben that, ''You just can't turn your back on subordinates. Give them a little and they'll take a lot. Pretty soon the whole operation's out of control.''

A 9,1-oriented leader is hardworking, prepared to spend whatever time it takes to grapple with problems that lie in his or her domain. The emphasis is on willpower exercised by an inflexible determination to master, control, and dominate. To do this, it may be necessary to tell subordinates, ''Do it or else.'' When production is on track, this person feels in charge. Appreciation of others is scant or nonexistent.

A leader oriented in a 9,1 way has little use for the suggestions, recommendations, advice, or guidance of others. If information is required, it is requested point blank, often on a ''yes''/''no'' basis. The idea is to quiz people for the information you need, making it appear to be more of a ''test'' for them than a lack of details on your part. When it comes to making final decisions, the goal is to rely on no one.

The 9,1 attitude toward the accumulation of money or other external indicators of power is, "The more I have, the better." But it goes a lot further than that. It is important for a 9,1-directed person to feel in complete control over everything that lies within reach. Approving spending authorizations, signing paychecks, double-checking performance evaluations, or managing direct reports are all ways of acquiring control over others. However, in time, the accumulation of control may so overload the 9,1-oriented individual that it becomes self-defeating. Rather than gaining the mastery and domination that is sought, it may lead to this leader's eventual downfall.

That brings us to the minus end of the motivational scale, which represents what a 9,1-oriented manager most fears—failure. Whether perceived or real, this is to be avoided at all costs. For a 9,1-oriented person, "fear of failure" translates to personal inadequacy. Experiencing failure causes such a person to feel unworthy, no good, incompetent. The thoughts that come to mind are, "How could I have been such a fool!" or "I'm a real loser! How could I be so dumb!" Morale plummets. The desire is to escape rather than face reality. The 9,1⁻ side of Ed was apparent when he blanched at Ben's remark about possible failure. This is Ed's greatest fear and his only defense was, "I haven't been wrong yet, have I?"

Feelings of mastery, control, and domination are replaced by anxiety and distress when failure does occur. The first reaction is to deny it by finding a scapegoat. In other words, blame for failure is placed on colleagues and subordinates, even bosses, leading to, "Next time I'll watch them more closely." The general conclusion is, "I am the reason for my successes; failure is caused by the actions of others. You just can't trust other people." Ed's reaction to Ben's remark about the last transfer shipment was immediate finger pointing: "That wasn't my fault! You go check with Engineering. They're to blame and I got Gil to admit it!"

Another by-product of 9,1⁻ is anger. This is when the 9,1-directed manager is "on the warpath," stalking the halls in search of an available target. The attitude becomes, "You can't get anywhere in life without a fight." As a result, such a manager runs roughshod over people.

What about activities in between, around the zero point? These are neutral, not particularly indicative of self-worth, one way or another. The neutral zone represents an equilibrium between the plus and minus poles.

The 9,1 corner of the Grid gains a fuller meaning when you consider the plus and minus ends simultaneously. The motivations fit and explain the basic assumption that, "Efficiency in operations results from arranging conditions of work so that human elements interfere to a minimum degree." This common denominator provides insight into why the 9,1-oriented person goes about daily activities as he or she does. These assumptions, of which the individual may or may not be aware even though they comprise the core of thinking about self and others, provide a basis for understanding the convictions of a 9,1-oriented leader.

When a 9,1 orientation spreads throughout an organization, it can produce an atmosphere similar to a guard-prisoner culture. This mentality leads to conditions of suspicion and distrust. Subordinates may salute the boss, saying "yes" when they really mean "no." The main idea is not to get caught doing anything wrong. This means that people begin to act in a closed and hidden way, not revealing their underlying thoughts and feelings and seeking to cover their tracks so that no possible mistake can be pinned on them. As a result, it becomes even more important to the manager directed in a 9,1 way to be vigilant and alert as to what is occurring in order to avoid errors. It may become necessary, as was the case with Ed, to single out a suspect employee for termination to set an example for others of what happens to those who dare to disobey. Such an atmosphere of management by fear and threat is unlikely to engender an organization culture that motivates employees to achieve high-quality results.

Conflict Solving

There are many ways a 9,1-oriented manager seeks to anticipate and short circuit conflict. Once a decision is made, it is communicated to subordinates for implementation. This may be done by saying, "Here's what I want you to do and how I want you to do it and you'd better get it right."

Conflict is seen as a threat to managerial control. The desired approach to dealing with it is to nip it in the bud or, should it blossom, to suppress it by beating others into compliance. Let's go back to Ed for a minute. He's told Ben that one of his employees is "going to get it." Here's what happens.

Ed stomps up behind his unsuspecting subordinate, "Phil, I want to talk to you, now!"

Phil does an about face. "Yes, sir, right away." Phil quickly hangs up the phone without even saying good-bye to the party at the other end. "What's up?"

"It's about that last report you turned in. I don't think the data's accurate and there are places that are incomplete. What do you have to say?"

"I'm sorry," stammers Phil. "It's not all my fault. Helen helped me with the research. She's partly responsible."

"No, you're responsible! When I ask you to do something, I expect you to follow orders. If you choose to delegate it to someone less competent than yourself, that's your problem. It doesn't let you off the hook."

"I promise it won't happen again . . ." pleads Phil.

"It better not!" Ed barks. "I'm putting you on probation and I'll be keeping a close eye on you!" With that, Ed turns on his heel and leaves the room before Phil, the flustered subordinate, can utter another word.

The negative side of 9,1 conflict solving is evident in the previous exchange where Phil, the subordinate, is denied any right to defend himself. Ed feels his authority has been undermined by Phil taking independent initiative. Such activity must be curtailed because it threatens Ed's 9,1 control not only over Phil but over Helen and others as well. Ed doesn't want to hear Phil's explanations. The 9,1 attitude is "I don't want excuses; I want results!"

Preventing Conflict

Instructions may be given a step at a time. It is presumed that this approach decreases the likelihood of confusion or error. Furthermore, it means that the 9,1-oriented leader is the only one with an overview of the entire project. This limits the potential for others having enough information to deliberate alternative ways of doing things. By keeping attention focused on the bare essentials, the leader hopes to eliminate questions. Even if the 9,1-oriented boss asks, "Do you understand?" the expected reply is "Yes." When subordinates don't understand, they have learned it is better to pretend that they do and to figure it out on their own.

Handling Conflict When It Appears

While such one-way supervision and step-by-step instructions are calculated to eliminate disagreement, this approach is not sufficient to eliminate conflict.

Conflict is a significant factor in organization life and is potentially present whenever two or more people interact. There are healthy and unhealthy ways of dealing with it. If handled poorly, it can be destructive to the people and to the organization. Figure 3-3 illustrates two contradictory points of view, with one person represented by vertical lines on an arrow pointing down and another by horizontal lines on an arrow pointing up. The solution the leader wants in this situation for dealing with a problem is a vertical one, represented by a half circle with vertical lines. The leader sees this as the most effective

How Is Conflict Resolved?

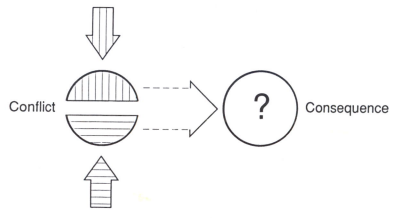

Figure 3-3. Two contradictory viewpoints result in conflict. The consequences of that conflict depend on Grid style.

way of dealing with the issue in question. The other person thinks a horizontal solution is the more effective approach, represented by a half circle with horizontal lines. Obviously, both vertical and horizontal solutions cannot be implemented simultaneously. One or the other or some third possibility must prevail, depending on how the leader exercises power and authority. The circle at the right of the figure represents the consequence of this interaction. The outcome is contingent upon how the conflict is managed.

Because a 9,1-oriented leader is likely to view disagreement as insubordination, the approach to resolving conflict is to suppress it by rejecting counterarguments as unacceptable and forcing his or her view onto others. This may lead to a fight, as illustrated in Figure 3-4.

Any difference of opinion constitutes a challenge. A 9,1+-oriented manager personalizes conflict by saying, "You think I'm wrong," not "You think that my position is wrong." It is difficult for this boss to distinguish between the issue at hand and the resulting ill feelings toward the disagreeing party.

A 9,1-oriented manager seeks to end the conflict by proving the opponent wrong. The approach is to win by forcing others to back off. All that matters is winning by showing who's in control; being liked by others is beside the point. The fact that adversaries may feel frustrated or degraded is irrelevant.

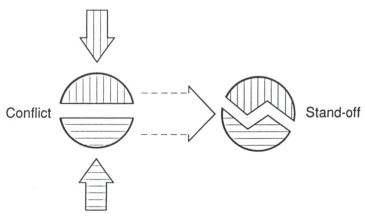

Figure 3-4. The 9,1-oriented approach to conflict results in win/lose fighting when the opponent resists. The outcome may be a stand-off.

If the subordinate continues to resist, counterattack ensues, revealing itself either as a well-intended protest or as "anti-organization" creativity in which subordinates consciously seek to sabotage some aspect of operations. Obviously, the latter is not carried out in the open. This might involve a shipment of poor quality where the culprit cannot be identified, the breakdown of equipment due to tampering, or no more than the "failure" of someone to tighten a screw. Slowdowns and foot-dragging are other typical responses designed to deny 9,1-oriented managers their objectives.

When agreement is not forthcoming, the 9,1-oriented leader uses rank and tells the subordinate, "I say vertical. You say horizontal. I have the final word. Vertical is it. Now do it, or else!" This is suppression, as shown in Figure 3-5.

Fear of failure to stay in control leads to management by fear and threat. Believing that rank is power permits a leader to act in an arbitrary manner. Subordinates are told what to do and expected to comply, no questions asked. Whether they continue privately to disagree is beside the point. "What you think is your business. What you do is my business." This describes the case of Ed and the disobedient subordinate. Suppression is a powerful means of extracting compliance and is widely practiced, driven by the leader's 9,1− fear of failure and caused by a perceived loss of direction and control.

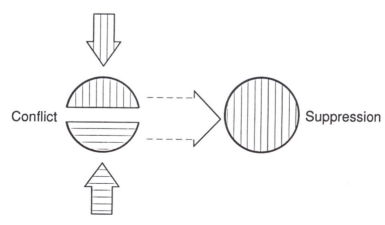

Conflict   Suppression

Figure 3-5. In 9,1-oriented conflict solving counterargument is suppressed and leader thinking prevails.

A 9,1-oriented boss uses threats to bring a subordinate back in line. If this fails, punishment is the result. Punishment may be indirect, for example, neglecting to invite a person to an important meeting or leaving someone's name off the list to receive an urgent memo. Transfer to another location is a second way for dealing with insubordination. Other forms of retribution include solutions as obvious as demotion or termination or less obvious alternatives such as assignment to unpleasant tasks or undesirable shifts. In any case these strategies are intended to bring an end to conflict and to eliminate those who fail to comply.

Another approach to gain compliance is to undermine an opponent's sense of confidence. By belittling a person or raising doubts about his or her ideas, even good ones, a 9,1-oriented person creates such an obstacle that the advocate is likely to lose faith and give up. For example, dogmatic, flat statements such as "You don't know what you're talking about," "That won't work," or "You'd be a fool to try that," are ways of bringing someone into line. The use of hard-hitting humor and sarcasm can also be used to suppress an adversary. This kind of humor carries a sting.

Several side effects may arise that were not anticipated by the 9,1-oriented manager. For example, the message that subordinates hear is that the boss has no confidence in them. Thus, they are reluctant to act responsibly on their own initiative. Creativity and initiative are stifled and potential contributions to the organization are lost.

The mistaken notion of a 9,1-oriented boss is that when disagreement is suppressed, so too is resistance. While suppression may settle the disagreement, it is unlikely the subordinate is convinced that the boss is right. A person's convictions are seldom altered by forced compliance. Therefore, suppressing disagreement is likely to result in information being withheld which in turn may lead to failure for the boss.

When Conflict Remains

Because of the resentment and resistance that suppression and losing in win-lose fights provokes, people either "go underground" to continue the crusade for their position or rely on other strategies, such as withholding cooperation. The 9,1-oriented leader may then try to reduce the intensity of conflict by indirect means.

Motivations and approaches to conflict solving shape how a 9,1-oriented person exercises leadership in the daily work of an organization. These influences are evident in the way this individual deals with the other elements of leadership.

Initiative

Giving directions is nothing short of unilateral exercise of initiative. It means telling others to do something, to stop doing something or to do something in a different way. The word for initiative in the 9,1 context is "hard-driving," i.e., "I drive myself and others."

How a 9,1-oriented manager exercises initiative is shown in the following conversation between Ed and his subordinate, Phil. We have turned the clock back to an episode that occurred prior to Phil's scolding.

"Phil, this is a critical project. I need this report as soon as possible. You know from previous tasks what I expect."

Phil responds, "I just had a thought. There are several others in our group who might be able to contribute something. I was thinking about Don and Helen. Any objections to my pulling them in?"

Ed glares at Phil and replies, "Did you hear me ask for your advice? If I wanted them working on it, I would have asked them instead. I asked you! Now, do I have to tell you again or are you going to do it my way?"

Phil has been shut out and he knows it.

This manner of exercising initiative rests on three shaky assumptions:

1. I already know the best way to undertake this task.
2. Asking for help would be seen as "weak" by others.
3. People operate better when you tell them what to do.

Operating by these assumptions may work in some cases. There are people who have lived in a 9,1 reign of tight control for so long that they have adopted the role of compliant followers. They ceased thinking or acting autonomously years ago. The last thing they want is responsibility. Therefore 9,1 leadership is embraced. In a sense, they have become good soldiers, willing to execute commands, but nothing more. This can result in a "weak" organization, vulnerable both to internal and external attack.

Ed's positive motivation for initiative can be summed up in the statement: "I control what happens by being on the spot and imposing my will on every situation." His negative motivation is revealed in: "I introduce a new activity only after I can assure myself that it will be successful." An example of the latter is a concern that often preoccupies Ed when he is contemplating a new venture: "This is a risky proposition. I can't afford a flop. Headquarters is watching my department closely. I need to keep my record flawless if I want to move up. I think I'll sit on this one for a while until I can get more data." It is not that a 9,1-oriented individual is afraid to take a risk; many successful entrepreneurs have come from a 9,1 orientation. The point is that there must be something to back up the wisdom of every action—for some, this may lie in facts and logic; for others it stems from gut intuition. In either case, it has the quality of one-alone initiative.

Inquiry

The phrase "knowledge is power" aptly describes knowledge as one of the important tools for exercising domination, mastery, and control.

Questions are one way of acquiring knowledge about operating situations; a person like Ed may interrupt and interrogate, taking little at face value. Questions are direct and limited to factual information. Numbers, volume, whether tasks are on schedule and up to specifications are the information sought; thoughts, opinions, feelings, or recommendations are not. "Just give me the facts." In this way, the 9,1-oriented leader retains the right to cross-examine, evaluate, and interpret. This decreases the need to acknowledge contribution on the part of others and allows the boss to take full responsibility.

Subordinates may regard such questions with suspicion. They know the 9,1-directed leader is in hot pursuit of problems, errors, failures, or weaknesses in trying to pin the one who "did it" to the wall. Naturally subordinates become very careful and guarded about how they respond. If the 9,1-oriented leader fails to get the information required by direct means, a trap may be laid by posing a leading question. No matter how the subordinate replies, trouble ensues.

Ed has just left Phil's office after reprimanding him. He marches down the hall and spots Helen walking into her office. Still angry about the fact that Phil took Helen away from other duties against his direct orders, Ed decides to ascertain the extent of her involvement in working on the report. However, he doesn't do this in a straightforward manner; rather, he sets a trap.

"Helen, catch me up on things. What have you been doing?"

Helen knows this is a loaded question. She pauses, carefully weighing her words. "Well, I finished the quarterly report and put it on your desk the end of last week. Didn't you see it?"

"Yes, of course. What about the stat study? Haven't you finished that yet?"

"I'm still working on it. I should get it done this week."

Ed squinted his eyes a bit and said, "I'm surprised it's taking you so long. Is that it? Anything else?"

Helen searches her memory. "No, I believe that's all."

"What about that report I had Phil working on? Someone mentioned you were involved in that."

"I forgot," Helen says, biting her lip. She has been afraid this might lead to trouble. "Yes, Phil did ask me to run up some numbers for him."

This is exactly the response Ed has been waiting for. Now the tone of voice becomes accusative. "Helen, you know that when I assign work I do it directly. Now, tell me, did I ask you to work on that assignment with Phil or did I ask you to complete a statistical analysis for me? I could have sworn it was the latter. Which one of us needs memory lessons?"

Helen's cheeks turn scarlet and she lowers her head. "I was only trying to help. Phil said it was important . . ."

Ed barks, "Next time someone asks you to do something, ask yourself just how important this job is to you. You take your orders from me! Is that clear?"

Such a question is not really intended to promote problem solving but instead to pin the victim. If Helen volunteers the fact that she was doing something other than instructed, she's in trouble. On the other hand, if she doesn't, she's in trouble. It's a no-win proposition; she's been "caught." If she balks, she's made aware that it could cost her the job.

A 9,1-oriented boss's inquiry is based on defensive listening and constant probing for indications of trouble. This is easy to understand when we remember that this boss dreads failure and therefore feels compelled to stay on guard to prevent its occurrence. In the situation with Helen, Ed can now use this episode as a justification for increased surveillance, and Helen knows it. Often a kind of tunnel vision occurs with the 9,1-oriented individual so focused on a single event that other critical information isn't heard. The leader becomes "deaf" to available input that might lead to a more successful conclusion.

Ed's credo is: "I investigate whatever I'm responsible for to the fullest, and I avoid being caught off guard by not having the facts."

Advocacy

A 9,1-oriented person lets others know exactly where he or she stands on any issue. This individual "says it like it is," no holds barred.

Things are black and white—no in-betweens. "Absolute" statements that convey the notion "always," "never," "impossible," or "everyone" are the rule rather than the exception. Convictions are not expressed in a way that invites discussion. Tentativeness is viewed as a sign of uncertainty. Alternative possibilities or counterarguments are resisted even when this means marshalling evidence that belies the facts. Other people have difficulty getting a word in edgewise.

The reaction to 9,1 advocacy is often, "What's the use? Why beat my head against a stone wall?" This means the benefits possible from exchanging viewpoints are lost, and the 9,1-oriented leader may sacrifice good results while being unaware of doing so. However, if someone confronted the person with that fact, it would immediately be rejected. The rationalization would be that people just aren't doing what they're told but it would not be attributed to problems in the domain of R_2.

Ed's position on advocacy is characterized in the following: "I take positions that stick regarding how things are to be done. I make sure others can't challenge me on what I say. I belittle other viewpoints to cast doubt on their validity."

Decision Making

A 9,1-oriented leader says, "I place high value on making my own decisions and I am rarely influenced by others." This approach comes from the belief that the leader alone has the required R_1 resources, whether that entails knowledge, experience, or authority. Others are unlikely to be consulted beforehand and are involved only in terms of carrying out the decision.

For a fuller picture of 9,1 decision making, let's take another look at Ed. On the plus side, he might proclaim, "I make decisions for others to implement without question." The negative side is revealed in: "I stay on top of things to make sure my decisions are carried out according to plan." Think back to Ed's interactions with Phil and Helen. Phil got put on probation for deviating from the letter of the law as laid out by the boss. Helen got her knuckles rapped and there is no question in her mind as to what is expected in the future.

Decisions made by a 9,1-oriented manager are individual and unilateral. Input from others is not solicited nor is it desired. Subordinates are expected to comply with the boss's demands and to carry out the 9,1-oriented leader's will.

Critique

Review and evaluation of performance is an indispensable aspect of 9,1 leadership. A 9,1-oriented leader wants to know that work is being done. This can be determined by patrolling the halls, inspecting ongoing activity, and on-the-spot interrogation. Remember the example where Ed "catches" Helen?

Critique in the 9,1 sense is more or less the same as criticism and correction. Seldom does it contain a constructive component. Rather it is one-way, fault-finding, and judgmental evaluation. Subordinates are not involved in thinking through the activity as a way of learning from it; that is not even an option.

What does a 9,1-oriented manager like Ed think about critique? On the plus end he would respond, "I don't hesitate to point out and correct performance problems. I tell people when they're wrong or where they've failed to measure up." On the minus end: "I avoid having mistakes pinned on me; rather, I take the offensive and seek to put the blame on someone else." Remember when Ben asked Ed about a mistake? Ed was quick to react, saying it was Engineering's fault and backing this up with the fact that he had gotten Gil to take the blame.

Subordinate Interaction with a 9,1-Oriented Boss

A 9,1-oriented boss is after results and subordinates are the means for accomplishing that end. This boss has little to say other than to tell subordinates what is to be done, by whom and by what time. Input is not tolerated. While compliance may be gained, 9,1 behavior often has an adverse effect on subordinates' level of commitment and ability to complete a task.

9,1 Reactions to 9,1

The only thing going for this combination is that both have a strong concern for results, but if they have different ideas about how to achieve them, watch out! The result is a win-lose fight and, because the boss has higher rank, he or she will win. But not really, because this subordinate "goes underground" and creates havoc. Such a situation is ripe for anti-organizational creativity on the part of the subordinate. "I'll show that boss!" Actions are taken in a secretive manner aimed at disrupting the boss's dictates. As a result the win-lose fight continues and productivity suffers. It is a battle of wits with intense involvement on both sides. There is little possibility of a meeting of minds.

1,9 Reactions to 9,1

This is the opposite situation because it represents a "weak" subordinate who is susceptible to a "strong" boss. Moreover, this subordinate wants to please the boss and is therefore a willing participant in the pressure to comply. The difficulty for the subordinate is that no positive reinforcement is forthcoming from the

9,1-oriented boss. You can do 99 things right and never receive a word of praise, but do one thing wrong and you've had it!

The subordinate tends to take what the boss says at face value and seldom questions the boss as to specifics or rationale. As a result, the subordinate is sometimes operating in the dark and is likely to do a poor job on an assignment. This sets the subordinate up for more criticism. Morale on the part of the subordinate continues to deteriorate and the outcome may be that this individual is eventually pushed into a 1,1 corner from which he or she is unlikely to emerge.

Paternalistic (9+9) Reactions to 9,1

A paternalistic subordinate dislikes 9,1 control but tends to bite his or her tongue rather than responding in kind and taking the risk of getting slapped down. The subordinate may voice doubts and reservations but offer to go along in the name of progress. In this way, the subordinate avoids future criticism for actions that fail by putting him or herself in a position to say, ''I told you so, but you didn't listen. I knew better.'' In some cases the subordinate may show off as a way of exhibiting to the boss a vast wealth of knowledge.

Often this combination of a 9,1-oriented boss with a paternalistic subordinate takes on the character of the junior or surrogate leader. The subordinate tries to be the boss's pet, by acting in his or her behalf. Then this subordinate is in a position to lord it over others on the team. This may be resented by colleagues, because the paternalistic subordinate has cast him- or herself in an unacceptable ''superior'' role, serving as the boss's stool pigeon.

It can be a ''win-win'' situation for both sides—but both win for wrong reasons. The subordinate may help the boss by advancing a desired end. In doing so, the subordinate comes to be seen as loyal and thereby gains the adulation and veneration that is sought, but this is not winning in the team or organization sense.

1,1 Reactions to 9,1

This is the classic case of avoidance and neutrality. The subordinate seeks to escape all contact with the boss as it is sure to result in pressure to do more work. Furthermore, the subordinate's lack of responsiveness is frustrating and the boss feels exasperated by a lack of answers. The boss may criticize the subordinate and demand improved results only to be greeted with excuses for delays, blame for nonperformance placed on other parties, or confusing arguments that have a quality of circular reasoning. It is sometimes difficult to make sense out of what a 1,1-oriented person is saying, and this is particularly disturbing to the rational-minded boss.

A boss who is mean may enjoy bullying this subordinate. The subordinate usually just "takes it," realizing that the fastest way to get rid of the boss is simply to remain neutral and accept the blows as they come. The last thing this subordinate wants to do is to start a fight. However, if the 9,1-oriented boss persists, it may lead to the emergence of a backup style by the subordinate.

The subordinate creates an impression of being compliant but because of a low concern for production and people, there is a tendency toward procrastination. On the other hand, to keep the job and stay out of trouble, the subordinate is likely to comply without question to the boss's instructions.

5,5 Reactions to 9,1

The force and drive of a 9,1-oriented boss puts an end to 5,5 tentativeness and ambivalence by clearly defining the way to go. However, when the course of action dictated by the boss deviates from the tried and true, the subordinate becomes uncomfortable and may balk, asking questions aimed at getting the boss to compromise. The boss continues to hammer on the subordinate until his or her will is broken and compliance is gained. The subordinate retreats with the intent to implement a plan as specified by the boss. However, during the course of implementation, actions may be modified to what is deemed to be more acceptable. On the other hand, because of this subordinate's fear of embarrassment, every effort is made to avoid criticism from the boss that might lead to a loss of popularity with peers.

This subordinate may find him- or herself disappointed much of the time because expectations are created between boss and subordinate that may not reach fruition. This is because the 5,5-oriented subordinate has only a superficial understanding of the situation and fails to confirm specifics with the boss. As a result, the boss has one set of expectations, the subordinate another, and conflict ensues when the results come in.

Opportunistic Reactions to 9,1

9,1-oriented bosses are unlikely to faze an opportunist. For this subordinate the issue is not right or wrong, sound or unsound, but rather, "What's the gain?" The subordinate's concern is whether he or she stands to get ahead. Therefore, the subordinate may buckle under or, alternatively, pass it by, or even resist. The answer is determined by where advantage lies.

The opportunist in a subordinate role seeks to manipulate the boss's thinking; playing the game according to what the boss seeks to achieve and fears. The subordinate goal is to enhance the boss's feelings of mastery, domination, and control, but also to "help" when gain comes from stimulating the boss's fear of failure, all the while playing up to a boss so as to project an image of strength and trustworthiness and to avoid being seen as weak and dependent.

9,9 Reactions to 9,1

This may be the most productive combination with a 9,1-oriented boss because both seek results, although a different approach to achieving this outcome may be sought. The boss is impressed with the subordinate's possession of the facts and, while the boss resists questions in general, this subordinate at least demonstrates in-depth thinking in those that are formulated. When this subordinate raises doubts and reservations regarding a course of action, the boss may seek to brush them aside without an answer. The subordinate, however, persists in discovering the rationale behind a proposed action and, to make progress, the boss may supply the underlying thinking to get on with the activity. The boss's tendency to move towards problem-solving behavior is partly because the 9,9-oriented subordinate does not polarize the situation into a win-lose fight. Even though the boss may be operating from a stance of "Who's right?," the subordinate continues to pursue "What's right?" When the subordinate takes this position, the boss does not feel threatened by "failure" or loss of face. As a result, it is easier to solve the problem than continue the impasse. It even becomes possible for these two to enjoy a good argument and to learn something from having done so.

When a 9,1-oriented person and a 9,9-oriented person continue to disagree, one of them may fall into a backup style. In the case of two colleagues, we saw Ben go into what appeared to be a 1,1 backup style when he shrugged his shoulders and told Ed, "Have it your way." This doesn't mean that Ben has lost his convictions about teamwork. It does suggest that he is frustrated by Ed's closed-mindedness and unable to move forward in a problem-solving way given the present circumstance.

Recognizing 9,1 Behavior

Many words and phrases describe a 9,1-oriented manager. No single one of them captures the whole, but as a group the words and phrases give an idea of how everyday language depicts this style of leading. Figure 3-6 illustrates the characteristic statements that describe 9,1 behavior, starting at the top with intense drive toward the plus motivation, extending down through a neutral

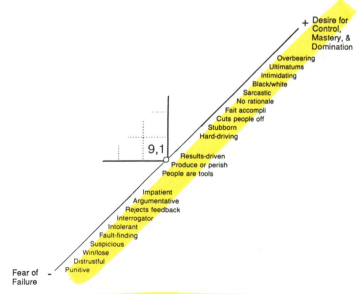

Figure 3-6. Words and phrases that characterize the 9,1 Grid style.

zone, and ending with words and phrases that describe the minus motivation.

Summary

The 9,1 Grid style represents a strong leadership theory that can be relied upon to accomplish results. It may work well in the short term—as long as the boss is right—even though it fails to capture the involvement of others. Beyond turning subordinates "off," it has the unfortunate result of shutting out their potentially crucial input when the boss is wrong.

The 9,1 Grid style comes in many variations. Our portrayal of Ed accentuates many of the "tough" features of this Grid style. It is important to keep in mind that the 9,1 Grid style reveals itself in more subtle forms. The key lies in examining the degree of concern for results, which is high, and the degree of concern for people, which is low.

What the 9,1-oriented person lacks is the knowledge, skill, or motivation to integrate a concern for people with a concern for production. Because it rests on the assumption of an inherent contradiction between the two, the 9,1 orientation becomes a black/white dilemma, where in order to achieve one (production) the other (people) must necessarily be sacrificed.

Once 9,1-oriented individuals become aware of the consequences of this style of leadership in terms of its impact on others, which extends also to its impact on long-term results, they are in a good position to rethink their basic assumptions about how to work with others. This is especially true when 9,1-oriented people realize that even greater productivity can be achieved through earning the input, the understanding, and the commitment of those who contribute to achieving corporate objectives.

Chapter 4

1,9: "Don't Worry, Be Happy . . ."

While Ben and Ed headed down the hall immersed in conversation about the pros and cons of participative management, Dan and Liz lingered in the conference room. The focus of their attention was the upcoming celebration dinner Al had proposed. Because it was almost lunchtime, they decided to continue their talk over a pizza.

"Yes," said Liz. "It's a wonderful lunch spot. I can't believe you've never been! Anybody who's anybody has been there. It's *the* place, you know."

"Well," chuckled Dan, "there's always got to be a first time!"

"Okay, okay," said Liz. "You'll love it. Come on. Let's leave our notebooks here. We can pick them up later."

"Since you seem to know the 'in' places, Liz," said Dan, "what's the scoop on this place Al's booked for our big dinner?"

"Oh, it's the best. Terribly expensive, though. That shows what Al thinks we're worth. He's proud of us for coming through on this last deal! Compare it to last year when we lost that major bid. I didn't think we'd ever hear the end of it. Al was so angry! I think he was disappointed in us; he felt we had let him down."

"Don't remind me," groaned Dan. "He didn't speak to me for a week. He looked so sad and hurt every time I caught his eyes. I felt terrible—even though I supported his position every step of the way. I did every single thing I knew how to do to get back in his good graces. I felt so rejected."

"You shouldn't take it personally," interjected Liz. "He wasn't any more disappointed in you than in the rest of us."

''Maybe not,'' mused Dan, ''but it sure seemed that way. I have trouble working in an atmosphere where people are so cool and distant. I function best when people are accepting of one another and feel appreciative of what I do.''

''Well, there's no reason to delve into all that,'' said Liz. ''It's over and done with. Let it go. We should focus on the present and see what happens. By the way, what do you think of Ed's proposal?''

''Proposal? What proposal?'' Dan looked perplexed.

Liz explained, ''You know, the one he submitted about mandatory work requirements for employees. The way I read it, it would mean much stricter supervision over sick leave, vacation, and so forth. If it gets approved, I think it would have quite an impact on human resources. What do you think?''

Dan groaned. ''That guy is so tough-minded. You'd think with all his years of experience he'd know the best way to get results from people is to be kinder with them. I don't know where he gets off, trying to whip his subordinates into shape. And now he wants to force his brand of totalitarianism on the whole division. Well, I can't support that. I'm not worried, though. Al won't go for it. He may listen to what Ed has to say, but Al's on our side. He knows how important people are to this operation.''

''You're right about that,'' quipped Liz. ''I can see Ed's point of view, though. He's a strong advocate for results, a true believer, so to speak. And the fact is we are in business to make money. I just think Ed ought to accommodate a bit. Everything's so black and white to him.''

''Oh, I agree with what you're saying,'' said Dan. ''Wait a minute, though. Let's get off all this serious talk. We need to lighten up. If anyone saw us right now, they'd think we were planning a funeral! Ed's projects come and go. There's no point in our getting upset over him. After all, it's our lunchtime and we need to relax a bit. Let me tell you about this new program I'm thinking about for our employees. The plan is to install it at all levels of the organization. It's called 'Coping with Stress.' '' Dan laughed and then continued. ''That's something we can really use, don't you think?''

Liz pondered the idea a moment. ''Well, I guess so. What do others think about that?''

Dan replied, ''Well, I haven't tested the waters with everyone yet, but the response I've had so far is pretty good. I'm going to scout around more before I say anything to Al. Al's got to be on board or it's no go. But it would be voluntary, of course. I certainly don't want to force anyone to participate. It's really quite interesting, though, and aimed at helping people work better by teaching them constructive coping skills. One of the personnel guys at headquarters described it to me. He's a really sharp fellow and pulls a lot of clout with the CEO from what I hear. I told him what a great idea I thought it was and that I was sure others would like it. He is so smart; wish I could think like him.''

After hearing this endorsement, Liz became more interested. ''Tell me more,'' she said.

Dan took his cue. ''Well, I was so excited that I had him sign me up. I attended this conference off in the woods and let me tell you, I came back one happy chap, peaceful and serene, ready for anything—even Ed. Now, that's a great program if you can feel relaxed in the face of a tough guy like Ed! What do you think about the idea now?''

Liz laughed. ''Well, you may be right. Let me sleep on it. Oh, I meant to ask you for your reaction to that marketing idea of mine. I'm still working up the proposal but I thought I should get some feedback from others before I put it in final form.''

''Anything you do meets with my approval,'' said Dan. ''I've never seen anyone work harder than you to do a good job.''

''Thanks,'' said Liz. ''You always seem to have something nice to say. I appreciate your support. It gives me confidence. Here we are. Let's get a table and then I'll place an order. What would you like?''

Dan smiled gratefully at his companion. ''Whatever you want is just fine with me.''

□ □ □

Figure 4-1 illustrates the 1,9 orientation in the upper left-hand corner of the Grid, where low concern for production, 1, is coupled with high concern for people, 9. It is based on the premise that production requirements and the needs and desires of people often interfere or conflict with one another.

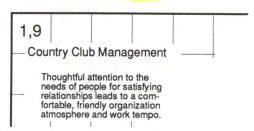

Figure 4-1. The 1,9 style Grid is located in the upper left corner of the Grid.

This kind of leader says, "People are the crucial element. They can't be treated like commodities, weighed in some production scale as an indicator of worth. Their feelings and attitudes are primary." As a result, conditions are arranged so that personal and social needs can be satisfied on the job. When these needs are jeopardized by production concerns, the 1,9-oriented leader is afraid that people will be unhappy, morale will suffer, and therefore production will decrease.

A 1,9-oriented boss leads in indirect ways that are intended to create friendship and camaraderie. This results in a lowered emphasis on productivity though this may be unintentional. The belief is that productivity takes care of itself as long as a congenial atmosphere is maintained. A leader with a 1,9 Grid style avoids imposing his or her will on subordinates, saying, "I'd rather be helpful to people than to push them for results." This attitude is reflected in the statement, "You can't pressure people into doing things—they naturally resist being treated like that. On the other hand, if you treat them nice, they'll do whatever you want." What this means in practice though, is not the same as in words. It is, "I find out what they want or think is okay and then try to make it come true. I think people should be helped, not goaded." This kind of supportive management unintentionally turns attention away from the task in the interest of warm and friendly relations.

A country-club atmosphere comes to prevail when a 1,9 orientation spreads throughout an organization. People work at an easy tempo with others whom they like. The spotlight is focused on areas of agreement and satisfaction. Creativity and innovation take a back seat because too often they lead to controversy and challenge.

Production tends to suffer in a 1,9 culture because problems that need to be solved are put aside "until later." Without resolution, these problems result in lowered productivity, unnecessary expenses, or both.

Motivations

The 1,9-oriented person sees the realm of R_2 as all important, but not in a way that leads to productive relationships in order to maximize results. Rather good relationships become an end in themselves. The 1,9-oriented boss has lost sight of R_1 and R_3. R_2

is cultivated because it satisfies the motivational needs of the 1,9-directed person in terms of fostering warm and accepting attitudes in which feelings of harmony can prevail. The rationalization is that somehow this will lead to productive effort. If productive effort is not the goal, however, it is unlikely to result.

Figure 4-2 illustrates the motivations underlying the 1,9 Grid style of working with others.

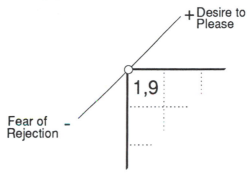

Figure 4-2. The plus and minus motivations of the 1,9 Grid style.

The 1,9+-oriented person feels secure when relationships are positive and when others are accepting and approving. The assumption is, "If I am nice to people, they will like me." This means being nice, helpful, kind, and sympathetic. These feelings are communicated and convey the fact that the 1,9-oriented individual is tenderhearted. This person is likely to be very sensitive to what others think and feel and therefore eager to receive signs of their appreciation. When others demonstrate their approval, there is a general feeling of oneness. For these reasons the boss seeks to create an atmosphere of warmth, caring, and approval. The words "deferential" and "ingratiating" are apt descriptions of the 1,9+ attitude. Look over Dan's comments to Liz to get the general flavor of a 1,9 approach to dealing with people. Dan's greatest desire is to establish an atmosphere of warm togetherness, one in which positive feelings may flourish. Concern for productivity is minimal or only a by-product of concern for people.

The negative side of 1,9 motivation is fear of rejection. Rejection leaves this individual "hurt or even deeply wounded." Because criticism is taken as one form of rejection, a 1,9-oriented person is constantly alert to signs of it in an effort to avoid it. A typical reaction to this is the desire to escape further hurt, which, however, results in separation from those whose acceptance and approval is sought. Because 1,9-oriented people enjoy being with others in preference to working alone, the true aim is not to flee but to go to any lengths to avoid the possibility of complete rejection. The result is pleading for acceptance. In our story, Liz reminds Dan of another occasion when Al was unhappy with the team. Dan groans and says, "I did every single thing I knew how to do to get back in his good graces. I felt so rejected."

The idea that "I'm not good enough" may stem from a 1,9-oriented person's feelings of low self-worth. In other words, "If I had tried just a little bit harder, had done just a little bit better or more, or just done it differently, you wouldn't be displeased with me." The person oriented in the minus direction may even experience feelings of guilt because obviously he or she did something wrong or else the negative feelings would not be present.

Conflict Solving

Conflict is abhorred because a 1,9-oriented individual takes disagreement personally. It is not the idea or proposal that is rejected; rather, it is the person him- or herself who feels discounted. In other words, "People must not like me anymore or else they would not reject what I say." What "I" say or what people think "I" have said is synonymous with *"Who I am"* for the 1,9-oriented person. This individual opts to be safe by avoiding conflict altogether, if possible, or going along with whatever others say rather than taking a stand.

Preventing Conflict

There are several ways in which a 1,9-oriented person may seek to stay out of harm's way. All are strategies to "defuse" the conflict before it has the opportunity to erupt.

One way to prevent conflict is to create a pleasant atmosphere in which, it is hoped, conflict will not have an opportunity to manifest itself. The 1,9-oriented person keeps relationships informal by expressing interest in people's personal lives—their families, hobbies, vacation plans. Co-workers are showered with compliments.

Actions such as these promote a sense of "warm togetherness" among people and help ward off the potentially disgruntled colleague or subordinate. This creates an atmosphere of harmony that makes it possible to ask people to accomplish organization tasks that might otherwise seem burdensome. By being gracious and over-solicitous, the 1,9-oriented manager anticipates a good-natured readiness to pitch in on the part of others. The idea is that harmony in R_2 brings about satisfactory results in R_3.

People are encouraged to talk about the things they like rather than focusing on differences. Because the latter tend to stay submerged, the manager can deal with people in a climate that—on the surface—appears free of tensions and frustrations. Such a person says, "I show my concern for people by being sensitive to their feelings and appreciative of whatever they do." The operating motto is, "Don't say anything if you can't say something nice." When surrounded by others who also accentuate the positive, problems that need to be solved tend to be ignored. Eventually, these problems grow to such proportions that they become crises.

Informal chats allow a 1,9-oriented boss to keep a close monitor on people's morale. Those who feel left out and lonely are brought back into the flock by the 1,9-oriented manager expressing positive interest in their well-being and granting special favors to lift their spirits. Work is more enjoyable and life more pleasant with an appreciative pat on the back, a friendly word, or a smile. These gestures create an attitude of sharing, a sense of warmth, and a balm of security.

Another way to avoid conflict is not to disagree. A 1,9-oriented person is reluctant to propose a different viewpoint because it might be challenged. This individual avoids making statements such as "I disagree," or, "You're wrong," or even "I take exception to that." Even if slighted, this person tends to say, "It just isn't worth a fuss." Therefore, opinions that might make it necessary to take a fixed position are not expressed. For example, instead of saying, "I saw a great new line of equipment today. I think we ought to do a cost/benefits analysis on changing ours out to make our operation more competitive," the comment is likely to be, "XYZ Corporation has just put out some leading edge equipment. Maybe we could take a couple of days to visit their plant in San Francisco for a demonstration. Besides it's a wonderful time of year to be in California. Doesn't it sound like fun?'' The latter opens up the discussion without taking a firm position. Rather it entices others to consider a new possibility by attaching the work activity with a pleasurable experience.

Another way to avoid disagreement is to get other people to talk first. ''Obviously, we can't disagree if I think exactly what they think—so the solution lies in knowing what they think!''

Deception also serves to avoid tensions with other people. When asked to explain some matter that might cause feelings of rejection or hurt, the 1,9-directed individual is unlikely to speak the whole truth. Bad news is glossed over or downplayed. When there is no way to avoid it, the conversation may start with an apology to soften the impact. ''I know it's not your fault, but . . .'' Although the 1,9-oriented person may not actually lie, the words are softened to make them as palatable as possible.

Handling Conflict When It Appears

There are two basic ways in which a 1,9-oriented manager handles conflict once it has surfaced. It depends on which end of the motivational scale is most active at that point in time. In order to understand this, let's take another look at Dan. His positive motivation, desire to please, is expressed in the following: ''I try to lighten up the conversation when conflict arises by telling jokes that take the focus off the problem.'' This may in fact irritate others like Ben and Ed who are eager to grapple with the conflict rather than avoid it. However, Dan's effort to ease the tension is based on the mistaken notion that everyone hates conflict as much as he does. Now, think back to Dan and Liz's conversation; when the topic turns to an area of potential conflict, Dan says, ''Let's get off all this serious talk. We need to lighten up. If anyone saw us right now, they'd think we were planning a funeral!''

On the minus side, we can sum up Dan's motivation as, ''I avoid generating conflict; when it does arise, I go to any lengths to placate those who disagree.'' When Liz supports Ed's concern for productivity, Dan is quick to say, ''I agree with what you're saying.'' Dan is an agreeable kind of guy. The motivational premise is that if you agree with everything others say, you'll never cross wires with them and you'll stay in their good graces.

Often, the 1,9+ approach to conflict is to interject humor into the situation. Humor itself, of course, is a laudable human quality. However, when used by a 1,9-oriented individual in situations of conflict, it becomes a way to divert attention from a serious subject to avoid conflict. It is a distraction that allows a 1,9-oriented person to shift the topic of discussion to one that is less controversial. Humor is used when a person's motivation is directed towards the positive end. It is consistent with a desire to please, and a 1,9-oriented person uses humor to avoid "displeasing" feelings.

Another characteristic of the 1,9-directed person is to explain away negatives. When others react angrily or in a hostile manner, this person becomes soft-spoken, even meek. Such reactions are rationalized by saying, "Al has been under terrific pressure" or "Ed must not be feeling well." In other words, any kind of potential conflict is discounted and minimized by attributing its real cause to some extraneous factor.

Sometimes, the 1,9-oriented person gets caught in situations where differences are unavoidable; for example, production records may indicate a down-trend for the last quarter. A way of defusing this issue is through the use of apologies and promises of "I'm terribly sorry. It will never happen again." Such promises represent an effort to avoid negative consequences stemming from one's actions. To escape feelings of rejection, the individual may ask for extra work in the hope of regaining whatever acceptance and approval may have been lost as a result of the mishap.

Another strategy of the 1,9-oriented person is to downplay the pressures. Distress may be experienced when the push for results comes down from above because this, in turn, means that the 1,9-oriented boss is forced to make demands on subordinates. It threatens the warm R_2 environment this manager has sought so hard to foster. For this individual, it is a no-win situation because either subordinates are frustrated by being asked to do more or privileges must be withdrawn to cut expenses. The 1,9-oriented boss may wish to avoid doing either, with the result that productivity falls still lower. In both cases, however, the atmosphere of harmonious relationships is threatened above and below.

Several tactics are used to deal with this apparent dilemma, such as coaxing and cajoling to motivate subordinates. What might otherwise have been posed as an inflexible command thus becomes an appealing request. Additionally, explaining production requirements a little bit at a time may alleviate resentment by subordinates. Inconveniences that cannot be avoided are "sugar-coated" to make the necessary work more appealing.

The minus side of handling conflict is to back down. A 1,9-oriented manager is quick to accept the position expressed by someone else rather than take the risk of disagreeing, although unexpressed reservations about a course of action may remain. Agreement and harmony, however, are maintained. The manager might say, "You've got a good point there," or "On second thought, I think you're right," or "Now that I've got it in perspective, I believe your way of thinking is better than mine." All of these are escape hatches that let the 1,9-oriented person off the hook even when holding different convictions.

Figure 4-3 illustrates the 1,9 approach to conflict. When a 1,9-oriented boss and a subordinate find themselves at odds on some issue, the boss sells out personal convictions by yielding to the subordinate's solution to gain the subordinate's approval and feelings of goodwill. This approach destroys effective participation, however, because it teaches arrogant subordinates that they can walk

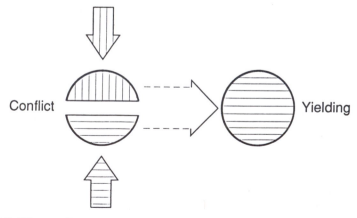

Figure 4-3. When conflict erupts, the 1,9-oriented individual backs off and yields to the other viewpoint.

all over the boss. If the boss fails to take an active role in arriving at effective decisions, subordinates are likely to fight among themselves—exactly what a 1,9-oriented manager seeks to avoid. As a result, this further undermines the boss's ability to exercise good leadership.

There are several other ways in which the 1,9-directed boss manages to defuse conflict when it occurs.

When Conflict Remains

With all these techniques for anticipating and defusing conflict before it has a chance to appear, or smoothing it over when it does, how does a manager like Dan deal with tensions that continue to cast a shadow on the corporate landscape? One way is by letting off steam. When a 1,9-oriented person feels tension and frustration, the negative feelings are discharged by complaining to third parties—colleagues, family members, and friends. In his conversation with Liz, Dan is able to vent his frustrations about Ed. Dan is unlikely to confront Ed face to face on reservations. It is less threatening to let off steam to a third party than to openly confront the problem at the source. While such venting may relieve the stress experienced by the 1,9-oriented person, it does little to correct the real problems. As can well be imagined, gossip is rampant in a 1,9 setting.

Forgetfulness is possibly more noticeable in the 1,9 Grid style than it is with others. It's the old dictum, "Out of sight, out of mind." Unpleasant subjects are put aside, perhaps to be dealt with later, but only if someone else brings them up. In Dan's conversation with Liz, he is at first "perplexed" when she mentions Ed's tough new proposal for tightening up the ranks. Once she provides enough background for Dan to recall the specific details, he groans and begins to express his dissatisfaction.

Forgetfulness also comes into play when a 1,9-oriented manager overextends him- or herself to please others. Here's how it happens. To gain affection and approval, particularly from someone who provokes fear, a 1,9-oriented manager bends over backwards to comply—even though this may promote intense resentment at having to follow through on the request. It is a case of the mind saying, "No!" but the words coming out of the 1,9-oriented manager's mouth are, "Yes, of course. I'd be glad to do that for you." As a result of the resentment experienced, however, the promise is often forgotten, blocked out of memory. When confronted with this forgetfulness, the 1,9-oriented individual is quite apologetic but that seldom serves to make the situation better. People oriented in this way are often difficult to depend on because you know they are saying yes when they may not be able to come through for you, either because of this hidden resentment or because they have simply overloaded themselves by saying yes to everyone.

Initiative

A 1,9-directed person is eager to be helpful and many actions are taken under this premise. Senses are fine-tuned. Eyes and ears pick up casual impressions and body language, and these are filtered through 1,9 attitudes to determine whether an action might gain quick acceptance. This individual is alert to initiatives taken by others; there is a desire to respond in order to gain approval. We might stress that this is not initiative in the self-starting or stopping sense because it is following the real or perceived leads of others rather than being taken on one's own volition.

For example, in the case of Dan, he is implementing a new program on stress management, because it was "suggested" by someone in headquarters. The positive motivation for initiative can be summed up as, "I take action that I think pleases others because that brings us closer together and earns me the acceptance I crave."

The negative side of motivation is, "I avoid introducing innovative activities because I might be personally challenged or criticized for my ideas." Dan prefaces his discussion with Liz by saying, "Well, I haven't tested the waters with everyone yet, but the response I've had so far is pretty good. I'm going to scout around more before I say anything to Al." Even on the issue of lunch, he defers to Liz, "Whatever you want is just fine with me."

Two kinds of initiative are particularly difficult for a 1,9-oriented person. One is bringing up an issue with which others may disagree. "I don't have the heart to say no" explains part of the reluctance. Additionally, taking initiatives may be seen as pushy and this could get a 1,9-centered individual into trouble. A rationalization is,

"Sometimes it's difficult to know what to do so it's better to listen to what others think about a situation before considering it myself." The manager hopes the situation will take care of itself as others deal with the problem.

The other difficulty in exercising initiative lies in ending a discussion because others might misinterpret this action as having their input cut off. It might imply disinterest or impoliteness. "If I end the conversation, they might think I don't care; it would hurt my feelings if someone felt that way about me." Or, "I don't want to interrupt. They might have an important point to make." As a result, meetings drag out, work doesn't get done, and everything piles up. Inevitably, the 1,9-oriented individual falls behind and suffers feelings of tension and stress and the pressure mounts. Co-workers feel frustrated or disappointed because expectations are not met. Thus, a basic contradiction exists because the 1,9-directed person, ever thoughtful, is unable to see the consequences of this reluctance to terminate a conversation, keep on schedule, and exercise sound time management. Instead of pleasing others, others become angry and rejecting, exactly what a 1,9-oriented individual seeks to avoid.

If 1,9-oriented people are characterized by low initiative, how do we reconcile this with the fact that they often appear to be so busy? The answer has been implied previously in that such people say yes to every request; it's no wonder that they have no opportunity to reflect on what might really need to be done. These requests may stem from bosses, colleagues, or subordinates, although bosses are given preferential treatment. This is because rejection by an authority figure is perceived as more threatening, being reminiscent of parent-child interactions. However, initiative in general is lodged in someone other than the 1,9-oriented individual.

Inquiry

People who are oriented in a 1,9 direction like to be "in the know" because this keeps them close to other people. However, this is not an easy task because this individual is reluctant to ask questions for fear of stepping on someone else's toes. As a result, 1,9 inquiry tends to be shallow. Sometimes, however, a 1,9-oriented manager is pressured by his or her boss to "get the facts." The manager hopes that the information will be volunteered and tends to hang around subordinates waiting for it to be offered. Rather than risk rejection by pressuring others, the 1,9-oriented person may draw inferences from the situation, usually positively-oriented, to provide to higher levels.

How is the 1,9-oriented manager motivated when it comes to inquiry? The following statement characterizes the plus motivation for Dan: "I seek to bring out the positive in others. I ask the kinds of questions that permit other people to talk about themselves. People like to blow their own horn once in a while and I encourage them to do that. It makes them feel good and as a result they like me." Dan does a lot of "management by walking around." Here is a typical remark that passes between him and a subordinate in the hall: "Hi, Joe. You're sure looking good. The world must be treating you right. By the way, I just read that last report you turned in. What a success story! I want you to fill me in on the details."

On the minus side, Dan might say, "I avoid asking questions that raise unpleasant issues. When I find myself dealing with negatives, I do everything I can to get the discussion back in a positive vein. There's no point focusing on disagreeable subjects." Let's say a disgruntled employee has come to Dan for consolation. His response might be, "Please don't be upset. We all make mistakes. I'm the world's worst! Tomorrow you won't even remember this happened. In fact, you'll be laughing about it. You know the old saying, 'Why cry over spilt milk?'" Because the 1,9-oriented individual is so approachable, he or she may soon become the repository for everyone else's complaints. In this role of "armchair counselor," the 1,9-oriented person provides comfort and support, but in doing so unwittingly undermines effective communication processes because true sources of complaints are not addressed.

A manager operating in a 1,9 way asks the kinds of questions that reveal what others want or need. For example, "Ask me anything and I'll be glad to do it," or, "When would it be convenient for you to meet? I'm at your disposal." Such remarks place responsibility with the other person and are unlikely to bring forth rejection. Sometimes a 1,9-oriented person goes out on a limb and asks another party a question for which there is no ready reply. This, of course, can lead to an embarrassing situation in which the 1,9-oriented person flounders until the situation can be brought back to an even keel. Those who are oriented in the 1,9 direction are obviously good listeners, alert to what others are saying, thinking, and feeling, even though what is reported is taken only at face value.

When inquiry takes the form of individual reading and study, it may be somewhat thorough provided the content is fairly positive. However, if the subject matter has a negative flavor, for example, reflecting organization tensions or problems in the market, this person finds it difficult to devote the attention it deserves. The reading material is put down with the intention of picking it up later, but later never comes. If this person does get around to completing the assignment, the goal is only to get the gist of it rather than to examine it thoroughly. The attitude is to learn a little about the issue in order to avoid an awkward situation but not to gain insight on how to solve present or potential problems.

Advocacy

When an individual expresses convictions as to what should or should not be done, others may be stimulated to take counterpositions. The discussions that follow may lead to misunderstandings and resentments. As a result, a 1,9-oriented person is unlikely to advocate strong convictions, particularly on subjects of a controversial nature. This means that potentially important input about how to solve a problem remains untapped.

What are the motivations that underlie this behavior? On the plus side, Dan's stance might be, "I take positions that reinforce the positive actions of others by using platitudes and compliments. If people are split on an issue, I stay out of it. Instead, I stand on the sidelines, unassuming, timid and shy." For example, Dan's response to a colleague's idea might be, "That's a great idea! I think the others will like it. You are so smart. I wish I could think like you."

The minus side of advocacy is, "I avoid taking positions that might be displeasing to others." For example, Dan's typical reply in a team meeting takes the form, "All of the ideas that have been presented sound good to me. Why don't we just keep tossing them around for awhile until we can agree on the best solution?"

The advocacy of a 1,9-oriented manager lacks force. When undertaken, it is likely to be tentative, nonspecific, or indirect to avoid a negative effect on others. Any points made are qualified so that attention to them is diminished. "Of course, I'm probably wrong, but could it be that . . . ?" Usually, reservations remain unexpressed with the 1,9-oriented person saying to him- or herself, "I'm not sure about this but the others are probably in a better position to see the solution so I'll just go along." Qualifiers such as these are to preserve good relations and to facilitate a friendly interchange. This is why 1,9-oriented people may be seen as gullible or naive. Common descriptions are "He's a 'yes man,'" or "She's too quick to agree." Problems that might have been solved remain unsolved, or solutions reached are less than sound.

Decision Making

Making decisions can be a pleasure when they are likely to be embraced by others. A 1,9-oriented manager sees decisions of this nature as opportunities for sharing. When decisions affect several people, group discussion is encouraged to consider and recommend the preferred solution.

For example, Dan likes to meet with subordinates to get their ideas. When he winds up such a meeting, he looks to others for the decision to be made. He might say, "I have really enjoyed this little brainstorming session. Who can sum up for us the way we need to go, based on everyone's input?" The statement that characterizes a 1,9-oriented manager when it comes to decision making is, "I try to ensure 'spontaneous' agreement before making decisions."

On the negative end of the motivational scale, the 1,9 stance is, "I avoid making decisions that are frustrating to others; if something comes up that is disturbing, I make sure others know it's not my fault." When Al asked the team to take on the last assignment, Dan reluctantly went back to his subordinates and said, "The big boss has called upon us to do a little project. I know how busy you are but it shouldn't take too long, and I'll pitch in and help all I can. There just wasn't any way I could say no. I hope you understand."

Some decisions of necessity are unilateral. The 1,9 approach to this is to engage in extensive consultation prior to formulating the outcome. When decisions involve taking unpopular action, the result is procrastination. Whenever possible, unpleasant decisions are delegated. Not only does this relieve the manager of potentially negative actions, but it also establishes a reputation of being a good delegator.

Decision making is particularly difficult when the person pressing for the decision is the 1,9-oriented manager's boss. The best way to stay in the boss's good graces is to do whatever is requested and then to let subordinates know that this decision was made at a "higher" level and is final. This lets the 1,9-oriented manager "off the hook."

Critique

A manager operating from the 1,9+ position reacts to critique as follows, "I try to make others feel good by putting a positive light on things. When people are happy, they are naturally motivated to do better." Dan tells Liz, "Anything you do meets with my approval. I've never seen anyone work harder than you to do a good job."

On the negative side, Dan's position is summed up in, "I avoid pointing out people's weaknesses or failures. That might make them unhappy. People won't like me if I'm critical." His response to a disappointed subordinate might be, "I'm sorry it didn't turn out like you expected. Don't worry about it. I'm not. I think you did just fine." The tendency is to look on the bright side by making comments that avoid disturbing aspects of performance. Positive reinforcement through compliments or encouragement creates a climate of approval conducive to better working relationships. One justification for shifting away from the negative is the premise that people probably already know their limitations and faults. Calling attention to them only increases frustration.

Negative feedback is avoided. When this is not possible, the 1,9 strategy is to attribute the points of critique to someone else. For example, "The boss asked me to tell you that . . ."

Subordinate Interaction with a 1,9-Oriented Boss

A 1,9-oriented boss is friendly and agreeable and from that perspective relatively easy to get along with. However, this individual's low concern for productivity tends to be frustrating for those subordinates with a strong focus on achieving results.

9,1 Reactions to 1,9

This subordinate's desire for mastery, domination, and control conveys hostility and rejection to the 1,9-oriented boss. As a result, the boss seeks to gain the subordinate's goodwill with friendliness, but the subordinate's abrasive attitudes provoke a hasty retreat. The tendency for the boss is to leave this subordinate alone. The subordinate's reaction may be one of frustration because it is difficult to get the boss to take necessary action. There is little in the way of trust and respect between the two parties.

The 9,1-oriented subordinate's reactions to a 1,9-oriented boss range from ignoring the boss through disgust to open contempt. The subordinate may take pleasure in meetings showing the boss up by asking questions the boss can't answer or contradicting statements the boss has made.

In operating with his own subordinates, Dan seeks to create an atmosphere of harmonious relationships. In some respects this creates problems for the team members because they must react in a stimulus/response way to the dictates from above. They are seldom prepared but are suddenly called upon to take action when Al issues an ultimatum and this is apologetically carried down through the ranks by Dan for implementation. Furthermore, despite the promises, they can't expect much help from Dan because he has his hands full, having overextended himself with promises to others.

The relationship is basically the same between two colleagues, one with a 9,1 orientation and the other with a 1,9 orientation. Just think of Ed and Dan. Ed feels disdain for Dan's attention to people and their feelings. Dan feels Ed is "too tough" and tries to stay out of his way. In the situation of equal rank, the 9,1-oriented person simply pushes past those who are considered weak. It is "survival of the fittest" played out in an organization setting.

1,9 Reactions to 1,9

This boss-subordinate pair get along quite well because both desire to be liked by and to please the other. It is a situation of mutual admiration; the boss's friendliness strikes a responsive chord with the subordinate. Work becomes an environment for socializing with productive effort taking on a secondary role.

This subordinate, like the boss, aims to please and sympathizes with the pressures placed on his or her boss. Together they lament the woes of the organization, taking little action to solve the deeper problems but fully immersing themselves in conversation about how "they would do it" if in a position to do so. The subordinate finds a cooperative ally in the boss for the planning of events such as birthdays, retirement parties, or welcoming new people on board. If you think hard enough, you can find a reason to celebrate on a daily basis. All this activity is aimed at improving employee morale and, although people may be happy, there is little fulfillment from productive effort because there is little by way of productivity going on.

Paternalistic (9+9) Reactions to 1,9

This subordinate "cozies up" to the 1,9-oriented boss by becoming an indispensable helper who is seen as appreciative, respectful, and one who conveys a sense of warmth and approval. Paternalistic subordinates have a need for adulation that is satisfied by the boss. The 1,9-oriented boss's kind and giving nature may lead to the subordinate being told, "What a wonderful subordinate you are" and in exchange the subordinate may offer helpful advice. The boss is appreciative of the subordinate's concern. It appears to the boss that the subordinate is keeping the boss on top of things. When the 1,9-oriented boss does something the paternalist doesn't like, however, the subordinate may trigger the boss's guilt by "playing the martyr." Such behavior continues until the boss comes around. 1,9-oriented people have a difficult time with guilt, and a paternalistic subordinate uses this to control boss behavior.

1,1 Reactions to 1,9

The subordinate oriented in a 1,1 way is not particularly interested in the friendly gestures of the 1,9-directed boss and would rather not be bothered. This subordinate finds it relatively easy to give the boss a noncommittal answer and thus escape involvement by indicating a lack of interest. This lack of subordinate responsiveness can be disturbing to the boss. A typical boss reaction is to continue the effort to develop a mutual social interest with the subordinate. But all the messages communicated by this subordinate say, "Don't push!'' The boss response is one of low pressure and apology. In this environment, the 1,1-oriented subordinate has an easy time of doing the bare minimum to get by and frequently offers excuses for delays. This subordinate quickly learns that the boss is unlikely to confront less than acceptable behavior and takes advantage of the boss's unassertiveness.

5,5 Reactions to 1,9

A 5,5-oriented subordinate is likely to have a good relationship with a 1,9-oriented boss, although there is some frustration with the low concern for productivity. It is important to the subordinate that an acceptable level of effort be maintained so as ''not to look bad.'' Thus the subordinate exerts a subtle pressure on the boss to keep things on track. In a conversation between Dan, a 1,9-oriented individual, and his 5,5-oriented colleague, Liz, Dan was expressing criticism about Ed's strong results-oriented approach. At this point, Liz revealed her 5,5 convictions by reminding Dan that the reason they were with the organization was to work. This is the 5,5 effort to balance the two concerns of production and people.

Generally, though, the rapport between the two (5,5 and 1,9) is good with the boss being responsive to the subordinate's need for popularity and prestige. The subordinate is responsive to the compliments offered by the boss as this builds a sense of confidence and well-being. Furthermore, both are tuned in to a need for togetherness and enjoy being part of the group, finding security in the presence of others. Because neither is fond of conflict, they work together to diminish tensions among people, which is accomplished by the 1,9-oriented boss seeking to cultivate harmonious relationships and the 5,5-oriented subordinate smoothing over any conflict that occurs.

Opportunistic Reactions to 1,9

Although an opportunistic subordinate may have little respect for the 1,9-oriented boss, these attitudes are likely to be disguised. By offering acceptance, appreciation, kind words, and a pat on the back in public, the boss is provided ''warmth and approval.'' However, this same subordinate may be critical of the boss's weaknesses in third-party discussions behind the boss's back. This may be particularly true in contacts with those of higher rank than the boss. An opportunist may want to undermine the boss by planting doubt in the minds of superiors about the 1,9-oriented boss's competence. The opportunistic goal is to supplant the boss. The implications of this for the 1,9-oriented boss is of little concern to the opportunist.

If the boss becomes insecure, the opportunistic subordinate may offer advice, exuding confidence that all will turn out well. The opportunistic subordinate feels free to take personal, self-serving initiatives. Should the boss question what's going on, the subordinate may provide a positive statement about all the good things that are being done for the boss, thus alleviating any fears. Despite the best efforts of the opportunistic subordinate, the boss's anxiety tends to run high.

9,9 Reactions to 1,9

A 9,9-oriented subordinate feels impatient with the irrelevancy and "soft touch" qualities—the slow movement and lack of solid data and facts—that characterize 1,9 leadership. It fails to meet the solution-seeking requirements of the 9,9-oriented subordinate. The subordinate may find it necessary to "take over" to exert some leadership in what appears to be a leadership void. While the subordinate is pleasant enough and responsive to the niceties offered by the boss, the boss feels rejected when the subordinate turns the conversation to work issues. There is an underlying tension as one seeks productive and involved effort, and the other seeks easygoing relationships in a harmonious work environment.

The gulf widens between the two in situations of conflict where the boss is anxious to escape and the subordinate is determined to get the disagreement out into the open. The boss essentially "drops out" as the subordinate wrestles with the problem and seeks a sound solution. If the boss is implicated, he or she backs off in an apologetic manner and tells the subordinate, "Whatever you want; whatever you say; I'll go along with you on anything." This has the effect of creating distance between the two because in the aftermath the boss feels rejection, whether or not this was intended by the subordinate.

This combination can, however, result in a more problem-solving approach because the boss is unlikely to confront the productive initiatives of the subordinate. However, it is frustrating for the 9,9-oriented subordinate because the boss often seeks to modify his or her initiatives in order to ''reduce the pressure.''

Recognizing 1,9 Behavior

The words and phrases in Figure 4-4 characterize a 1,9-oriented manager's actions and indicate how this Grid style is described in everyday language.

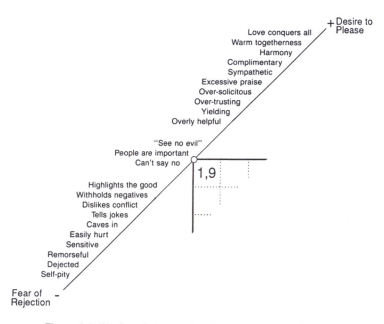

Figure 4-4. Words and phrases that characterize the 1,9 Grid style.

Summary

This chapter has focused on the behavior of a 1,9-oriented manager and its impact on an organization. While such a boss may be liked and appreciated by those with whom he or she works, it is unlikely that this manager gains the respect of others.

The harmonious atmosphere promoted by a 1,9-oriented manager encourages R_2 relationships that are friendly and pleasant. However, the likely result is that productivity—R_3 results—suffers. The idea of learning from experience to improve future performance is virtually nonexistent.

The next chapter examines the interesting combination of the 9,1 and 1,9 approaches to managing people and results—paternalism.

Chapter 5

Paternalism, 9+9: "Getting People to Worship the Ground You Walk on"

The paternalistic Grid style, or 9+9, comes to life in Al Jennings, the leader of the team. We have already seen several examples of Al's behavior, but let's revisit an episode that occurred at an earlier time. Dan and Liz referred to this incident during their luncheon, recalling the time when the team had been unsuccessful in obtaining a major bid. Al's response to this failure provides a sharp contrast to his present experience of success.

☐ ☐ ⊡

Dan walked hurriedly toward Al's office. He had just been handed the bad news. The deal had fallen through. "It's just amazing," he said under his breath. "I thought we had this one in the bag." As he approached Al's door, he looked around for his colleagues. He certainly didn't want to be the first one to arrive and end up taking the heat for this misdeed. He saw Liz and Ben turning the corner, and he walked a little faster to catch up with them.

"Hi, I was hoping I would spot you. I thought there might be safety in numbers," Dan said, laughing awkwardly.

Ben cast a solemn glance at him and proceeded into Al's office. Ed was already there, standing at the window with hands in his pockets, glaring at the street below. Gil was seated at the side of the room and Al hovered over his desk. Dan observed that his face was redder than usual, and he imagined Al as a time bomb ticking toward its predictable outcome.

Al was irritated. He had anticipated a victory on this one, something that could not fail to be noticed by those above. A lot had been riding on this deal, much more than the rest of the team realized. If they had managed to come through, it would have opened doors that offered tremendous payout, putting them on the leading edge. There was another proposal in the offing that Al had been considering but, without this victory under his belt, he was unwilling to take the risk. The odds would not be in his favor and he feared another loss might damage what credibility he had left. This missed opportunity for what could have been a feather in his cap was what disturbed him most. On the other hand, things could be worse. He had planned to contact headquarters just this morning on the new proposal, but then, based on instinct, he had delayed. This had been a wise decision as they didn't stand a chance of getting it now, in light of this afternoon's rejection. "At least," Al thought to himself with some relief, "I didn't go that far. My neck would really be on the line!" With this, his attention was drawn back to the matter at hand.

"You may all be seated," Al directed.

Al cleared his throat and continued. They waited for the explosion. Usually, Al was good at controlling his temper. They even joked sometimes that he should patent his brand of what the team called, "controlled anger," because he was so good at it. But not today! The team sat and waited for the blow-up.

"By now I suppose the news has come your way that we lost out on that major West Coast deal. I don't need to remind you how important that was to me." Al's eyes were black as coal as he surveyed the room and its contents, waiting for this to sink in. "I want you to know how disappointed I am. How could *you* let this happen?"

Dan and Liz shifted awkwardly in their chairs. Ben looked agitated, and Ed sat brooding. No one spoke in response to Al's question.

Gil got up to get a cup of coffee, but Al stopped him in his tracks by saying, "There's no coffee today, Gil. So why don't you just sit down and pay attention." Gil literally jumped back in his chair.

Finally Dan, unable to tolerate the deadening silence any longer, raised his voice in reply. "What a tough break! We worked so hard to get those figures together. I just knew we had it. And then this."

Al boomed, "How many times have I told you never to count on a deal until you see the signature on the dotted line! Why did you ease up? I was depending on you, and you let me down! Now I'm gonna catch hell from headquarters. And I can promise you that any heat I take for this is going to be passed right along to you!"

Ben continued to look agitated. He wanted to believe that everyone had done the best job possible. The problem was that Al had each of them on a short leash with no leg room to do his or her job. They were at Al's beck and call, always running to obtain the little details he requested. Ben surmised that if the members on this team had felt a greater sense of freedom to exercise their own initiatives, critical facts might have been surfaced. Al's exercise of leadership tended to be cloaked in secrecy with Al trying to maintain the big picture and only revealing bits and pieces of information on a need-to-know basis to others. This was Al's way to maintain his control of the team and be the "omnipotent leader." Ben felt this was a key problem in the team. Information tended to get bottlenecked in Al's office.

"One of these days," thought Ben, "we're going to get in real trouble because we don't have all the facts. I'm not sure there was any other outcome to today's deal; we just didn't get the bid—period. But I know I wouldn't feel so frustrated if Al would operate in a more open manner. I dislike all this secrecy. It's as though he thinks we're children who aren't old enough to be told the facts of life. If anything, it's time for him to grow up. I'm tired of working with my hands tied."

Al lowered his voice and proceeded into his tirade. "Well, no one seems to have any answers. I'm not going to let you slip by on this one, though. I want each of you, on your own, to go back to your offices and figure out what went wrong. We need a good story for the folks upstairs. I've got some ideas, but I want to see what you come up with. We'll meet back here later today and work through the night if need be. We're not going to let go of this one until I have it solved."

"Al, I'm still planning to take off the rest of the week for a short vacation," Gil chimed in. "If that's okay with you . . ."

"What do you think, Gil? Here I am pouring my heart out to you about how miserable I feel. This is nothing short of a calamity. And you want to take a drive into the mountains. This is serious business. Now you tell me, what's more important to you, to take some little jaunt into the woods with your family or to stay here and work this matter out with the rest of us?"

Gil looked sincerely distressed. On the one hand, he had a wife at home who was bound to be upset if he reneged on his promise. On the other hand, he was less than six feet away from a mountain of a man who wielded control over whether or not he kept his job. He pondered which was the lesser of the two evils and cast his vote to stay with the team. "I'll talk to the family about waiting until the end of the month. I'm sure they'll understand."

"I think that's a good decision," said Al, and then added somewhat sarcastically, "I know we're all relieved that we can count on your support."

Ed interrupted the conversation abruptly. "Let me say a word in our defense."

Al's gaze slowly focused upon Ed. "Go ahead. I'm listening."

Ed cleared his throat and continued. "Just from what I've heard about that competitor bid, it's way below industry average. There's no way that they're going to be able to meet it without losing money. This job may land in our laps yet!"

"That's probably wishful thinking," responded Al. "Furthermore, I'm hesitant to believe that headquarters is going to see it from your perspective. What you can do, Ed, and perhaps you, too, Frank, is a little undercover investigating to dig up the impressions at higher levels. It would be good if we could plant some doubt in their minds about the position of our competitor on this project. Know what I mean?"

Ed hesitated momentarily considering the ramifications of such action, but Frank jumped right in. "Sure, no problem. I can do it. Actually there are some people upstairs who owe me one. I'm more than glad to help you out by calling a few favors due."

Al settled back in his plush leather chair and folded his arms across his chest. He seemed to soften up a bit and the glimmer of a smile returned to his face. "This may just be one of those tough breaks but we need to do everything we can for damage control. Furthermore, I need to know that you're behind me and that I can count on you to present a united front." He looked around the room for some acknowledgment.

"What a question!" exclaimed Dan humorously. "You know we're behind you all the way."

Frank concurred, "I'll get on the phone right away. Don't worry about a thing. We'll make it through this."

The rest of the team acknowledged their support with a nod of their heads, with Gil looking up long enough to add his approval.

"Well, then, I'll see you back here at 4:30," said Al. "Anyone have a problem with that?"

□ □ □

The paternalistic orientation, shown in Figure 5-1, is a simultaneous exercise of the 1,9 and 9,1 Grid styles. It is represented numerically by 9+9 to illustrate the joining of the soft "9" of 1,9 with the tough "9" of 9,1. Elements of these two styles are used "simultaneously" or in such quick succession that they blend into a new style, unlike "pure" 1,9 or 9,1.

9+9: Paternalistic Management

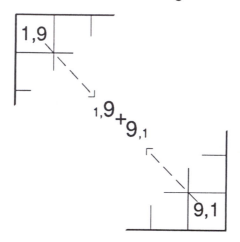

Figure 5-1. Paternalism, or the 9+9 Grid style, is a combination of the tough "9" of the 9,1 style and the soft "9" of the 1,9. A paternalistic person assumes reward and approval are granted to people in return for loyalty and obedience; failure to comply leads to punishment.

One critical distinction between 9+9 (paternalism) and 9,9 deserves mention. Paternalism is a complicated style, but quite easily understood once the underlying dynamics are revealed. The reason is that a paternalist portrays behavior from two apparently contradictory Grid styles. It is a way to get people to produce through reward and punishment, being stern and demanding in a 9,1 manner, but at the same time kind and benevolent in a 1,9 way. This is quite different from the 9,9 Grid style, which seeks to "integrate" the two concerns of production and people.

A paternalist, by virtue of operating from a style that has "added" the two 9's, tends to be over-solicitous regarding the welfare of others yet at the same time over-demanding of them to carry out his or her wishes. This person may go overboard in complimenting subordinate behavior and then in the very next breath criticize the same actions. Subordinates soon discover that no matter what they do, it just isn't good enough. The paternalist may delegate work to subordinates but then fails to give them autonomy within which to accomplish it. The paternalist is often looking over the shoulders of subordinates, correcting them or warning them of possible errors, explaining how they *should* be performing if they cared enough to do a truly excellent job. As a result, real spontaneity is lacking and taking initiatives outside "approved" areas is seen as risky and not worth the possible punishment for failure.

A paternalistic leader may appear as a parental figure, benevolent autocrat, kindly despot, mentor, or teacher. The statement that typifies this person is: "I own you and I feel responsible for you. I want to help your career along, much as if you were my son or daughter. That's why I expect your loyalty as a matter of course." This leads to a "family atmosphere" that stresses team and corporate values—as defined by the paternalist.

The paradox for the paternalist can be summed up as follows: "My subordinates are bright and capable, with plenty of know-how, but they check with me first, even when there is no need to do so. They are reluctant to accept responsibility. They don't take the ball and run." It is likely that subordinates feel this way because the executive may unwittingly undercut their confidence by questioning every action they take if they seek to act autonomously. Ben expressed frustration in his silent thoughts that Al kept them so busy fetching bits and pieces of information that they rarely if ever had time to exercise independent initiative. Primarily, this team operates in a reaction-response mode to Al's dictates.

These contradictory ways of relating to others may cause people to see the paternalist as pompous, presumptuous, self-important, and sometimes self-righteous. The paternalist may project him- or herself as the standard of reference—"I know best!"—using his or her own knowledge as the sole source of authoritative information and opinion. Often, the paternalist comes across to others as a pain in the neck.

Motivations

Paternalistic behavior can be understood through a more complete evaluation of its motivational dimension. What is it that the paternalist desires, the (+) side of motivation, and what does the paternalist fear, the (−) pole, that which is avoided? Figure 5-2 illustrates paternalistic motivations.

Paternalism

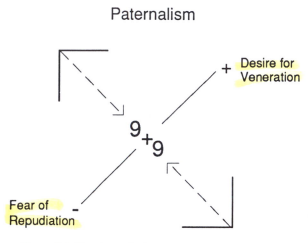

Figure 5-2. The plus and minus motivations of paternalism.

The positive motivation is to enjoy the veneration of others and to have others emulate the paternalist as their model. Generally, paternalists strive diligently to gain the admiration of subordinates by offering the benefits of their experience, counsel, and guidance to those for whom they are responsible. Often, there is a tendency to preach and pronounce.

A paternalist tends to stroke subordinates, showing acceptance and approval for a job well done to get them to do more of it. Projecting him- or herself as the standard of reference, the paternalist is in effect saying, "Copy me." This communicates a sense of self-importance and conveys a certain self-righteous quality. It makes the paternalist appear god-like but may also lead him or her to being seen as a "stuffed shirt."

Taken into the work setting, veneration means the paternalist projects the picture of a strong, self-determined person, committed to sound human actions that make the corporation a better place to work and allow the talents of its individuals to blossom. The latter, unfortunately, is only present as a good *intention*. It seldom comes into actual practice. Instead, innovation, creativity, and the development of initiative are stifled in favor of cloning subordinates that are essentially copies of the paternalist him- or herself. In the absence of paternalistic guidance, people become like children, not knowing which way to turn. They have become dependent on someone to tell them what to do and how to think.

The image a paternalist seeks to convey is the apparent selfless desire to serve with no thought of personal gain but simply a desire to act in the interest of making life better for others. The paternalist may believe this to be true, but he or she is self-deceived in thinking there is no personal gain. The gain that is sought is the dependence of others on the paternalist and the respect and admiration for this "all-knowing" leader.

The negative side of paternalism is fear of repudiation. When the paternalist is heard to say, "I told them what to do but they didn't listen," he or she is indicating that they were *wrong* in ignoring the wise counsel or the precautionary warning so kindly provided. When someone who has understudied the paternalist decides to leave and take another job, the paternalist expresses deep hurt and remorse, saying, "How ungrateful people are!" Inwardly what is experienced is the repudiation by one's own child. The "child's" view might be quite the opposite: "I gave indication after indication that I couldn't take it any more, but my boss never seemed to get the message. I felt suffocated. I had no choice but to seek escape for my own wellbeing."

The less extreme forms of fear of repudiation include the avoidance of disappointment, being let down, or losing the admiration of one's loyal following. This kind of disappointment is the basis for Al's treatment of team members in the unsuccessful bid proposal described earlier. His exact words were, "I was depending on you and you let me down."

A key observation about paternalists is that they remain blinded to the smothering effect they have on subordinates because they measure themselves by their generous and kind "intentions," rarely if ever stopping to allow others to provide constructive feedback and critique on how the actual behavior may affect them. Perhaps there is a fear that input from subordinates might expose their "clay feet" and result in feelings of humiliation. At any rate paternalists rarely tolerate honest feedback from subordinates, seeing it instead as "insubordination" and ingratitude. This attitude effectively shuts out the only real opportunity available for thoughtful self-appraisal. The greater dilemma is the misconception harbored by paternalists that they are great people-developers. Quite the opposite is true. By cultivating dependency in subordinates, paternalists stunt the growth and development of those beneath them. Creativity and innovation are stifled. Even taking "safe" risks becomes too risky. The organization, although it may appear strong under the guidance of a paternalistic leader, is actually weak because leadership has not been encouraged to develop in subordinate groups. There is as a result no back-up, no potential for succession.

Conflict Solving

How does a paternalist handle conflict? The basic tool employed is "reward for obedience" and control through "punishment and reprimand." Most subordinates realize that it is not in their own best interests to stand up to the boss. As a result there is much subordinate behavior called "boss-think," shown in Figure 5-3. Subordinates quickly learn that reward comes from venerating and

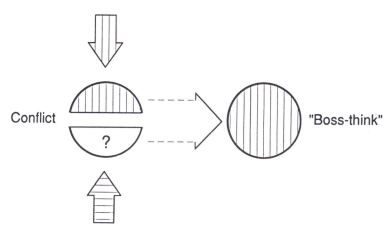

Figure 5-3. When a paternalistic boss and a subordinate disagree, the subordinate soon learns that it is best to think like the boss.

copying the boss's positions. Subordinates also see that they benefit by giving the paternalistic boss whatever is desired rather than resisting, even though what the boss wants may not be the best for the organization, the work team, or even the boss in the long run.

The goal of every paternalist is to create subordinates in their own image and likeness, people who have learned to think as the boss thinks, to do as the boss does, to enjoy the same outside activities as the boss enjoys, even to dress in a similar manner. At some point along the way, subordinates may resist this parent-child model as too constraining and begin doing things independently of the boss. This is difficult for the paternalist to tolerate. As a result, paternalistic bosses have their own distinctive ways of dealing with conflict.

The 9+9+ side of conflict solving can be expressed as, "I tolerate disagreement among unruly children because this allows them to blow off steam. But when it comes time to get down to work, I cut it off, letting them know that I appreciate what they have said. I want others to embrace my point of view and I seek to cajole them over to my way of thinking." In the first meeting with Al and his team following the successful bid proposal and the announcement of the celebration he has planned, Al allows his subordinates to quibble among themselves about issues of teamwork, but finally he seeks to draw them back to the issue at hand, first by showing Ed "a stern look," and then by using a remark that makes it clear to them that he is growing irritated: "You don't want to rain on *my* parade, do you?" When the conversation gets off track a second time, he takes control of the meeting, refocuses his issue, states firmly, "I won't take 'no' for an answer" and then terminates the conversation with "So, that's settled." He effectively cuts off further input.

The negative side of this is, "I expect agreement based on loyalty and I don't hesitate to use guilt and reprimand to bring people into line." An example appears in the second meeting of Al's team following the rejected bid. Dan makes a feeble remark that, considering how hard they had worked, he can't imagine what went wrong. With this, Al unleashes his wrath and in no uncertain terms lets the team know that they have failed to act in a responsible manner and they have let him down. His words are designed to induce profound guilt on the part of team members as punishment for their failure.

Preventing Conflict

Conflict is avoided by reinforcement of obedience through praise and compliments. Once the subordinate has come to expect and feel secure with this positive support, the paternalist can then withhold praise as an indication of displeasure. If resistance or disobedience continues, the boss may exercise reprimand, letting the subordinate know that bad behavior is not to be tolerated. The boss then reiterates his or her expectation of the subordinate and provides encouragement in anticipation that compliance will be forthcoming.

Handling Conflict When It Appears

When conflict does arise, one way to reduce it is to divert attention from disagreement by changing the subject or placing the problem in an alternative context. Then the subordinate is subjected to subtle pressure until he or she "sees the light" and becomes willing to accept the boss's solution.

When the conflict involves two or more subordinates in disagreement with one another, the paternalist might say, "You two get in a room and work it out. Don't come out until you can reach mutual agreement or one of you prevails." This terminates the conflict from the boss's viewpoint, leaving responsibility for the unruliness with the ill-mannered children.

Control is again restored when subordinates express appreciation and gratitude for all the boss has done. Controlling subordinates through reward and punishment is the model of paternalistic child-rearing extended into the company. This is vividly portrayed in Al's dealings with subordinates.

When Conflict Remains

When conflict persists and control cannot be reestablished, the subordinate is "disowned" and rejected. This is evident when the boss says, "I can't believe it. Think of all I've done for her . . ." Vengeance and retribution may be sought when "genuinely" volunteered help has been rejected. Once a break occurs, it is likely to be permanent, with little the subordinate can do to get back in the boss's good graces.

Initiative

A paternalist exercises strong initiative until it is felt that subordinates can be trusted to do what is expected without further instruction. Then, the boss may ease up based on the assumption that subordinates will continue to obey and follow through in the desired manner. If anything out of the ordinary arises, however, the boss insists that subordinates check back rather than acting on their own. Thus, at first glance, there appears to be a degree of delegation when in fact there is none. It is a form of "pseudo-delegation" where subordinates are not free to exercise independence of thought and judgment or to define their own solution to a problem. Rather, they are merely present as extensions of the boss's will. Subordinates in a paternalistic environment become dependent on the guidance and direction of an authority figure. They prefer to follow and to be told what to do and, when they comply, such behavior is rewarded. Having been so indoctrinated by a paternalistic boss, these subordinates lose the capacity for thinking and self-initiative. They have learned to pattern their behavior on the boss as a means for staying on track. Subordinates are reluctant to take action on their own and instead wait for those above to make the first move. When, for whatever reason, the boss is no longer there, they are helpless because there is no model for them to copy.

The plus side of 9+9 initiative is, "I help others embrace my initiative and educate them in my thinking so they can follow in my footsteps." Think back to the celebration meeting Al called at the beginning of the book. He was promoting the idea of a victory dinner and seeking endorsement by other team members. He told them numerous times that "this was something they needed to do," that it would be "good for team spirit," "it represented a new beginning," and so on. It is important to Al that other people come around to his way of thinking.

The negative aspect for 9+9 initiative is reflected in the following: "I avoid introducing activities that are shaky and might run the risk of causing me to lose credibility and respect." The price paid is that innovation and creativity are sacrificed. An example of this occurred earlier in our story. As everyone waited for Al to start the meeting, he was thinking to himself about another bid he wanted to make.

However, in view of the current failure, he determined it was too risky to make such an overture because he was unwilling to suffer any further loss of credibility. This is $9+9^-$ initiative involving a fear of risk and therefore a reluctance to take action except on a sure thing because failure could place one's leadership in question and thus risk a loss of following.

Inquiry

Because the paternalist is in charge, telling people what to do, guiding their actions, and counseling their every move, much inquiry is focused on ensuring that things are going according to expectation or to previously formed conclusions or judgments. It may not be direct in the sense of asking for reports, but questions are intended to let others know what is expected of them. Indeed a paternalist often relies on questions as a primary teaching tool to determine if the other person can respond correctly. It's "Socratic supervision" in a fashion. This indicates whether the lesson has been learned; if not, further instruction is needed. Much inquiry is also indirect through listening and observing to establish that things are being done as they should be.

There is a high degree of "need to know" because the paternalistic manager cannot afford to be wrong or to let it be known that there is something to be learned from subordinates. Thus, written information may be heavily relied on to stay up to date. The information may be concerned with technical matters, rules and regulations, or machinery and equipment—anything that plays a critical role in supervision. Thus, the paternalistic boss is likely to be known as one who is abreast of the issues. No detail is so small that it can be skipped over because the paternalist feels compelled to "know everything."

The $9+9^+$ inquiry statement is, "I ask questions designed to bring others around to my way of thinking. Then they will come to respect me for my wise counsel." Sometimes this can take the form of rhetorical questions when subordinates are wandering off in the wrong direction. For example, when Al was pushing for a victory party, he brought people back to "his" purpose by saying, "You don't want to rain on *my* parade, do you?" The safest use of such leading questions, however, is in the preferred one-to-one meetings with subordinates because it is easier to sway an individual's thinking than that of a whole group. All it takes is one divergent opinion to cast doubt on the paternalist's gospel.

The 9+9⁻ statement is, "I avoid being caught without the facts because this may result in lack of respect or loss of following." This is part of the reason for Al's vehement outburst when the team learned they had lost out on an important job. Al, who always considered himself on top of things, was caught short, which threatened his credibility with levels both above and below. He told his team to go back and study the matter in order to unearth all the details. The thought is that armed with enough data they could rationalize their position and thus be protected from external criticism.

Advocacy

The paternalist has strong beliefs and advocates them intensely, often with an overtone of moralism as in *should*'s and *should not*'s, or *ought*'s and *must not*'s. Veneration comes when others admire and respect the convictions the paternalist embraces. They realize the paternalist is wise and profound and therefore worthy of their loyalty.

A paternalistic boss motivated toward the plus end might say, "I take positions that build my image of credibility; in this way the likelihood is increased that others will accept my viewpoint." This is demonstrated by Al in his celebration suggestion; it is for the purpose of letting Al bask in his own glory; other team members are there to help him do so and to pay him tribute. He has strong convictions about carrying through with his suggestion and essentially forces team agreement.

The 9+9⁻ perspective is, "I avoid taking positions that indicate uncertainty or doubt or that may prove damaging to my credibility with others." This is evident in Al's decision to postpone undertaking a new proposal because he does not view it as a safe risk. He is unwilling to put his convictions on the line.

Decision Making

The paternalistic boss is the sole decision maker, although subordinates may be led to believe that they have some degree of autonomy. In making these decisions, however, the paternalist doesn't bark them out as commands to subordinates. Rather, once it is determined what a subordinate should do, the paternalist uses teaching, coaching, counseling, and guidance to ensure the task is fully understood and accepted. As a result the paternalist doesn't come across as abrasive and harsh but rather as kind, warm, and helpful, even though the subordinate is learning in an imitative or rote way to do whatever has been taught. This may create the need to check back rather than to operate on personal initiative. Thus, the subordinate is carrying out what the boss expects and in this sense may never become an independent thinker based on individual analysis and judgment.

The 9+9+ statement for decision making is reflected in, "I make my decisions and then let others know what they are, allowing discussion although the decisions are not subject to change. I provide convincing arguments that demonstrate how these decisions are for everyone's own good and that reflect favorably on my wisdom and judgment." In describing Al's approach in Chapter 1, it is said that his decisions came through as ultimatums. At the same time, "Team members knew they could try to argue, but the easier, softer way was to acquiesce to their leader's will." For example, several of Al's subordinates question the usefulness of a celebration dinner, yet they go along with Al's strong desire for this event because it is easier than fighting him on it.

The 9+9− statement is, "I avoid making decisions that might be challenged by others in a way that could lead to loss of respect." This negative feature is apparent in Al's deliberation on a new bid. He started to initiate the process but then wisely decided to await the news on the current proposal before taking this step. When it became clear that the group had failed to procure the first one, Al was angry but felt relieved that he had not been hasty on the second. Protecting his credibility is all important.

Critique

The paternalist cannot afford to be open to feedback from others because anything of a negative character might suggest weakness, and the paternalist takes pride in what is thought to be infallibility. Thus, personal feedback is one-way, from the boss down, or even from one colleague to another. In the case of subordinates, they understand where the boss is coming from and limit their reactions to weaker or stronger applause. After all, if "parents know best," there is little or nothing to learn from children. Therefore, their safest move is "to be seen and not heard" rather than risk giving constructive critique, even when it might be pertinent.

The paternalist, however, feels little or no reluctance to give feedback to subordinates through discussion of their performance. It is the boss's obligation to pass on to them whatever subordinates need to know for their own good. This permits them to benefit from the boss's wisdom and guidance.

The approach to feedback is praise and reprimand. A subordinate is given instructions and then, upon successful completion of a task, rewarded by compliment. If the subordinate fails to comply, reprimand is the result. Following this, compliments are once again provided, telling the subordinate that, "You're really okay, so let's move on. You'll do better next time—but only if you follow my lead."

The plus motivation for 9+9 critique is, "I spoon-feed critique points to subordinates to make sure each point is digested and appreciated before I introduce the next one." In other words, critique is from boss to subordinate, one-way, never the other way around. When the team successfully obtained the bid, the critique offered by Al is full of praise and compliments, and the expectation is that the comments in return will be of a nature that applauds Al's own leadership. For instance, he says to Liz, "I especially appreciate your vote of confidence." On the other hand, he becomes irritated and uncomfortable with Ben's probing for problems in team interaction and eventually puts a halt to this discussion. In the context of the team failure, he puts it on the line to subordinates and is unwilling to hear their rationalizations or defensive statements, such as that offered by Ed. However, Al winds up the meeting by rationalizing the failure himself, saying, "This may just be one of those tough breaks . . ." Nevertheless, there is no doubt in any team member's mind how Al wants things done in the future. His "critique" has been heard loud and clear.

The minus motivation is, "I show disappointment when subordinates don't follow the rules. I remind them of the benefits of being in my good favor." For example, in the lost bid, Al criticizes the team severely for not following the rules: "How many times have I told you never to count on a deal until you see the signature on the dotted line!" Near the end of the meeting, he allows a bit of a smile to return to his face, indicating that they just might be able to get back in his good graces. Nevertheless, Al reinforces that he is counting on them to present a united front and awaits their acknowledgment of this. In short, there is no real critique of what happened to thwart their plan. The blame has been put on subordinates who must now double their efforts to make it up to the boss.

Reward and Punishment: A Key to 9+9 Control

The use of reward and punishment in acknowledging subordinate compliance or reducing non-compliance has already been mentioned as a hallmark of the paternalist orientation to leadership. Less has been said about punishment, but it is of equal importance in comparison with reward because punishment is how disobedience is handled.

Inducing Feelings of Guilt

Classically understood, punishment means scolding someone, handing out demerits, or in some other way blocking or reducing a person's sense of self-esteem. In dealing with subordinates, the paternalistic method is much the same though its manner of execution is unique. The boss relies on communicating his or her personal disappointment in the subordinate's conduct or effort so that the subordinate feels small and contrite. The most common way of achieving this is to induce feelings of guilt.

How does a manager accomplish this? There are many variations on this theme but the following exemplifies one in particular.

When a subordinate does something wrong, i.e., anything contrary to the paternalist's expectations, the paternalist may say to this individual, "I am really disappointed in you for having done that. I have done my best to make it clear to you that this is unacceptable.

Yet, in spite of my warnings and efforts to help you, you have disregarded my advice. How could you do this to me—your benefactor? I feel deeply hurt. Your behavior shows a total lack of appreciation for my efforts to help you along in your career. You bite the very hand that feeds you. I feel as though I have been slapped in the face."

In this situation, it is a rare individual who can come away without remorse. When the subordinate acknowledges the mistake, the paternalist may add, "I'm glad you can admit that your actions were unsound, inappropriate, and ill-advised. I'm thankful that you've seen the error of your ways. Next time I feel sure you'll listen to my advice and not repeat this behavior. I'm relieved this little matter is settled and that our working relationship is back on a good footing." The paternalist has sent the subordinate spinning on a guilt trip but, then, at the last moment, reinserted the hook of dependency by promises of favor in return for compliance.

What about the subordinate who does not fall for this trap, who refuses to feel guilty for having taken initiative? More drastic measures are called for to punish such behavior. Rewards are withdrawn; a moratorium of silence is imposed; little or no help is forthcoming; any semblance of supportive relationships is lacking. Furthermore, the line is drawn. The peers of this subordinate are faced with a choice, to side with the paternalistic boss or to align themselves with "the rebel" and thus suffer similar retribution. The "in"-subordinate soon finds him- or herself the "out"-subordinate. Because most of our jobs are dependent to some extent on the collaboration or assistance of others, this outcast, unable to operate under such adverse conditions in a productive way, may soon be out of work.

Guilt is a powerful way of seeking to exercise control over another person. Unfortunately, it has the potential of being very destructive in that it tends to undermine a person's sense of self, thus reducing autonomy and initiative. It has the long-term effect of creating an enduring dependency in which the subordinate fails to "grow up" or mature. This leads to a "weak organization," one that lacks the necessary talent for promotion and must go "outside" in order to find competent leaders.

Subordinate Interaction with a Paternalistic Boss

A paternalistic boss is so controlling that subordinates find it difficult to deviate from what is prescribed. The extent of adherence depends upon the particular Grid style of the subordinate.

9,1 Reactions to Paternalism

This boss-subordinate pair is most likely headed for a fight because, in their minds, there is only enough control to go around for one person and both would like to have it. As a result, the 9,1-oriented subordinate is limited to those actions to which the boss subscribes. This subordinate may seek to win the boss over with the strength of his or her convictions but unless the boss's equally strong convictions lie in the same direction, the subordinate is unlikely to be successful.

Generally, they operate well together because this subordinate serves to enhance the boss's image by virtue of the results achieved. Consider Ed and Al. Ed feels a need to let Al know that he is on top of things. Ed turns to Al to confirm he is right to the rest of the team, such as in the example where Ed spotted the deadline mistake in a conversation with Frank. Ed wants credit for spotting the inconsistency, but at the same time he is careful not to implicate Al as part of the reason for near failure. They operate with a shaky truce, aware that if either steps on the other's toes a disruptive fight may ensue.

1,9 Reactions to Paternalism

This combination works out well, at least for the boss. The subordinate is eager to please the boss and provides adulation and respect for the boss's wealth of knowledge. The boss couldn't ask for a more willing and supportive worker. However, there are a few shortcomings. Because this subordinate is likely to accept any directive issued by the boss without question, the quality of the work may suffer simply because the subordinate is overloaded or because the subordinate has inadequate knowledge to carry the task out. Even here, though, the positive motivation of the paternalist may be gratified by stepping in and demonstrating his or her expertise to the subordinate in how to undertake the activity in a "better way," the boss's way, that is.

Dan feels a strong sense of loyalty and support toward Al and remarks to Liz that he would never counter anything Al said to his face. While this may serve to enhance Al's public image, it does little by way of ensuring that decisions are sound and correct.

Paternalistic (9+9) Reactions to Paternalism

The paternalist-paternalist pairing can develop into a mutually satisfying relationship, particularly if the boss serves as mentor to the younger subordinate. Older paternalists tend to surround themselves with younger people, taking them under their wing, so to speak, and helping to move their careers along. Younger paternalists, on the other hand, tend to be extremely sensitive to and appreciative of their elders whom they perceive as hands helping them up the ladder of success. When older paternalists and younger paternalists get together, a symbiotic relationship is formed that may prove beneficial to the pair. They "speak the same language" so there is no difficulty in communicating needs. They are often seen patting each other on the back for a job well done. Sometimes it's difficult to ascertain which of the two is most complimentary in adulating the actions of the other.

What happens when they disagree? This is less pleasant as both feel determined to bring the other around to his or her way of thinking. It is a carefully controlled contest of wits as to who gets the last word. The boss is going to win, of course, by virtue of greater power and authority, which causes the minus side of motivation to intensify for the subordinate. Besides "losing face" with the boss, the subordinate may have lost respect from his or her colleagues. Because the push for loyalty is so strong, however, the subordinate is unlikely to fight back or try to retaliate, preferring instead to take a low profile until his or her reputation can be rebuilt and some modicum of superiority regained.

1,1 Reactions to Paternalism

This subordinate operates similarly with a paternalist as he or she does with other Grid styles. The objective is to remain invisible, present but not seen, doing the bare minimum to comply, and walking a thin line between obedience and insufficient effort.

A 1,1-oriented subordinate like Gil carries this out fairly well with Al, for the most part, remaining unaware of his presence. When Gil does speak up, there is so little content to what is said that it fails to stimulate much attention. A paternalist finds it difficult to discipline such a subordinate because threats and even actual punishment are taken as par for the course without much hint of reaction. It is difficult in fact to stimulate much of any reaction in this subordinate and the boss can only presume agreement by virtue of the subordinate's silence.

5,5 Reactions to Paternalism

Such a subordinate operates on a fairly even keel with a paternalistic boss because the paternalistic need for respect and adulation is only a step removed from the 5,5 desire for status and prestige. Furthermore, a 5,5-oriented subordinate strictly adheres to protocol, which means obedience to an authority figure. Thus, disagreement is unlikely. Unless the subordinate feels the presence of a strong majority pull in another direction, he or she tends to keep doubts and reservations undercover.

In situations of conflict between the boss and others, this subordinate may take the initiative to serve as mediator, seeking to draw extremes to a happy medium. This is one of Liz's key functions on Al's team. She smooths out disagreement in an even-tempered way. If the conflict gets out of hand, however, she bows out and leaves it to the contending parties to resolve. She seems to operate by a "live and let live" attitude with her paternalistic boss and with the Grid styles of her colleagues.

Opportunistic Reactions to Paternalism

The opportunistic subordinate and the paternalist can be another symbiotic combination. When operating well together, they might characterize their interaction as "win-win." The apparently "loyal" subordinate plays to the boss's ego needs for veneration and adulation by buttering the superior up. "I'm your right-hand," or "I'm your Person Friday—just call on me." This subordinate may warn the boss in private of potential errors, but seldom if ever embarrasses the boss in public. All of these are manipulative ploys in order to advance a selfish personal cause. The desired opportunistic gain is advancement.

Frank thinks of himself as Al's confidant and emissary, proud of the influence he wields, or at least thinks he wields, with higher levels and colleagues as well. He offers to put in a good word here and there for Al, which is playing on the boss's plus motivation. All of this is at a price, however, and that is an anticipated promotion. Unlike the eager-to-please 1,9 style, an opportunist operates on the basis that there is something in every action undertaken to get him or her to the top.

9,9 Reactions to Paternalism

This subordinate is frustrated by a paternalistic boss for several reasons. Perhaps the primary one is the secrecy that characterizes a paternalist with this individual seeking to stay in control by keeping others in the dark. This is in direct contradiction to a 9,9-oriented person who strives for openness and candor in relationships. Additionally, the paternalist tries to keep tensions subdued whereas a 9,9-oriented person seeks open confrontation to discover the soundest solution. The latter is not permissible in a paternalistic culture, because it threatens control over others and is interpreted as disobedience. From a paternalistic perspective, it is the parent's role to adjudicate the squabbles of the young. A good parent would be unlikely to leave something as important as decision making up to uneducated or uninformed children.

The interplay between these two is illustrated by Al, the paternalistic boss, and Ben, the 9,9-oriented subordinate. Ben persists in expressing his convictions about what he sees to be ineffective team interaction despite Al's efforts to change the subject. Such action on Ben's part entails considerable risk because the paternalistic boss could come down on him. However, a paternalist usually displays "controlled anger," that is, emotions are kept in check and generally not revealed in their full force. To lose one's composure is to risk loss of face; parents are not supposed to fall apart in front of the children. As a result, the 9,9-oriented subordinate can often get his or her opinion aired.

Nevertheless, such a boss is difficult for this subordinate to operate under because true consensus is seldom achieved.

Recognizing Paternalistic Behavior

The words and phrases in Figure 5-4 give the flavor of paternalistic behavior.

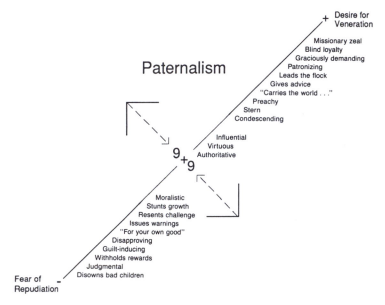

Figure 5-4. Words and phrases that characterize paternalistic behavior.

Summary

A paternalist treats other people as part of the organization family by telling them how to perform any new activity and rewarding or reprimanding as needed and desired. Others are encouraged to be responsible, but they are likely to be slow in taking initiative. They soon learn the paternalistic boss is only happy with them when they are handling problems in the prescribed manner.

The motivation of a paternalist is domination, mastery, and control exercised in a way that gains admiration. This means those with and through whom leadership is exercised become dependent. When subordinates behave and comply, they endear themselves to the paternalist, who may then become more motivated to steer their every move. This kind of helping weakens the ability of subordinates to exercise independent initiative and to contribute to organization goals. Readiness to guide their every action is unlikely to aid subordinates to become autonomous and self-reliant corporate members.

The key to change lies in gaining an awareness of the implications of this increasing dependency on the part of subordinates. The organization grows weaker by virtue of lost creativity and innovation. Needed initiatives are postponed until receiving the go-ahead by the paternalist. The solution is to stimulate more open participation among subordinates, thus earning their respect and encouraging the development of problem-solving skills.

Chapter 6

1,1: "Sorry, But It's Not My Problem . . ."

As the meeting broke up, Gil closed his notebook and looked around the room as others paired off and dispersed. Before he could get out of his chair, however, Liz caught his attention.

"Gil," said Liz. "Gil?"

Gil raised his head and met Liz's gaze.

Liz moved closer and kept her voice low as she continued. "Gil, I was wondering what you thought about today's meeting, particularly the discussion between Ed and Ben?"

"Why?" replied Gil.

"You might say I'm taking my own little survey," confided Liz.

Gil scratched his head and answered, "Frankly, I think that kind of thing keeps us in a state of agitation. We sure do know how to polarize issues around here but not how to neutralize them. That's the key! Neutrality!"

"Go on," said Liz, looking interested in what Gil had to say.

"I'd like to see us cool off and not be so personal about these matters. We all know that everyone has idiosyncrasies, quirks, and limitations; I'm not sure this thing between Ed and Ben isn't just as basic as that, if you really want to track it. They just rub each other the wrong way. If you take a close look at many of our arguments, they are hollow and without substance. Instead of trying to fill our glass with conflict, we ought to try to empty it."

Ed, who was walking past on his way out, interrupted, saying, "Sounds like double-talk to me, Gil!"

Gil responded to Ed, "If you hear it that way, so be it. I know it's impossible to change your mind."

Liz tittered good-naturedly.

Ed turned around and responded, "Look, Gil. Ben and I have a genuine difference of opinion. I happen to think he's wrong, and he thinks I'm wrong, but at least we respect our right to be different. We may not solve our disagreements, but at least we keep talking and airing our different viewpoints. It's better than not giving any opinion at all—Gil!"

Gil just stood there in silence.

Ed sneered at what he considered to be Gil's lack of backbone and walked away.

Gil said, "Liz, I've got to go. There are a million matters for me to attend to."

"Okay, Gil," responded Liz. "See you later."

Gil slipped away as quickly as possible and headed down the hall.

"Well, that knocks off half the day," he thought to himself. "I wonder what's gone wrong in my office."

Gil had come to the company 28 years ago as a young man. He had known Al through a community fraternity and, although they were not close, they shared many mutual friends. Gil had been courted to leave his position with a quasi-governmental body to serve as head of engineering in Al's group. While not unhappy in the previous post, his wife had encouraged him to take advantage of the opportunity. He submitted his resignation and made the move.

When Gil first took over, he found the company an exciting place. In contrast with the somewhat dull agency work, Celarmco was in a period of rapid growth and expansion. A whirlwind of activity kept his adrenalin flowing at top speed all of the time. Al had taken Gil under his wing and made him part of the family. At first Gil felt a certain degree of freedom to exercise new initiatives. His goal was to create a tight and cohesive network among the engineering groups under his control. Gil brought in some talented young people—high caliber, recent graduates—and transformed the unit into a state-of-the-art operation.

Before long, however, Gil felt a growing pressure from Al to coordinate his every move with other members of the group, even on matters that had little effect on the team. Gil sought to comply and brought his ideas to team meetings, asking for input and approval. He discovered that Al would chip away at his proposals until they bore little resemblance to his initial ideas.

Gil had never been one to assert himself, always being much more likely to go along with what others saw to be the soundest approach. He tended to cave in to the pressures of his peer group and his newly found convictions grew weaker and weaker until they disappeared from view. Soon Gil came to depend on Al to issue the word from on high, operating in a reaction/response way to comply with whatever was requested. This resulted in less conflict, and because Gil didn't like conflict, it became his style of choice in interacting with others. Even at home, Gil preferred for his wife and kids to rule the roost, giving in and allowing them to have their way rather than take a strong position.

Over the years Al had moved up a couple of notches and Gil had moved with him. As Gil saw it, they had an "understanding" of sorts. Al issued orders and Gil complied and, for the most part, they tried to stay out of each other's way. This suited Gil just fine.

Gil had been reminiscing over the "old days," but the sound of the noon whistle quickly brought his attention back to the present. He sauntered down the hall towards his office.

Passing the message board, he noticed there were three calls, two of which had requested a callback. Gil shrugged his shoulders and collected the notes, laying them on the edge of his desk. "I'll answer them later," he thought to himself. Normally, he would get his secretary, Rita, to do it but these required his personal attention.

Gil opened his drawer and fished out the lunch he had brought from home. He had started brown bagging it years ago. The rationale was that it saved money, and there was always the possibility that Al might take pity and give him a raise. The real reason though was that Gil didn't want to get tangled up with people and, if he ate in the cafeteria, no doubt others would try to draw him into conversation. "I don't need that," thought Gil. "I have to attend enough 'meetings' as it is. Lunch should be a time for peace and quiet."

The phone rang and Gil pondered whether to answer it. He decided to ignore the repetitious buzzer. He took the latest issue of *Sports Magazine* out of his top drawer and started thumbing through it. Focusing on a mountain lake, he recalled last summer's vacation. "Boy, that was a beautiful trip! The bass were so thick they almost carried the boat across the water."

Gil was startled by a knock on the door. "Your wife is on line 3, sir. Do you want to take it?" Rita stood awaiting his reply.

Gil groaned and then took a deep breath. "Yeah, sure. Line 3, did you say?"

"Yes, sir," replied Rita as she made a hasty retreat.

"Hello," said Gil. "Yes, dear . . . I know, dear . . . I'd be glad to, dear . . . Not at all, dear . . . Yes, me too, dear. Bye." He sighed and wrote himself a note to stop by the grocery store on the way home.

The phone rang again and Gil jumped. "Damn, that thing won't stop!" This time, concerned that it might be Al, he picked it up.

"It's who? Well, I don't know any Mr. Ramsey. Why don't you see if you can get rid of him. Yeah, thanks." Gil shook his head and took another bite of his sandwich.

Gil's thoughts returned to the morning. "What a meeting! I really laid it on the line to them, though. Imagine! Two grown men acting like little boys. Why didn't Al nip that in the bud? Well, at least I managed to stay out of it, for the most part anyway. Ed is such a bully! I wish he'd leave me alone! If people could just learn to stay out of each other's way, we'd all be a lot better off." With this, Gil unwrapped his chocolate chip cookies and a smile came to his face. "My favorite part!" he grinned as he chomped into the first one.

□ □ □

Gil had lost his interest in the organization and its people a long time ago. You might say that he got pushed into the 1,1 corner and, now that he's been there so long, he's comfortable with just staying there.

The 1,1 leadership pattern is located in the lower left corner of the Grid, as shown in Figure 6-1.

The 1,1-oriented boss experiences little or no contradiction between the need for production and the needs of people. Concern for both is at a minimum. As Gil remarked in the story, "If people could just stay out of each other's way, we'd all be a lot better off." While this may seem an unlikely style for a manager to possess, it is more common than most of us realize. It takes talent to be a

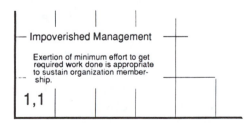

Figure 6-1. The 1,1 Grid style is located in the lower left corner of the Grid.

successful 1,1 and we'll show some of the specific tactics employed to stay invisible while still being present. You may already have picked up a few from Gil.

Motivations

The motivations of a 1,1-oriented individual like Gil are shown in Figure 6-2.

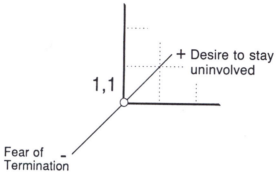

1,1

+ Desire to stay uninvolved

Fear of Termination

Figure 6-2. The plus and minus motivations of the 1,1 Grid style.

The positive motivation is a desire to stay uninvolved, to fulfill the requirements of your job, exposing yourself to as little contact with others as necessary. A 1,1-oriented individual feels emotionally drained and withdrawn. While there may be underlying feelings of concern for the organization and its members, it is viewed as "not worth it" to get involved. Getting close to people ultimately spells trouble. Getting committed to organization purpose only leads to disappointment. There is a realization, however, that one must demonstrate sufficient presence to maintain employment. This means doing the minimum necessary to build seniority with no real regard for making a contribution. The need to keep one's job is what leads to the minus motivation.

The 1,1⁻ motivation is fear of termination, or fear of losing organization membership. This happens if people see you as a non-performer, deadwood, or a drag on the organization. It can spell the beginning of the end for a 1,1-oriented person. This individual may be bored to tears with the job routine but he or she never reveals it, hiding feelings of discontent and restlessness from others.

Although work does offer little sense of purpose or fulfillment, it promises the benefits of financial security and retirement. There is an underlying rationalization that "the organization owes it to me." It is important to be present but inconspicuous because this enables a 1,1-oriented individual to avoid controversy. Other people are kept at a distance, so the 1,1-directed person doesn't have many ene- mies—but neither does he or she have many friends. This is the organization isolate who does not stand out; he or she is the conference room wallflower. The degree to which such an individual can remain unobtrusive and nonresponsive is governed by the minimum that others are prepared to tolerate while at the same time not attracting their attention.

Presenting oneself in this low-key and colorless manner is the secret to maintaining neutrality. A 1,1-oriented "leader" occupies a position of authority in name only. The nonchalant attitude is expressed in the motto, "See no evil, speak no evil, and hear no evil." In this way you are protected by not being noticed. The 1,1-oriented individual glides through the organization, leaving no permanent mark. But, as in the case with Gil, the organization has left its mark on him by "pushing" him from a more active Grid style into the 1,1 corner. Now his days consist of watching the minutes tick by until he can claim his retirement.

Conflict Solving

By holding the title of boss, yet not acting like one, 1,1-oriented managers remain relatively uninvolved in conflict. This is the "ostrich dynamic," keeping your head buried in the sand in order to avoid "seeing" problems. Disagreeable situations may even be noticed but are ignored, and sometimes they actually disappear for lack of attention. However, situations of potential conflict do arise from time to time, and these must be dealt with. How does a 1,1-oriented individual react to conflict?

A person oriented in the 1,1 direction takes a bystander or laissez-faire approach to leadership and responds to conflict by seeking neutrality, shown in Figure 6-3. Neutrality implies less commitment than 1,9 yielding. When a subordinate sees the 1,1-ori- ented boss in this neutral stance, the reaction is often one of disdain. When subordinates need help, it doesn't take long for them to learn

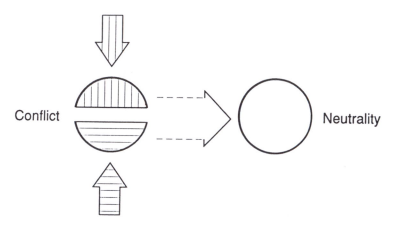

Figure 6-3. A 1,1-oriented individual responds to conflict by seeking neutrality.

to go elsewhere, because they know they won't get it from the 1,1-oriented manager. The boss's neutrality is a real impediment to progress; he or she is a weak link in the hierarchical chain.

What are the motivations underlying such behavior? The positive side of the 1,1 approach to conflict is expressed in the phrase, "I try to 'turn off' conflict by waving the white flag or turning away from those who waste their time arguing over the issues." In the story, when pressed to reveal his point of view on the Ben/Ed argument, Gil carefully avoided taking either side and instead made a joke that his co-workers were acting like children and wasting the team's time. The 1,1– side of conflict is, "I avoid getting implicated in disagreements by making myself scarce, either disappearing completely or blending into the woodwork. If pushed, I respond with 'I don't know.'"

Preventing Conflict

The 1,1-oriented individual avoids conflict by engaging in a disappearing act. There may be differences between what you see and what you don't in terms of 1,1 behavior. When you look at a 1,1-oriented manager's behavior, it appears to conform to the requirements of a job description because this person always tries to do enough to get by and to stay within acceptable parameters of conduct. In other words, the 1,1-oriented person is on time because being late attracts attention. When you walk by this individual's office, he or she appears to be busy and absorbed in the work at hand. You won't catch this person leaving early or working less than the specified number of hours. Sick leave is within normal standards and vacations are checked out with the necessary parties in advance. Occasional expressions of mild interest serve to lessen the apathy and boredom this manager may feel. Furthermore, they give the appearance of involvement in the deeper objectives of the organization so that the 1,1-directed individual doesn't stand out as a loner.

The behavior you don't see is likely to be different. It reflects the depth of resignation and indifference that characterize the 1,1 orientation. One way to avoid trouble is to be sure to return phone calls but to do so when the other party is unlikely to be available. Contact with others is not initiated unless the 1,1-oriented person is specifically asked to take such action. Memos not marked "Action" are filed in the wastebasket.

When participation is expected, the tactic is to be seen but not heard. In a group setting, a 1,1-oriented manager seldom participates in a spontaneous manner. Comments are made from time to time, but nothing is said to reveal thoughts (or the lack of them) regarding the issue under discussion. "Could be," "Possibly," "I guess so" casually acknowledge some point but with little or no commitment intended or conveyed. You just don't know what this person values because it is never disclosed. Acting in this passive way is acceptable only as long as others fail to notice it. If and when others do observe this behavior, the 1,1-oriented individual may become the target of outrage and disdain.

Another tactic used by the 1,1-oriented person is message passing. This is designed to evade involvement in the affairs of others. Orders from above are moved down the line so as not to get caught "holding the bag." Messages from below may or may not be conveyed to those above. It depends on whether failing to do so might draw the ire of higher-ups somewhere down the road. It is dangerous to get pinpointed as the weak link in the communication chain. The preferred strategy is neither to add to nor to subtract from what others have said. Instead, repeat, repeat, repeat. This is the safe way to pass a message without becoming entangled in the interpretation of its contents. If a subordinate asks, ''What does that mean?'' the 1,1-oriented manager replies, ''Look, you know as much as I do. I'm giving it to you verbatim.''

The flavor of the 1,1 orientation is seen in the following example with Gil. Al has just held a weekly staff meeting where changes in procedures and policies were discussed and where team members have been asked to initiate the appropriate changes within their own areas of responsibility. Gil's behavior was acceptable during the meeting itself; he had listened, taken notes, nodded as key points were raised, all indicative to Al of his ''interest.''

> Gil returned to his office and told Rita to inform his subordinates of a 1:00 meeting. He started the meeting promptly although only four of the five had arrived. Gil carefully read the notes and conclusions so that no one could later accuse him of not communicating the full story. Upon finishing his recitation, he dismissed the group and filed the dated notes in his drawer.
>
> Several of the subordinates lagged behind. The one who was late said, ''Boss, I missed the background on that first point you made. Can you fill me in?''
>
> Without looking up, Gil replied, ''Bob, why don't you ask one of your teammates? OK?'' That was the end of that.
>
> A second subordinate mustered up courage. ''Boss, when is the actual deadline on the government project?''
>
> Gil scratched his head. ''They didn't say. Maybe I'll hear more on that next week.''
>
> Rita stuck her head in the door and interrupted the conversation, ''Mr. Phillips, they just delivered 15 boxes of supplies to our department. What should I do with them?''
>
> ''I don't know,'' Gil answered in a monotone voice. ''Al said to order them. Just let them sit until we find out what to do.'' With that, he grabbed his notebook and said, ''I've got to go.''

This incident describes a typical 1,1 approach. The ''facts'' as this manager heard them from above were delivered to subordinates. If Gil ever gets called on the carpet, he can say in all honesty, ''I told them what to do. If they haven't done it, it's because they didn't listen. It's not my problem.''

What happens when a subordinate makes a mistake? Gil might mutter to himself, "Oh! They are always causing me trouble. But what in the world can I do?" Responsibility finds no home with the 1,1-oriented manager. The finger is always pointed at "them."

Handling Conflict When It Appears

When conflict arises, there are many ways for a 1,1-oriented manager to create the appearance of responding without actually presenting a point of view. This is consistent with the basic strategy of maintaining neutrality in order to stay safe.

A grunt is the best reply of all. It can mean "Okay," "Sure," or "Whatever . . . " When pushed up against the wall, a 1,1-oriented person's retort might be "It doesn't matter to me" or "It's no skin off my back," but both of these replies invite controversy, whereas "hmm" is an absolute dead-end. How do you respond to the latter? About all you can do is drop the subject.

The 1,1-oriented individual is an artist when it comes to giving responses that say nothing: "I'm not a mind reader . . . ," "I haven't heard anything . . . ," "I just don't know . . . ," "Sorry, I wasn't there . . . " If pressed further, the 1,1-oriented individual exercises some real creativity: "It's up to you. . . , " "Whatever you say . . . , " "Well, that's in your job description—not mine," "You're asking the wrong person. I'm no expert on that matter." When challenged at a later time on the lack of input, a typical response is, "If you wanted to know what I thought, you should have asked!"

Although 1,1-oriented people give up easily in an argument, it is important not to convey the impression of backing off. Neutrality is best maintained by responding to disagreement with a quip like, "Fine! That's your opinion and you're certainly entitled to it." When Ed pins Gil to the wall, Gil's response is, "Well, if you hear it that way, so be it. God knows I can't change *your* mind."

Many times a 1,1-oriented person answers in vague and general terms that reveal little or nothing. A comment such as "I suppose so" or "Who knows?" is one way to pass on a contentious point without making enemies. Although others are unlikely to be satisfied with such a reply, the 1,1-oriented manager feels safe because no obligation has been created. Saluting is preferable to resisting and may take the form of "Whatever you say . . . " or "Yeah, I think that might be true." There is implied agreement without explicit commitment.

Complaints are dealt with by remarks aimed at downplaying their significance or delaying action. "It'll probably work itself out." The "it" becomes "Out of sight, out of mind," the hope being that "it" will soon fade from view.

Written complaints in the form of a letter or memo are filed and forgotten. "There's no use worrying about that." If the issue arises again, the 1,1-oriented manager can plead ignorance and say, "I can't answer you right now. I need to look it up and get back to you."

When a 1,1-oriented manager realizes that subordinates are working at cross-purposes, the general approach is to ignore it and stay out of the way of the contenders. If the conflict becomes severe enough to endanger future security, the negative motivation clicks on and the 1,1-oriented manager may try to quash the conflict. This can be done in a matter of fact way by shifting assignments or separating people, arranging for transfers, and other seemingly neutral actions.

The double-talk tactic can be especially useful when there are two points of view, each supported by an important faction. Not wanting to offend either party, the following may be offered: "Well, Liz, your idea sounds pretty good and the evidence you have offered supports it but, on the other hand, there are some strong points in favor of Ben's position," or "I can see that it would be possible to do it Liz's way but I can also see the possibility of doing it Ben's way." A sympathetic message is conveyed to both sides and the 1,1-oriented manager is free to go in either direction once a final course of action is determined.

Another way to live with conflicts is to free yourself of the burden by mentally walking out on them. If others press for resolution, a 1,1-oriented manager might say, "Everything will work out. Just give it time." The days slip by; the weeks turn into months. This is one more way to dampen resistance, and it allows the 1,1-oriented manager to live with conflict by just hoping it will go away.

Initiative

A 1,1-oriented person is apathetic and unlikely to develop, much less initiate, new ideas or courses of action. The intent is sit back and to let things run their course. The most characteristic action of such a person is the effort put into doing the minimum. Even here, actions are passive and nonassertive.

When outright avoidance is not an option, the strategy is to throw the problem in someone else's lap. If you can delegate the matter to a subordinate, by all means do so! For example, if another department files a complaint with Engineering, Gil quickly acknowledges it through a third party or in writing. He might get a subordinate to study the matter and determine how to alleviate the complaint. However, once Gil's subordinate accepts this responsibility, he or she has also assumed responsibility for implementation.

When a 1,1-oriented manager must supervise several facilities, self-initiated visits to each location are avoided through the rationale: "I just can't get to them all and it would be unfair for me to visit some and not others. Those that I missed would feel ignored. So . . . "

A basic assumption for the 1,1-oriented individual is the "can't do" attitude. The passivity stemming from this prevents even reasonable initiative. Caution becomes extreme. There are a thousand excuses for not taking initiative: "It just wouldn't work." "The boss might get upset." "It might make subordinates angry." "They said 'no' last time." There are 9,999 more, but all take their character from the same origin. The 1,1 "can't do" attitude has its roots in "Don't upset the apple cart." Initiative spells risk for a 1,1-oriented person. Risk can lead to failure, which draws attention to the individual who took the risk. Then comes the assault: "Why in the world did you do that?" "You should have known better." "Won't you ever learn?" All of these can be avoided by not putting oneself in a position to be hurt. The easier, softer way is to glide along and live with an attitude of "can't do" rather than risk the consequences of disagreement and conflict.

The plus motivation for 1,1 initiative is, "I put out enough effort to stay out of trouble but I get rid of work by delegating to lower levels whenever possible." The minus side is, "I don't initiate action unless I have to." When Gil returns to his office and discovers several phone calls have been taken in his absence, he considers the possibility of delegating the task of a return response to Rita. This is the standard procedure. However, because these calls require personal attention, he begrudgingly accepts responsibility.

Inquiry

The 1,1 attitude toward inquiry is, "The less I know about it, the better. That way I can always plead ignorance." In other words, it is better to be like a turtle with your head pulled in, looking neither right nor left.

Such an attitude is unlikely to be acceptable to others at any level. Therefore, inquiry is carried out to position the 1,1-oriented manager at the minimum "need-to-know" basis. Information is a defense rather than a means to solve problems. What knowledge is obtained is of such a superficial nature that the 1,1-oriented manager still risks being seen as uninformed. When asked a question for which he or she has no answer, the manager simply responds, "I'll see if I can find out." This avoids the criticism that might be forthcoming if the reply were "I don't know." It may even relieve anxieties felt by the inquiring party.

The 1,1+ statement for inquiry is, "I seek to stay informed enough to be in the know, but I certainly don't stick my nose into anyone else's business." For example, before Gil goes to one of Al's meetings, he carefully reviews the agenda and studies memos relevant to his department. However, it is only a review, done to stay out of trouble with no intent to discover new information or ideas. The goal is not to get caught off guard. This is reflected in the 1,1- side: "I avoid getting caught short due to lack of information. That could jeopardize my job security."

In summary, a 1,1-oriented manager is rarely well enough informed to respond effectively. In a situation of crisis, actions are perfunctory at best because this manager's knowledge is so limited.

Advocacy

When it comes to advocacy, the 1,1-oriented manager is noncommittal and reticent, avoiding spontaneous comments that might reveal some conviction. The private attitude is, "You have to be very careful what you say because it can come back to haunt you." Subordinates weigh your words to discover their meaning, trying to focus on hidden implications. Better to keep what you think to yourself than to risk an objection.

If a colleague asks, "What's new?" the 1,1 reply is, "Nothing." If the question is, "How are things going?" the response is, "Okay." Further discussion is not encouraged by this kind of answer, yet at the same time there is nothing negative about a nice, bland "okay." A 1,1-centered person is likely to let it drop there, not reciprocating with "And how are things with you?" Although this might be common courtesy, it simply prolongs the conversation. It's much easier to drift along, subscribing to the opinions of others and seeking to avoid, if possible, any further interchange.

When required, convictions are expressed in terms that don't hold the 1,1-oriented manager to a fixed point of view. On close examination, phrases such as "perhaps," "maybe," "I'm not sure," "You may be right," characterize 1,1 conversation. All are statements that provide the flexibility to go either way if forced to take a stand. The same is true of "That's not a bad idea," or "That might work." These enigmatic statements appear to endorse a position of another person, and yet later the 1,1-oriented manager can claim, "I didn't say I liked it" or "I never said it was a good idea."

The positive side of advocacy is, "I acknowledge the directions set by others without taking a firm position." In a typical Al meeting, Gil might say, "Well, whatever solution we go with, the results are what count." In this way he appears to be productivity-oriented yet, in fact, he has said nothing. The 1,1−statement is, "I avoid taking positions that draw attention to me or carry my signature." When the team is seeking to make a decision and all eyes turn to Gil for his reaction, he might respond, "I like the sound of Ed's idea. I think he's got a real handle on this thing. So I cast my vote with Ed."

Decision Making

A typical 1,1 remark is, "Decisions? That's not my problem. I only work here." This communicates a total sense of withdrawal from responsibility. The 1,1-oriented manager believes that if decisions are postponed or delayed, maybe the problems will take care of themselves or just go away. The approach is to be patient and to let circumstances dictate the outcome. When a decision must be made or is forced on the 1,1-oriented manager, it just happens. It becomes history, no longer subject to further thought, whether right or wrong, good or bad, sound or unsound.

If possible, a 1,1-oriented manager defers rather than decides. The idea is to leave well enough alone. One way is to write it off as a matter that lies in the future, "It's not here-and-now so why worry about it?" or "It's a waste of time to try to answer that. We don't have the information" or "I'll do it tomorrow."

Delegation is considered a virtue in that it is a good way to pass the buck. The rationalization is, "Giving subordinates problems helps them grow," and this may be true when subordinates have the necessary competence to work it out. Such a climate breeds a "Do your own thing" mentality in that subordinates learn to initiate activities that they want to do. Rather than delegation, this is indicative of 1,1 abdication of responsibility. No one is being led.

The 1,1-oriented boss may subscribe to "teamwork" when pressured by others to operate in this manner. But it is teamwork by appearance only. Subordinates are brought together and told, "Here's a problem for you to thrash through and deliberate. Make a decision and report to me," or "I don't want to influence you so I'll just listen." Without sufficient leadership, the group may struggle aimlessly or just fall apart. On the other hand, there may be one subordinate with leadership qualities who picks up the gauntlet and commandeers the group to resolution. The 1,1-oriented manager accepts the conclusion as self-evident. When levels above look down on this, they may think they are seeing teamwork.

Gil provides a good example of 1,1 delegation and teamwork in the following monologue: "I hold a team meeting at 10:30 every Tuesday morning. They are informal and relaxed. I ask my subordinates if they have any agenda items or matters to communicate to the group. Quite often, there is nothing and I call the meeting to a close. If I have a report from Al's team, I read this, of course. When a problem arises, I let them argue it out and come to agreement. If an impasse is reached, we just drop it. I usually accept what they say. Al thinks we're a great team."

While Gil may extol the virtues of his co-workers he has effectively removed himself from participation by abdication of responsibility. He has eliminated any real possibility of teamwork.

The positive motivation of 1,1 decision making is expressed in the statement, "I let others take responsibility for making decisions whenever possible. When I can't delegate this chore, I make decisions that reflect what is already known." The minus side is, "I avoid making decisions that might draw attention to me."

1,1-oriented managers are hard to spot because, although they are present and occupying space, you tend to look right through them as if they were invisible. They might as well be the office plant except that the plant has no negative repercussions on the organization and its people.

Critique

A 1,1-oriented manager would never think of doing critique—it's not avoided, it just never even comes to mind. There is no motivation to examine something you care so little about. As far as giving feedback to others, whether colleague or subordinate, the reaction is, "Why start a fight? Anyway, people should judge their own performance. Each individual is in the best position to judge how he or she is doing. It shouldn't be my problem . . ." So, subordinates are free to do what they want and, unless their actions lead to conflict, they are given the go-ahead by the 1,1-oriented manager. If they don't pan out, maybe they will try something different next time. At any rate, that's their business. If subordinates request feedback, the 1,1-oriented manager may feel compelled to reply, but the content of the answer is so vague and shallow as to be worthless.

The 1,1+ side of critique is, "I seek to make other people responsible for their own evaluations; I'd rather not get involved. If I have to respond, I make it neutral or tell them I need more time to think." Gil's motto that he uses with subordinates is, "The best learning is self-learning!" Subordinates are left to figure it out by themselves. The negative motivation for critique is depicted in the statement, "I steer clear of situations that might put the spotlight on me; the best way to avoid becoming a target is to stay invisible. You know what I always say, 'See no evil; hear no evil; speak no evil'—in other words, stay out of the line of fire!"

Origins of a 1,1 Orientation

A dominant 1,1 orientation does not always originate at an early point in life. Its origins may be in the adult years and related to the work situation itself.

Consider Gil's case. He did quite well academically. When he graduated from college, he took a post with the government. Then something happened. He lost interest.

Gil moved to Al's organization and found renewed purpose. He greeted his job with enthusiasm and sought to institute creative and innovative ideas within his area of responsibility. Slowly but surely, however, Al squeezed the life out of him, pushing Gil into what was seen to be the safety of the 1,1 corner. You can't get in trouble for what you don't do, unless the boss is telling you to do it, and then you comply. Otherwise, just rock along and roll with the punches.

Another case is managers who get in over their heads. A manager might have an outstanding record and receive several promotions. Suddenly this individual is responsible—and highly visible. Personal competence to operate with initiative is exposed, possibly for the first time in this person's career. The manager becomes immobilized, unable to make a move. Formerly operating under precise instructions from higher levels, this individual is now asked to act autonomously. The pressure is too great and the manager retreats to the safety of the 1,1 corner.

Once upon a time Gil was committed to his job but then he withdrew. Quite likely, 1,1 was his backup style. When the dominant style, let's say it was 5,5, no longer worked, Gil relied more and more on the 1,1 strategy. Eventually, all elements of 5,5 were completely phased out and 1,1 took over. Gil withdrew from the fight, rationalizing that his contributions were not appreciated so "Why try?" Sometimes this is called "burn-out." The previously eager individual has lost interest and the job has become empty and without challenge. Such withdrawal often results when a person can neither fight back nor afford to leave and seek employment elsewhere. The 1,1 corner offers a safe harbor that protects one from having to sail against unfavorable winds. It is the easiest way out.

Organization membership is preserved to ensure the benefits of retirement. While the 1,1-oriented manager withdraws from active participation, the appearance of acceptable behavior is maintained. There is a vacuum within but the exterior trappings remain the same. The individual conforms, not in the 5,5 sense of being one of the crowd, but simply to blend in and hang onto the job. The organization has become the means for maintaining a socially acceptable role by discharging the minimum requirements. Position, status, and pay come with minimum effort given in exchange.

Subordinate Interaction with a 1,1-Oriented Boss

The 1,1 leadership style is unlikely to be effective with subordinates, regardless of their Grid style. Some Grid styles just circumvent this boss and go on about their business. Others look to the boss for guidance but it is not forthcoming. Those who are talented seek escape. A team or department led in this manner drift towards doing less and less. The probable outcome is failure.

9,1 Reactions to 1,1

The last thing a 1,1-oriented boss wants is trouble. So, when conflict erupts with a 9,1-oriented subordinate, this manager runs for cover, taking whatever action is necessary to prevent combat. The subordinate will have to go elsewhere for a fight because the 1,1-oriented boss isn't interested. Hostile comments have little impact; this boss is indifferent. Orders conveyed from above are passed along to the 9,1-oriented subordinate. The boss's job is finished. The subordinate's job has just begun.

1,9 Reactions to 1,1

The warm and loving 1,9-oriented subordinate doesn't understand the apathy that characterizes a 1,1-oriented boss. This subordinate seeks ways to be helpful and to establish a closer relationship with the boss; the boss's reaction is to continue to dodge these efforts, feeling somewhat frustrated that the subordinate won't go away. However, the bright side for the boss is that there is no conflict here. The boss does the minimum to pass along necessary information. This subordinate is particularly useful from a standpoint of delegation because he or she accepts whatever task the boss wishes to pass along. Otherwise, the boss strives to be patient and tolerant with this subordinate.

Paternalistic (9+9) Reactions to 1,1

A paternalist has no time for a 1,1-oriented boss who is invisible. As a result, this subordinate acts as though the boss doesn't exist, even though he or she may follow lines of protocol. The subordinate may tell the boss, "This is how we're going to do it. I'll take charge." For example, perhaps the boss needs to sign some papers. The subordinate says, "Here, I've read these, and they need approval. Just sign on the dotted line." The fit is beautiful because the paternalistic subordinate wants control and all the 1,1-oriented boss wants is to abdicate responsibility without suffering pain. One self-rationalization offered by a paternalistic subordinate is, "This is for the boss's own good"; the subordinate taking the position that he or she is "protecting" or "taking care of" the boss.

1,1 Reactions to 1,1

Do you know the sound of silence? When indifference meets indifference, very little by way of productivity is likely to occur. Everyone is going through the motions, doing the bare minimum to keep things going. When problems arise, this boss and subordinate may get together and complain about how "they" are to blame. A climate of negativity surrounds this pair. Their "can't do" attitude may effectively block innovative and creative effort on the part of others. This duet actually maintains a fairly close relationship considering they are both 1,1. They find a certain "force" in numbers and others tend to avoid this wall of resistance, which is exactly what this alliance seeks to achieve.

5,5 Reactions to 1,1

The 5,5-oriented subordinate feels a certain degree of frustration with a 1,1-oriented boss because this leader is not involved in the group and up to date on company affairs. The disinterested and mechanical ways in which a 1,1-oriented boss operates do little to stimulate interest on the part of this subordinate. The unfortunate outcome of such leadership is that it operates by norms and standards that reflect "doing the minimum." This tends to drag 5,5 performance down to meet the norm. In other words, people with acceptable performance begin to achieve less and less. The result may be that they themselves land in the 1,1 corner.

Opportunistic Reactions to 1,1

In contradiction to the 1,1/paternalistic pair, the opportunistic subordinate feels no need to protect the boss and he or she may even manipulate higher levels to get the 1,1-oriented boss fired or moved out of the way. This can be done by aiding those above to see the 1,1-oriented boss's clay feet without the boss ever knowing or recognizing what is going on. Disparaging remarks are offered about the boss to others, but not to the boss directly. Such comments can be ruthless, particularly so because the opportunistic subordinate presents this as, "Being in the best interests of the organization."

The opportunistic subordinate tries to take charge and run the show. As a subordinate, he or she can be condescending to the boss because there is so little respect for the boss's non-performance. This is presented as outward acceptance and inward disdain. It is a subjugating attitude turned upwards. The boss is treated like a "subordinate." The opportunistic subordinate considers the boss on the way out. In other words, "Clear the way for the future—the 'me' generation."

The opportunistic subordinate may offer to "help." For instance, "I'll stand in for you. Just stay here and relax." The opportunistic subordinate represents his or her own interests, not the boss's, and the opportunist is sure to take credit for any moves that are made and any positive thinking that results. In other words, the subordinate becomes a boss replacement and thereby usurps control. This alleviates the boss's concerns about his or her own absence, but ultimately the boss may get axed by virtue of not being present and responsible for team action.

9,9 Reactions to 1,1

This subordinate obviously has difficulty understanding where a 1,1-oriented manager is coming from—no concern for people and no concern for production. The subordinate may think, "There's nobody home inside this person! Where is the leadership supposed to come from?" The shallow and superficial knowledge do little for a subordinate who is seeking sound solutions based on thorough understanding. The subordinate pressures the boss for involvement to no avail. Any efforts to "develop" the boss are stifled as the boss leans back on authority to disengage him- or herself. If the subordinate seeks self-development, the boss doesn't encourage it but neither does he or she stand in the way. The probable outcome is that this subordinate will leave the organization or find some recourse through higher levels to escape to a more productive environment.

Recognizing 1,1 Behavior

Figure 6-4 illustrates the many words and phrases that are commonly used in describing 1,1-oriented behavior and leadership style.

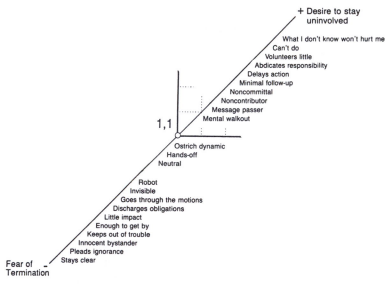

Figure 6-4. Words and phrases that characterize the 1,1 Grid style.

Summary

The Grid helps us understand how the underlying 1,1-oriented assumptions reveal themselves in a person's behavior. Foremost among these is the game of "sham" where an individual goes through the motions of being involved while lacking any true commitment. The objective is to be visible but mentally this person is absent. If you find yourself in the 1,1 corner, you are always present and on time. You don't abuse organization rules. You don't intentionally inconvenience others. You may be a nice person and other people may like you. Obviously, you're not a "zero," or you would probably have lost your job a long time ago. Sooner or later, however, the fact that you are not "really there" and that your absence, or presence, makes little or no difference becomes known. Then you're in trouble, because the organization may decide it wants more.

It might seem impossible for an individual like Gil to get away with being such a drag on the organization. However, as we have shown in this chapter, there are many creative ways for remaining present with little or no visibility. What a boon for the organization it would be if this creativity could be turned to productive purpose!

Chapter 7

5,5: "I Can Live With That . . ."

Frank was just leaving a meeting at headquarters with Joe Thompson and Harriet Turner.

"Thanks for coming by, Frank," said Harriet. "We appreciate the background. It was very helpful."

"I feel that way, too," said Joe. "You can count on us. We'll treat what you've said with the utmost confidence. Without this perspective on Al and his people, we might suffer repetition of the same problem."

Frank accepted the expression of appreciation in a dignified way and left, thinking to himself, "Sounds like my turn may be coming up."

When Frank was gone, Harriet turned to Joe and said, "What do you make of it? What's really going on?"

"Beats me, Harriet," replied Joe.

Harriet said, "I hate thinking what I'm thinking but it seems to me Al is in over his head. We've seen his tendency to slip into complacency and then to live with the tempo-in-progress that the rest of the team has come to accept. This may be Al's backup weak spot and, if it is, we can't risk it again."

Joe was quiet but finally responded, "The problem is in my bailiwick."

"I don't want to influence you one way or the other," said Harriet, "but why don't we look at the options. If you decide to move on it, which direction would you take?"

Joe pondered the question, "Well, you and I have just reviewed personnel across the board. There's no better time than now while it's still fresh in our minds."

"We have some good talent that could be transferred into Al's team," mused Harriet. "I can think of two specifically who could benefit from such exposure."

"Who did you have in mind?" asked Joe.

"Before we do that, let's look at Al's team and see what resources we have there."

Joe jumped in and remarked enthusiastically, "I like the way Frank came forth. You know, he keeps us in the know. He's very helpful in a dignified sort of way, and he seems to have good intentions."

"Well," said Harriet, "you can look at that another way. He might also be trying to undermine Al. Frank seems to operate undercover, rather than in the open. Sometimes I think he's talking out of school. If the information is so important, we should be learning it directly from Al. Coming from Frank, it could be interpreted as backbiting."

"Maybe so," said Joe. "This is a high-risk game we're in. To tell you the truth, I feel like I need all the help I can get."

"We might be better off just leaving Frank where he is," said Harriet. "Regardless of who is put in Al's slot, good or bad, Frank will undoubtedly continue to keep us informed."

"What about Liz?" said Joe. "We put her in there to give them a real shot of IQ. How's she been doing?"

"You heard what Frank said," replied Harriet. "She's pleasant, a good team player, although she plays up to Al a bit. But she's not leaving much of an imprint. That's been my impression as well. Nothing has changed by virtue of her being there. She hasn't contributed much in terms of deep thinking. Nor has she done anything to hasten their tempo. She's a 'live and let live' type of person. She makes a reasonable contribution to team effort. From what I understand, she provides balance. She helps them stay on track and to perform in a fairly smooth way."

"What about Ed?" said Joe.

"That guy's a tiger," laughed Harriet. "All you have to do is aim him at whatever you want and he'll hunt it down and chew it up. The trouble is he's a poor team player. He doesn't know how to work with people, only through them, using them as tools. He fails to take advantage of the valuable resources from other people for input by letting them express their viewpoints. He's impatient and unwilling to hear any argument other than his own. He's a great crisis manager, but otherwise a loner. He doesn't see the problems he creates for others, or, if he does, he doesn't seem to care. Like I said, he doesn't consult and he seldom offers rationale to his people. He just says, 'Here's the way it's to be done and if you don't like it, too bad.'"

"Is there anybody else among the current group?" asked Joe.

Harriet thought and then answered, "Well, we've seen Ben come up and up and up. He's been called a boy wonder. I think Ben is a real self-mover. He doesn't wait to be told what to do. He has a sense of urgency and seems to operate by high standards. When it comes to people, he's the opposite of Ed. Ben discusses, listens to arguments, consults. He doesn't back off from his own convictions just because they're different from others. He confronts people, but not in a provoking way. I wonder if he's ready to take on more responsibility. He seems very mature for his years. The more I think about it, he just might be the solution to our problem with Al's team. At least we ought to consider that possibility."

"Well," said Joe, "given all of that, what about Al?"

Harriet responded, "I think we've got to face up to him. Al is a good guy. He means well. He's sincere to a fault, and really wants to be acknowledged and appreciated for his good deeds. But he's content with the status quo and he's reluctant to get outside his comfort zone."

"I know," said Joe. "I get a stomach ache every time I think about how close they came to losing that deal. If you and I hadn't tipped Frank off . . . "

"Exactly," said Harriet. "Al tends to be too secretive and he's reluctant to share information with others. He's smart enough and he's certainly loyal and dedicated."

An idea occurred to Joe. "What about a staff assignment, with a bunch of good high-techies to work with him and keep him on a steady diet of facts and data?"

"That might work," answered Harriet. "What about the new Global Business Committee we're putting together?" There was a glimmer of recognition in Joe's eyes but Harriet went on to explain. "The one responsible for monitoring our emerging presence in the EEC as well as maintaining a corporate orientation as to risk and opportunities emerging from changes in Eastern Europe."

"Oh, yeah!" said Joe. He paused and reflected. "Do you think Al should head it up?"

"Probably not," replied Harriet. "Al would have his hands full just being a member. They would all have equivalent status anyway—one vote per person. It's an advisory board. And I think it's something Al would be good at. Plus he could make a real contribution to this new effort."

"I definitely like the idea," said Joe. "It would relieve Al of his current responsibilities without causing him to lose face. It's the kind of assignment he would interpret as an indication of our appreciation for his dedicated service and deep corporate loyalty."

"Okay. When would you talk to Al?" asked Harriet.

"According to Frank," said Joe, "Al's having a victory celebration over the successful bid. If I make a decision to go this way, and I'm leaning in that direction, we could review them with Al and whomever we select as his replacement, and from what you say, I guess Ben is it. Then we could use the occasion of the banquet to make a formal announcement. Al loves to be acknowledged and honored. I feel reasonably certain he'd see that as a heart-felt expression of our appreciation."

"That sounds like a good approach. Think about it some more, Joe, and get back to me. Do you want me to go with you when you talk to Al?"

Joe nodded. Then he said, "I'll explore it with the boss in the meantime and see how the wind is blowing up there."

□ □ □

Liz and Dan were absorbed in conversation when suddenly she became aware of the time.

"It's almost 1:00 o'clock! Dan, I'm sorry, but I've got to run. I have a meeting with my group in 30 minutes."

"Okay," said Dan. "Let me clean this up and we can be on our way." He picked up their trays and quickly deposited the garbage in the nearest trash bin.

Liz smiled as he returned to the table. "Dan," she said, "you're so meticulous in everything you do!"

"Oh," he blushed, "not really. It's only because the waiters are so busy. I just thought I'd help them out. Well, are you ready to go?"

They walked across the street and back into the high-rise complex that housed their offices. Liz spotted a business acquaintance across the lobby. "Oh, Dan, you go on. I have to stop and say hello to someone."

"Sure, Liz," said Dan. "Thanks for lunch. I enjoyed our little chat. You really helped me to think out my approach to that new program."

"Let's do it again soon. Okay?" Liz beamed. Then she made a beeline toward a gentleman dressed in an expensive blue silk suit.

"Brad! How are you? Liz Carlson, remember? We met at the City Business Convention last fall."

The young man looked puzzled and then suddenly a smile of recognition came to his face. He met her extended hand with his own. "Yes, I do recall. What a pleasure to see you again."

"What are you doing here?" Liz inquired. "You know, this is my office building. We occupy the tenth floor."

"That's right. I had forgotten you were with Celarmco," Brad replied. "I'm on my way up there right now."

"Oh, really?" Liz looked surprised. "What's up?"

"The legal firm I represent just took on your headquarters group as a major client," said Brad. "They sent me over here to check a few things out."

"Could you fill me in on the details?" Liz asked expectantly.

"Hmm, I'd really like to," Brad hesitated, "but I can't. You understand?"

Liz looked disappointed. She was always eager to be "in the know" on things. "Sure. It never hurts to try, though," she winked. "Are you going up?"

"In a minute," said Brad. "I'm waiting for someone. Nice to see you again."

Liz smiled and got on the elevator. A man and a woman stepped in behind her. When they got to the tenth floor, Liz scooted out, followed by the two strangers. She turned and smiled but kept on walking, thinking to herself, "I wonder what they're doing here." Liz stopped at the front desk and watched the two enter Al's office.

"That's curious," she thought. "I know I've seen them somewhere before." She searched her brain to place them, but nothing came to her.

Frank walked up behind her and said, "Hi, what's going on?"

"Not much, I'm on my way to a meeting," said Liz. "By the way, do you know if Al was expecting visitors today?"

"Why do you ask that?" Frank looked concerned.

"There are two people in there right now. I just wondered who they were," said Liz.

"No, I don't know," Frank replied, but he stared at the closed door.

"I've got to go," said Liz. "See you later."

□ □ □

"Joe Thompson, how are you doing?" Al jumped up from his seat and shook Joe's hand. "And, if my memory serves me, you are Harriet Turner," he said, turning to the woman.

"Yes, how are you?" Harriet asked. "We met last year at the Christmas party."

"That's right," Al recalled. "Have a seat, please. Joe, your secretary told me you were on your way over. What can I do for you today?"

"Al," Joe started, "I think we've got some good news for you."

Al looked puzzled, and Joe continued.

"You may remember that we've been deliberating the launch of a special task force to study Celarmco's relationship with the EEC for several months now. We're finally ready to move on that. The biggest slowdown was in finding a person qualified to lead this effort, and you're our first choice for the position. What do you think of that?"

This abrupt announcement caught Al somewhat unaware. He fidgeted in his chair, searching for a reply.

"Well, I feel honored by your confidence, but why me? Surely there are others more suitable for this job," Al responded nervously.

"No, Al, I can't think of anyone in whom our trust and confidence might be better placed," said Joe. "We're really counting on you to do this."

Al was fairly content with his current kingdom and wasn't sure he wanted to start over in a new situation. He pleaded, "What about this department? They're a young group. They need me, too."

Harriet entered the conversation at this point. "We've given that a lot of thought, and I think we've come up with a sound solution."

Al looked on expectantly as she continued.

"Joe has decided to move Ben into your slot."

"Ben?" Al looked surprised.

"Yes," continued Harriet. "Your evaluations of him have been good although you state that he's still young and somewhat naive. But we've kept an eye on him and he seems to show unlimited potential. We like the way he deals with us and the manner in which he operates with his people. His results have been outstanding. But, of course, you know that."

"Well, yes," said Al. "I can't deny that." Al looked worried. He had always told Frank that someday he would step into this position. Al continued, "Did you look at the others, like Frank? I would have expected you to name him as the primary candidate, or, if not Frank, then Ed."

Joe jumped in, "Both of them were close contenders but due to the circumstances, we want to keep them in place right now. They're valuable resources for this team and perhaps their greatest contribution at the moment is in their current positions."

"So this is all decided?" asked Al. "You know, as honored as I am by your recommendation, I'm still reluctant to leave."

"Of course you are," said Joe. "You've done a lot for this department, just as you did in your previous assignment. I haven't forgotten! But you can make a real difference in this new post."

Al looked uncertain.

Joe went on, "You know, the president himself approved my nomination of you."

Al perked up. "You're kidding? The president wants me?"

"You bet!" replied Joe. "It's quite a prestigious assignment."

"Well, in that case," said Al, "there's no way I can turn you down."

"Good," said Joe. "I'm really glad you see it that way."

"When does this all take effect?" asked Al, remembering the upcoming celebration dinner. "I had a little party planned for my subordinates."

"Excellent idea!" exclaimed Joe. "And what a wonderful time to make the announcement. Although I know they'll be sorry to see you go, at the same time they can't help but feel excited about your promotion."

"I don't know," said Al, wondering how this news would impact the team.

"Just leave it to us," replied Joe. "In the meantime, keep this under your hat. Before we leave, we'd like to have a word with Ben. Is he still in the office down the hall?"

"Yes," replied Al. "Straight down the corridor. Would you like me to show you?"

"No, thank you, we can find it." Harriet extended her hand and said, "Best wishes, Al. We have high hopes for this new group. I'm looking forward to working with you to select the right mix of people."

"Thanks," said Al. He turned to Joe, "Are you sure . . . "

"Don't worry," laughed Joe. "You're going to love it. I'll be in touch to coordinate plans for the dinner. In the meantime, just relax! You earned this, Al. Trust me!"

Al watched them leave, suddenly overwhelmed by a feeling of sadness that was quickly converted to elation. He had made it and this promotion expressed their great admiration for his ability. The years of hard work had paid off.

□ □ □

Frank saw the two as they left Al's office. They hadn't noticed him and he watched them go down the hall. He felt dismayed as he saw them enter Ben's office. "Oh, this can't be happening!" Frank thought to himself. He darted toward Al's door and nearly bumped into Al who was just stepping out.

"Excuse me, Al," said Frank. "I need to talk to you, right now."

In view of what had just transpired, Al didn't particularly want to talk to anyone, least of all Frank. Frank was persistent, however, and Al relented.

"Sure, come on in. What can I do for you?" The two men walked in and Al shut the door behind him.

☐ ☐ ☐

Joe and Harriet hailed a taxi and headed back to headquarters.

"See, I told you it would work," Joe said.

Harriet paused, "I think it would have been better to confront the issue than to shade the truth and make things sound so positive. Al will never know his limitations. How can he hope to improve?"

"It's better to let things settle down," said Joe. "Some people don't like the truth, you know, so why rub their noses in it? Besides, Al will be out of the way now, so why bring up a negative?"

"I still think it may backfire on you. And, I'm not sure I agree with your telling Al that the president gave the stamp of approval. You know that's not the way it happened, although I'll grant you that it's half true in that he didn't veto the recommendation either. But if my memory serves me right, you had to do some pretty fast talking."

"Well, it was the most expedient thing to do without making waves. And, I only said that to Al because he looked so tentative," said Joe. "I had to say something to pull him over the edge. There's no harm done. Just a little white lie and Al will never know the details."

"You and I don't see eye to eye on this matter. I think it would have been best to be candid with him. How is he ever going to get better if you don't give him accurate feedback?" asked Harriet. "Anyway, it's a moot question now, but I needed to voice my dissent. I just don't think the best way to run an organization is to keep promoting problems up the ranks."

"I hear what you're saying, Harriet," said Joe. "But I've always operated on the basis of being flexible. 'You've got to give a little to get a little.' Business life is a series of adjustments, you know. It requires a little shifting around to keep everything on an even keel. Sometimes it doesn't pay to be too open and candid."

"That's your opinion, not mine," countered Harriet. "Anyway, I do like Ben. I think he'll be a real asset to this company when he takes over Al's team."

☐ ☐ ☐

Both Liz and Joe portray the 5,5 Grid style at different levels of the organization hierarchy. Unlike the 1,9 orientation, the 5,5-oriented person doesn't yield but rather seeks a compromise or accommodation that everyone can live with. Like Joe said, "You've got to give a little to get a little."

The 5,5 orientation, shown in Figure 7-1, is located in the middle of the Grid where an intermediate degree of concern for production (5) is linked with an intermediate degree of concern for people (5).

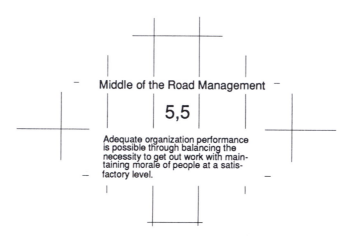

Middle of the Road Management

5,5

Adequate organization performance is possible through balancing the necessity to get out work with maintaining morale of people at a satisfactory level.

Figure 7-1. The 5,5 Grid style is located in the center of the Grid.

As in the previous Grid styles, a basic contradiction between the needs of production and the needs of people is inherent in a 5,5 orientation. The 5,5 solution to this production-people dilemma is to compromise or trade off, to give up half of one in order to get half of the other. It seeks a balance between the two rather than seeking an integrated result.

A 5,5-oriented manager only pushes for a moderate level of productivity and in return provides an acceptable amount of consideration for the attitudes and feelings of the people who implement this work. The underlying assumption is that extreme positions promote conflict and are therefore best avoided. Because of this compromise and willingness to yield on some points to gain an advantage on others, a moderate level of progress can be maintained. The expectation is that "We'll do a little bit better than last year."

A 5,5-oriented individual seeks to make reasonable progress within the system by following specified rules and regulations to maintain status as a member in good standing. "I want to look good and to be accepted by my peers." This person wears the right clothes, stays up to date on current events and other topics of interest, keeps up with management and market trends, reads the best sellers, and talks the jargon of the day. In other words, a person oriented in the 5,5 direction is a good conversationalist, friendly and outgoing, a "hail-fellow-well-met." At first glance, 5,5-oriented people seem to be on top of things and to know what's going on.

A 5,5-oriented person operates according to the rule of give and take: give a little to get a little. This whole mentality is extrapolated to teamwork—à la 5,5. It's positive reinforcement as a group norm. People become a cheering squad for one another to create a "can do" team spirit of enthusiasm and excitement. The problem, however, is that negativity is not tolerated and the team may lose sight of reality. Complacency sets in. People have been so busy building each other up that they have lost sight of the true objective.

When scrutinized more closely, it is clear that people who are motivated in a 5,5 way tend to take their cues from others. If you operate from a 5,5 orientation, the prevailing attitudes of the organization become your guiding light. If they like it, you like it; if they reject it, you do likewise. Your tendency is to embrace traditions, precedents, and past practices in a non-critical manner because "That's how things are done around here." This is seen as the safest road to travel because it's tried and true, and if it worked before, there's always the likelihood that it will work again.

The 5,5 motivational motto is, "If I think, look, and act like everyone else, I'll be seen as a member in good standing." People with a 5,5 orientation tend to identify with wealth, power, and status, or with those who have it, seeking to gain prestige by association.

Motivations

Figure 7-2 shows the motivational underpinnings of the 5,5 Grid style, which revolves around a need to "belong." For a 5,5-oriented manager, this comes from being "marketable," having those qualities that make a person a desirable and sought-after commodity. The

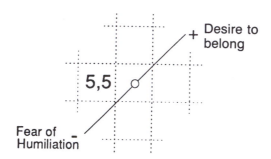

Figure 7-2. The plus and minus motivations of the 5,5 Grid style.

group wants you and values you as a member. This is where your sense of well-being comes from, not just membership as a numbered unit of the company, but membership in the group of people you work with to achieve common ends. As a 5,5-oriented person, you hope this group extends beyond the work environment itself into the realm of social activity, thus providing an added source of pleasure and satisfaction. In other words, these are people you can be safe with; you are like them and they are like you. No one is out of step.

The 5,5⁻ motivation is to avoid being humiliated or embarrassed. The greatest fear lies in finding oneself the target of ridicule and then suffering the risk of being cut off from the group. When a 5,5-oriented manager falls out of favor with peers, for whatever reason, hurt and shame are experienced. Being out of step can lead to loss of friendship and place one's membership in jeopardy. This fear of ostracism can result in intense anxiety because the 5,5-oriented person *needs* other people in order to know how to think. When this individual doesn't feel the support of the group, he or she becomes more and more anxious, uncertain about which way to turn. At the 5,5⁻ end of the scale, the manager feels totally dependent on others to know what direction to take.

When Liz first joined Al's team, she felt very self-conscious because she didn't know the "rules" by which the team operated. Her negative motivation, fear of embarrassment, was in full swing. She was very cautious about what she said and did, fearful that it would be perceived as "different." She looked for signs of appropriate behavior and as she became more comfortable with others on the team she loosened up and her positive motivation took over. Although she did so in a gracious manner, she allowed others to know that she had attended all the right schools and even knew some of the right people. She used her influence whenever possible to help other members of the group. Although a very intelligent woman, she soon learned the group norm of "good enough": Carry your weight but don't over-excel. As a 5,5-oriented manager, she knew it was important to do as well as others on the team, but not better. A good middle-of-the-road approach is the safest way to ensure group membership.

A person's IQ does not determine his or her Grid style. We can test this out in the case of Liz. If we conclude that Liz is probably an intellectual whiz kid with her Harvard MBA, MIT PhD, and whatever further honors are due her, then we can ponder questions about how intelligence and Grid style are interrelated in this given case. There is little throughout the story to suggest that Liz is capable of developing and gaining acceptance of an independent or original line of thought. This is reinforced by what others have said of her, including Harriet Turner at headquarters. Yet Liz's academic achievements tell us she is capable of understanding and succeeding in intellectual terms at an advanced level in the academic environment.

An explanation is that Liz's 5,5 orientation "prevents" her from seeing and promoting ideas that others have not yet embraced. She takes the lead on what is seen to be acceptable, with "acceptable" being defined by those with whom she interacts. She does not rely on her own ability to identify, develop, and advocate possibilities based on independent thinking. That is too risky for a 5,5-oriented person.

This suggests that any Grid style can either suppress or encourage a person's capacity for independent, creative, novel thinking, thus preventing or permitting potential contributions to the organization. In other words, Liz's intelligence is muted by her 5,5 Grid style.

Conflict Solving

How does an individual oriented in the 5,5 direction view conflict? There is an internal logic that says, "Because conflict is inevitable, a manager must deal with it, and that means cover it up or make it go away. There is an art to doing this that involves special skills of adaptation that permit people to find a middle ground all can accept." While this approach may not lead to any winners, it does ensure that there are no outright losers.

When you look at the motivations underlying the 5,5 approach to conflict, the plus side is, "I look for a compromise that everyone can live with." Remember how Joe dealt with Al's "promotion"? He knew he had to get more responsible leadership in Al's team, but he didn't want to hurt Al's feelings. He found a spot in the organization where Al would be unlikely to have a negative impact and then he told Al that he was the only one for the job. According to Joe, it satisfied all the requirements in an acceptable way. The fact that he had to shade the truth a little to avoid a situation of potential conflict with Al was beside the point.

The underlying negative motivation is, "I avoid disagreeable tension by shifting slightly to accommodate other points of view."

Preventing Conflict

The ideal situation for a manager like Liz or Joe is one that is conflict-free. Therefore, much effort is expended to avoid it. Several strategies of conflict prevention are employed.

The first involves careful adherence to traditions, precedent, and past practices. The idea is that these are deemed to represent "the safe way of doing things" and therefore they are unlikely to lead to disagreement. Furthermore, they take the focus off people. You can always say, "That's just the way we do it." When history can be relied upon, no personal decisions have to be made. Launching off in new directions is risky. A 5,5-oriented manager prefers the "better safe than sorry" approach.

Another conflict prevention technique is to structure the relationships of people according to pre-set conventions. This is conflict management by protocol, which dictates what people are to do in situations of uncertainty. By adhering to protocol, it may be possible to avoid embarrassing actions that produce criticism from others. As a result, self-expression and spontaneity are sacrificed to organization conventions that attempt to maintain status, hierarchy, and the privilege of seniority.

A third avoidance strategy is reliance on rules and regulations as a substitute for sound managerial action. In an organization rules establish what is regarded as acceptable and proper behavior, thus reducing the need for people to act on their own discretion. As a result, disagreements are unlikely to emerge. Those who fail to conform with these guidelines soon find themselves targets of powerful peer pressure. This further relieves a 5,5-oriented manager like Joe or Liz from having to confront the situation. When rule making is used on an organization-wide basis, the result is a massive bureaucracy with its roots in the avoidance of person-to-person conflict.

Another way to dodge potential conflict is not to take an unpopular stand on an issue. This means checking things out in advance to discover the consensus or putting out anonymous signals to see how people react.

Managers like Liz and Joe employ the tactic of minimizing differences and maximizing similarities. This reduces the need to confront underlying disagreements that might lead to conflict. When people have vested interests, the 5,5 approach for gaining agreement is to meet with each person on a one-to-one basis to "bend" people's thinking toward a majority point of view. If enough agreement is gained, the issue can be brought up in public for group decision making; if not, it can be postponed or dropped. This is a time-consuming process by virtue of repeating the same conversation with several people, and it stifles the creative thinking that the exposure of ideas can stimulate in an open, problem-solving discussion.

Handling Conflict When It Appears

A 5,5-oriented manager doesn't go out looking for conflict but sometimes it comes up and can't be ignored. There are several ways in which it may be dealt with in a 5,5 orientation. Because the 5,5-oriented person sees a basic contradiction between the needs of people and the needs of the organization for productivity, confronting conflict directly is seen as a situation where someone wins and someone loses. Therefore, the 5,5-oriented manager is likely to back off until tensions are allowed to cool.

The primary 5,5 strategy for conflict resolution is compromise, accommodation, and splitting the difference. This reasonable approach is shown in Figure 7-3. Both boss and subordinate give up something to get something back. The resulting compromise is shown in the diagonal solution of Figure 7-3, which represents something in between the original positions of the two parties. This bureaucratic approach can play havoc with effective performance from the standpoint of organization achievement.

The 5,5-oriented manager's approach in a situation where several different viewpoints prevail is to incorporate a piece of each idea into the final solution. This means everyone "gives a little to get a little." No one wins, but no one loses. Obviously, the final position doesn't fully meet the needs of anyone, but it does provide a middle ground that everyone can live with rather than continue to fight.

In a 5,5 orientation, this is seen to be a reasonable point of view, reflecting adaptability and flexibility. The true goal of managerial competence, however, is to achieve the best result in terms of production through people. The best is rarely defined by something that is in the middle, intermediate, or represents a split between divergent points of view. That is why 5,5 is only average, not excellent, performance. It is trapped in the constraints of status quo rather than rising above the current level of expectations. And much of this failure to strive for more is rooted in the 5,5 perspective on conflict.

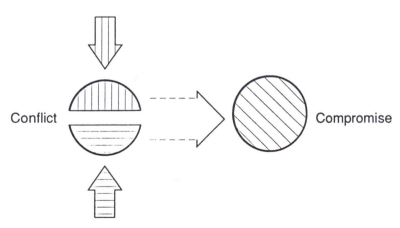

Figure 7-3. The 5,5 approach to conflict resolution is compromise, accommodation, and splitting the difference.

What happens in a situation when a 5,5-oriented manager like Liz finds herself caught between two layers of hierarchy, Al on one side and a pushy subordinate on the other? Al is saying one thing and Liz's subordinate something else. Liz relies on protocol that views it as inappropriate to bring all three levels together. Her only recourse is to act as the go-between, running back and forth from one side to the other until a final course of action can be agreed upon. This same approach is used when two subordinates disagree. The 5,5-oriented manager may separate the two parties and become an intermediary until some form of agreement and reconciliation can occur. Once again it is a time-consuming approach in which no one comes out ahead.

All of these 5,5 approaches serve to reduce tension but fail to solve the problem that created conflict in the first place.

When Conflict Remains

When conflict persists, there are several 5,5 techniques designed to smooth it over and promote the appearance of harmony. The first is the naive strategy of "We'll agree to disagree." This is like throwing your hands up in the air and saying, "Let's forget the whole thing!" The idea is that it's better to live with disagreement than to struggle with the underlying causes. The "agree to disagree" maxim is a popular 5,5 approach that provides a rational excuse for inaction.

An extension of the separation tactic between warring parties is to physically distance the two. This can mean anything from putting people at opposite ends of the building to arranging a transfer to another location or unit. This doesn't solve the conflict, but it does bring it to a standstill.

A similar approach is drawing the lines between departments. Think of Al's team. If we used the "compartmentalization" strategy, we could say, "If it's a production problem, go to Ed. If it's marketing, go to Liz. If it's personnel, go to Dan." And so on. By assigning responsibility to the different departments, conflict between departments can be bypassed. Such an approach can sometimes be justified by the complexity of an activity, but usually it is an arbitrary decision meant to provide a convenient rather than a sound way of relieving differences or avoiding tensions.

Initiative

The status quo is the arena of action for a 5,5-oriented individual. Effort is maintained at a steady pace within acceptable and orderly limits. Managers like Joe and Liz avoid novel and experimental approaches as these are viewed as too risky and could lead to loss of popularity. Innovative ideas not endorsed by the majority are dealt with by 5,5 remarks such as, "We'd better not . . . " or "That sounds a little radical . . . " or "I'll bet it's easier said than done . . . " If the creative source of such ideas persists, the 5,5-oriented manager looks for precedents: "Tell me who else has done it," "Were they successful?" or "Exactly how did 'they' do it?" If the answers are not forthcoming, the likely 5,5 reply is, "No, we'd better not."

The guiding light for 5,5 initiative lies in traditions, policies, and company practices. These "rules" provide the means for safe and risk-free conduct. By strictly relying on traditional ways of doing things, a 5,5-oriented manager feels safe and secure to initiate responsibility within acceptable limits. It forms a "comfort zone" in which to operate. The plus side of 5,5 initiative is summed up in the statement, "I only introduce activities when I know they will gain majority support." The other side of this, 5,5−, is "I avoid initiating novel ideas that have not stood the test of time."

Inquiry

Inquiry for the 5,5-oriented person is cautious and shallow because this person doesn't want to rock the boat. Inquiry can lead to conflict which, as we have already seen, people like Joe and Liz seek to avoid. However, 5,5-oriented managers like to know what is going on and therefore they frequently use the informal organization to keep apprised of the latest news and gossip. Such channels of communication are a gold mine for inquiry concerning morale and satisfaction. This lets the 5,5-oriented manager know how people are reacting to the dictates of upper management.

We often say that the 5,5-oriented manager uses the company grapevine to keep a finger on the organization's pulse. This permits the individual to observe others and to listen to what they are saying. As a result, the 5,5-oriented manager often gains popularity because he or she is always in step, rarely missing a beat. Relying on the status quo is preferred to searching for deeper understanding of issues that might lead to sounder solutions.

Questions are tentative and indirect. This enables the 5,5-oriented manager to rephrase the question or modify its content if the question provokes resistance or anxiety. "Oh, I didn't mean it that way" or "You misunderstood what I said. Let me rephrase it." Sometimes this leads to problems, however. For example, when Liz receives information about a customer complaint that has placed the company in a bad light, she may try to find out how her subordinate, John, is dealing with it. Rather than asking him directly, though, she may go to one of his peers and say, "Mike, do you know where John is? I haven't seen him today and I was wondering what he's up to." Unless Mike is a mind reader, he is unlikely to give Liz the information for which she is searching, that is whether John had successfully handled the customer complaint.

5,5-oriented listening means being alert for clues to stay in the know. For example, Liz is anxious to learn who is in Al's office and procrastinates with regard to her own commitments in an effort to discover this information. When she spots Frank, she questions him in a matter of fact way, "Do you know if Al has visitors today?" She acts similarly with others on the team, asking questions about who is doing what with whom, who is in line for a raise or a transfer or termination, and so on. All of these provide guidelines as to who is "up and coming" and who is "down and out." Liz sticks with the winners and avoids association with losers because, according to 5,5 thinking, reputation depends largely on whom you associate with.

Technical and written documents only receive a superficial reading or cursory review. Rather than waste time studying such material, a 5,5-oriented manager sees this as a good opportunity for delegation. "Here, read this and bring me back a capsule summary." This keeps subordinates busy and out of trouble and leaves the 5,5-oriented manager free to focus on more interesting areas of concern.

What are the underlying motivations for 5,5 inquiry? The 5,5+ side of inquiry is, "I try to stay up to date on all information concerning the organization and its people, but I seldom make it a point to study any particular item on an in-depth basis." The 5,5− side is, "I avoid getting caught in the embarrassing situation of not knowing what's going on." Liz asked Brad why he was visiting Celarmco. She was disappointed when he refused to break a confidence because she was always eager to be "in the know." That's how Liz maintains her popularity with the group. She is a good conversationalist, a skill she employs to further her knowledge about company affairs. The more she is able to discover about where others stand on the issues, the better able she is to ascertain the safe, majority point of view.

Advocacy

Managers oriented in a 5,5 direction are unlikely to be strong advocates of any position. If they are challenged, the tendency is to back off or to become evasive, sometimes allowing the convictions of others to override their own private judgments, because it's "in the interest of progress." The convictions of managers like Liz and Joe are usually shallow and vague.

A 5,5-oriented person may advocate in a reasonably strong manner when speaking in behalf of the boss or company. For example, Liz might say to her subordinate, John, "This company has stood for customer satisfaction for 35 years! It's our job to live up to that reputation!" In other words, when there is an established position or party line, the 5,5-oriented manager feels free to express convictions in support of it. That's because "The *company* is behind me on this!" While these are not personal convictions in the sense of being internally derived, they may be interpreted as such by others.

If you fall in the middle of the Grid, advocacy is not determined by your convictions but by what is politically safe or workable; what sells. Expedient positions are embraced, frequently at the expense of a sounder solution. This has important implications for corporate ethics. A 5,5-oriented manager is motivated only to do what everyone else is doing— right or wrong! The result is an erosion of principled thinking, thereby undermining equity and justice because no one is prepared to question prevailing attitudes that are unsound.

A further look at 5,5 behavior reveals that bending the truth, half-truths, or white lies are justified as acceptable tactics for getting results. Candor is sacrificed as a way of getting cooperation or because it is "the practical thing to do." Remember how Joe dealt with Al. Joe knew he had to move Al out of his current position to one that was "safer" for the company, but he didn't confront Al on his limitations because this might be demotivating. Joe's position would be: "Some people don't like to be challenged." It was easier to bend the truth and withhold information in order to accomplish the desired objective with the least amount of tension. The problem with doing this is that it weaves a web of contradictions and after a period of time the person practicing such behavior may get "caught." It is not intended to be a destructive manipulation of people; rather, the 5,5-oriented manager is "just tailoring the facts" to make them more palatable to others.

The 5,5+ motivational statement is, "I take positions that reflect the common point of view. I keep my finger on the pulse of the organization so that I know where people stand." For a 5,5-oriented manager like Liz, what happens when she isn't sure what position to take? She might say, "Based on what Al, Ed, and Ben have said on this matter, I'll throw my support to that camp." That certainly sounds like the safe path.

The 5,5− motivation for advocacy is, "I avoid taking positions that would make me stand out. I don't want to rock the boat and embarrass myself by looking different!"

Decision Making

Decisions are quick and easy in a 5,5 orientation because you rely on precedent to tell you what to do. If it hasn't been done before, don't do it! In reality, of course, a manager may have to make decisions that have no previous road to follow. This becomes a difficult process because the 5,5-oriented manager is afraid of the unknown. Therefore, this individual resorts to a variety of "techniques" for guidance.

For example, opinion polls and surveys are a good way to find out what people think without exposing your own thoughts on an issue. Once the results come in, you can say, "Well, that's exactly where I stand. Right with the majority." A decision is made without ever putting your own judgment on the line. If it turns out to be a bad decision, "We all go down together."

A 5,5-oriented manager delegates on the basis of equity and fairness. This means carving up responsibilities so that everyone gets a fair share. No one should have to shoulder more than anyone else. While it works out quite nicely on a mechanical level, it may be far removed from a sound approach that looks for solutions from those best qualified to contribute.

Popularity is the key determinant of decision making rather than objective evidence. The idea is that, "If the majority of us think this is the right answer, it *must* be right." This is a common mistake in many management circles today, but it is the preferred approach when people don't know what to do. It defines a situation where individuals prefer to go along with group opinion rather than engage in thorough inquiry, strong advocacy, or confrontation. The danger is that the majority overwhelms opposition and pushes a "unanimous" decision through to implementation. If group thinking has been based on unchallenged faulty assumptions, chaos may result. The excuse is, "But everybody else agreed that it was the right way to go!"

The underlying motivations for 5,5 decision making are "I make decisions within the confines of precedent, past practice, or protocol" for 5,5+ and "I avoid decisions that could turn around and bite me" for 5,5−.

Critique

The 5,5 approach to feedback is positive reinforcement. If you encourage subordinates to do well by offering praise, this keeps them motivated to do an acceptable level of productive work. Negative feedback, on the other hand, is risky because it can backfire. Like the 1,9-oriented individual, a 5,5-oriented manager doesn't like giving people bad news. He or she would much prefer to play up the positive. However, the 5,5-oriented manager realizes that people need to know their weaknesses in order to stay in step with the group and keep their behavior consistent with others. As a result, this manager has a clever technique called the "sandwich approach." When Liz sits down for an annual performance appraisal with John, she starts by telling him several positive aspects of his performance, then interjects several negative pieces of feedback, and concludes with compliments and praise for John's effort. In other words, she "sandwiches the criticism" in between positive statements. Once again, this is all in an effort to accommodate the employee and to make the necessary "medicine" more palatable.

Another technique is to offer a suggestion in a roundabout way. For example, in working with Al, Joe, the 5,5-oriented headquarters manager, might say, "Do you think it might be better to frame the report in this way? I know that's what they did last year and the president loved it." Although Joe has not specifically told Al what to do, we all know Al is not stupid. Undoubtedly, he has gotten the message about the "right" way to do it.

The 5,5 approach to feedback is superficial and shallow. It is not candid, open, or straightforward. The likely result is that those who receive it misunderstand what is being said or interpret it in a way that permits them to ignore it.

The 5,5+ statement of critique is, "I balance the bad with the good, but I make sure the scale tips in the latter direction. After all, I won't be very popular if I go around criticizing people."

Let's examine how Liz critiques John when he shows her a report he is working on. "John, about that report. I enjoyed the way you put that together and particularly your concluding remarks. I think it presents our unit in a good light. However, before we submit it, how about checking those specs out with some of the other marketing analysts. They seemed a little bit off track to me. Anyway, keep up the good work! I look forward to seeing the final." Liz has sought a balance of bad and good. John won't feel offended and he'll be motivated to correct any potential weaknesses.

The 5,5− side of critique is, "When I offer critique, I try to do it one on one. This way, I have more control and, if I get challenged, I won't be embarrassed in front of other people."

Subordinate Interaction with a 5,5-Oriented Boss

The 5,5-oriented leader is largely controlled by tradition coupled with adherence to rules and regulations. Team tempo depends on how rapidly a 5,5-oriented manager can get others to jump on the bandwagon because such a person adjusts his or her speed to the speed of the group. Making moderate progress is a primary objective, so the 5,5-oriented manager employs various techniques of persuasion to elicit people's support.

Subordinate reactions to such leadership varies depending on the Grid style orientation of the subordinate. Let's review the different possibilities.

9,1 Reactions to 5,5

It doesn't take a 9,1-oriented subordinate five minutes to see through a 5,5-oriented boss. When the boss starts to speak, the subordinate can immediately perceive the superficiality of 5,5 convictions. A 9,1-oriented person disdains 5,5 behavior, seeing it in its true light as a compromise, an accommodation, and a sacrifice of productivity to placate people.

A 5,5-oriented manager's knowledge, as evidenced in boss/subordinate interaction and responses to questions, is not sufficiently deep to demonstrate confidence that the boss really knows what he or she is talking about. Subordinate reservations are parried and deflected rather than being resolved with facts and data. When a 5,5-oriented boss is delegating a task or giving instructions, an attempt is made to stay on track, ignoring interruptions that may occur. When the boss does respond, it may be with, "Yes, but . . . ," an attempt to sell the subordinate a reasonable point of view. Because the 5,5-oriented boss is so "flexible," however, the subordinate oriented in a 9,1 way feels extremely frustrated at finding no way to "pin" this wishy-washy person down.

A 9,1-oriented subordinate usually continues doing things his or her own way regardless of what the boss says. If challenged, the subordinate may suggest they go to a higher level for arbitration, which generally has the effect of getting the boss to back off. The faster the subordinate can get out from under the 5,5-oriented boss, the better, as far as the subordinate is concerned. The problem with this kind of leadership is that the organization may lose some very talented people through the inability of this leader to successfully funnel the talent into productive team effort.

1,9 Reactions to 5,5

A 5,5 orientation works a lot better with a 1,9-oriented subordinate because the boss wants subordinates to be happy and tries not to arouse anxiety. Whenever a 5,5-oriented boss asks a 1,9-oriented subordinate to do something, the likely response is "Yes" because the subordinate is motivated to seek approval and to avoid rejection. Unfortunately, a 1,9-oriented subordinate often agrees without fully understanding the nature of the task to be done. If the subordinate asks questions, the boss replies with shallow answers and circular reasoning, leaving the subordinate even more confused. But this subordinate is unlikely to challenge the boss; rather, he or she goes off and does a mediocre job or waits for the boss to come and provide further direction. Additionally, because this subordinate says "yes" regardless of ability to comply, it may soon be apparent that the subordinate has taken on more than he or she can handle. This leads to resentment by the subordinate for being "pushed so hard," but it is not expressed and as a result leads to poor morale and low motivation to do a good job.

Paternalistic (9+9) Reactions to 5,5

The paternalistic subordinate with a 5,5-oriented boss is portrayed by, "I'm your ears and eyes." This subordinate becomes indispensable by keeping the boss posted on formal and informal organization issues and relationships. This is done by feeding the boss's positive motivation of wanting to belong while at the same time bringing into play the intense minus motivation, fear of embarrassment. Soon the subordinate has the boss under firm control, with the boss feeling a need to check every action to maintain the status quo and to avoid actions that might bring disfavor. The paternalistic subordinate has essentially assumed the role of the 5,5-oriented boss's alter ego.

As a subordinate, the paternalist derives a sense of importance from all this responsibility and relishes the confidant relationship with the boss. The subordinate sees him- or herself as the likely successor, because the subordinate already has indirect control of the team.

1,1 Reactions to 5,5

A 5,5-oriented boss experiences uncertainty and tentativeness when dealing with a 1,1-oriented subordinate. This subordinate, with low interest in the boss or the task per se, generally responds with silence. The subordinate is seeking to do the minimum to get by; the boss is attempting to get that level of performance up to acceptable group norms. In the case of a 1,1-oriented individual, it takes more active effort on the part of the boss. The boss must initiate conversation to see if the subordinate is on track. Seeking to motivate the subordinate through enthusiastic remarks has little or no effect. Because it is difficult to elicit a response of a positive nature from this subordinate, the 5,5-oriented boss tends to react from a negative motivational orientation of uncertainty and doubt. Once the boss understands where the subordinate is coming from, interaction becomes fairly routine, with the boss passing messages to the subordinate and then periodically checking for understanding and progress. Nothing is done to help the subordinate gain more commitment to organizational goals.

5,5 Reactions to 5,5

The 5,5-oriented boss and the 5,5-oriented subordinate provide a good model of the relationship of reciprocity. You do for me and I do for you. Everything operates according to a system of checks and balances. This extends into negative as well as positive supporting action in that the expectation is that you *cover* for me, too, hiding my mistakes from the eyes of others. It is a subtle collusion between two individuals whose primary interest lies in maintaining the status quo.

These two are a natural, with both sensitive to prestige-centered values. Boss and subordinate enjoy each other's company and appear to work well together, deliberating and discussing the issues to form a conclusion. The difficulty is that neither one has an in-depth knowledge of the real issues. As a result they tend to reinforce each other's superficial understanding and disregard that which appears to be complicated. Criticism and negative feedback from others is discounted as the jealous whinings of malcontents. They tend to live in a closed world of self-deception, both patting themselves on the backs for the good work they are doing. The eventual outcome of such complacency is often failure, leaving the 5,5-oriented pair startled and confused—wondering where in the world they might have gone wrong.

Opportunistic Reactions to 5,5

This subordinate is likely to work on the boss's 5,5⁻ motivation until the boss is sufficiently insecure that no move can be made without checking it out prior to taking action. While the paternalistic subordinate does this also, in the case of the paternalist, the motivation is to create a strong dependency. In contrast, the opportunist views the 5,5-oriented boss much as the 9,1-oriented subordinate does, with disdain and disgust. Therefore, the opportunistic motivation, to get on top, comes out in a carefully planned scenario to undermine the boss. The more effectively the opportunistic subordinate is in bringing out the 5,5⁻ motivation of the boss, the more dependent the boss becomes. The boss is afraid to make any move for fear of embarrassment and begins to avoid all risks. This can be destructive in that the subordinate has now set the boss up to fail. When the axe begins to fall, the boss suddenly finds him- or herself alone, the most distressing condition for a 5,5-oriented person. The opportunistic subordinate has disappeared from sight. Once the 5,5-oriented boss is out of the way, the subordinate hopes to assume the role of leadership.

9,9 Reactions to 5,5

The 9,9-oriented subordinate feels frustrated with the shallow convictions and lack of depth that characterize the 5,5-oriented boss. The subordinate soon discovers that he or she must take initiative to search out the facts and data necessary to make sound decisions and to implement a task in the best manner. The subordinate may press the boss for information by posing questions and offering alternative suggestions. This subordinate is unlikely to accept a "brush off" from the boss. The interchange is not aimed at being destructive but rather has a constructive quality of engaging the boss in thinking more deeply about the issues at hand. In this way both parties may gain a better comprehension of the work to be done.

The 5,5-oriented boss prefers one-to-one meetings with subordinates as a way to sell an approach and to avoid situations of conflict, but this is likely to be challenged by the 9,9-oriented subordinate who sees the desirability of getting all the cards on the table. The subordinate pushes the boss to take greater risks by bringing issues of controversy out into the open. Therefore, the overall effect of a 5,5-oriented boss working with a 9,9-oriented subordinate may be good in that the boss begins to expand his or her outlook, taking some guidance from the strong expression of convictions, both for task and people, from the 9,9-oriented subordinate. While the 5,5-oriented boss may not change Grid style, the 5,5/9,9 combination may bring team interaction to the level of problem solving. Other members of the team begin to look to the 9,9-oriented individual for guidance and, in order to avoid being "shut out," the 5,5-oriented boss may find it necessary to develop stronger convictions regarding productive effort.

In the situation of a heavy 5,5 organization culture, an individual with a 9,9 orientation is likely to feel continually stifled and frustrated. Several outcomes are possible. Those at the top may recognize the abilities of the 9,9-oriented individual and promote this person to higher levels, leaving the 5,5-oriented boss behind. Alternatively, the 9,9-oriented person may leave the organization for more productivity-minded ventures, thus representing a loss of leadership and talent for the organization.

Recognizing 5,5 Behavior

Figure 7-4 contains words and phrases that characterize the 5,5-oriented manager.

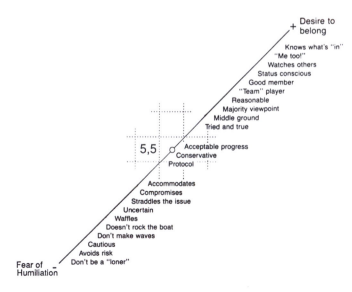

Figure 7-4. Words and phrases that characterize the 5,5 Grid style.

Summary

A 5,5-oriented manager seeks a delicate equilibrium between the needs for production and the needs of people. Conformity is the name of the game because when you pay attention to the rules laid down by the group, it ensures that you are in step with others and keeps you from looking different. A key to the 5,5 style of management lies in the approach to conflict, which is basically one of compromise. An individual motivated in this way sees conflict as disruptive of team spirit and therefore acts as a mediator to get things back on an even keel. The potential gain that can be had by exploring alternative points of view is sacrificed rather than taking the risk of disagreement.

What does this mean for the organization? The network of rules and regulations put in place to define acceptable behavior lead to a stultifying bureaucracy. Because protocol is the guiding light, one's advancement in the organization is based on seniority rather than merit. Decisions follow the majority point of view. Creativity is stifled because it is "different." Politics, favors, and trade-offs reduce the organization's capacity to respond to needed changes. Obviously, such an organization is bound to encounter difficulties in a rapidly expanding global marketplace and the likely outcome is that it will be left behind and the 5,5-oriented manager along with it.

Chapter 8

Opportunism: "What's In It For Me?"

"What a day!" thought Frank. "Everything is going wrong!" He reflected on the events as they had transpired. Al's victory meeting—that's where it had all started.

□ □ □

As soon as Al called the meeting to a close, Frank moved directly to his side and added his own private words of praise. Frank knew it was important to give his boss support and encouragement as well-placed influence in such areas could be critical for future success. This time, however, it was more than that. Frank was particularly anxious to avoid further challenge from Ben and Ed until he could get his story straight. There was no useful purpose to be served in antagonizing colleagues. He had made a mistake; somehow he had slipped up in his conversations and gotten "caught." Normally, he prided himself on his good rapport with people. He must have let his guard down in a moment of preoccupation; or, maybe they had put words in his mouth. That was the only explanation. "Oh well," thought Frank. "They'll get over it."

Frank's approach, when he disagreed with colleagues in a meeting, was to sit back and keep quiet, the idea being that it was to his advantage to ascertain the positions of others while they were still unsure of where he stood. When he did participate, he tended to endorse what he saw to be positive aspects of others' positions and then to express in a tentative way reservations about viewpoints contradictory to his own. All the while he sought to maintain the appearance of a neutral stance. Once the competition was removed, he could introduce his own plan and help others to buy into its merits.

Of course, with Al and others in key positions of power, he took a slightly different tack. He listened intently and avoided comments that might invite disagreement. Whenever Al convened a meeting, Frank knew the course of action had already been determined. Still, Al threw the issue out on the table for debate and asked subordinates to contribute their best thinking. Then he systematically shot down suggestions one by one as they were offered until only his own plan remained intact.

Frank usually just observed this parleying until he knew where Al stood. He was careful to let Al pose the recommended solution and then he would direct a couple of pertinent questions to Al that served to draw out evidence supporting the soundness of the idea. This made Al look good and brought other people's thinking into line with that of the boss. Then, Frank would embrace Al's solution, saying he was convinced by the wisdom of the arguments.

This interplay between Al and Frank occurred on a fairly regular basis but it was so subtle that most team members were unaware it was taking place. The others, seeing a person like Frank grapple with his convictions, ask pointed questions of the boss, and then come to a conclusion based on what appeared to be sound insight, were provided with a demonstration and reinforcement of the validity of the boss's thinking. The only two who sometimes balked at this were Ed and Ben, particularly if they had strong convictions in another direction. Additionally, Frank felt Ben was wise to this strategy, sensing that Ben was skeptical of any position Frank took. Ben had kidded him more than once about being slippery and evasive.

As Al proceeded toward the door, Frank trotted by his side somewhat like a friendly puppy, continuing his laudatory chatter. Al was enjoying every minute of the praise. Frank was just biding his time and preparing Al to be fully receptive before launching into his true agenda. With Al, it was necessary to establish warm and friendly relations before getting down to business.

"Al, the celebration dinner is an excellent idea," began Frank. "Just what this team needs to boost its morale and good spirits after a long, hard bout. You always manage to think of the perfect culmination of an effort. How do you do it?"

"Years of experience," Al chuckled lightheartedly and a bit playfully. "Someday, if you pay close attention, you'll be able to do the same with your people. Some of us have it, and some of us don't. Seriously, though, it's a combination of talents—cultivating a sense of loyalty and obedience in people that results in their striving to do well to carry out your directives. I can't think of a better way to run a business. It makes for one big happy family."

"You can say that again," beamed Frank. They walked on in silence as Frank looked over his shoulder to ensure they were not being followed. Once they were alone, Frank began to pry Al for information. "Say, how did that division managers meeting come off last week? Any big news?"

"News?" asked Al. "No, not really. Just a typical rehash of what we already know." Al was unaware that Frank had been doing some personal campaigning in connection with this. Frank had actively pursued several leads above Al's head to stay on top of the situation. Through one of his contacts, Frank had learned that there was an item involving the formation of a new marketing unit to deal with international strategy. Frank had honed in on this, seeing it as a way to move into the higher echelons. It would be an influential and highly visible group. When he had been alerted to this development, Frank had indicated his personal interest in the assignment. Frank felt fairly sure his liaison had gotten the message, but he was hoping Al might have some further word on the matter.

Al kept walking in silence, however, apparently immersed in his own thoughts. Frank broke the trance by offering to take Al to lunch.

"What?" Al returned to the present moment. "Lunch? No, thanks. I'm trying to cut down."

"We could get a light salad . . . " Frank persisted.

"No, not a thing for me," Al smiled, appreciative of Frank's concern. Frank looked so forlorn that Al almost changed his mind.

"Well, I guess I'll go check my desk," said Frank. "Might have missed some important messages this morning."

"You do that, my boy," Al replied warmly. "Remember, dinner at my house on Friday evening. My wife has promised something special. That's what I'm saving my appetite for."

"I wouldn't miss it for the world!" Frank perked up a bit. "I'll see you later."

Al disappeared and Frank started back towards his own office. He felt disappointed he hadn't learned anything more about the executive meeting. Sometimes he wondered if all the effort expended on Al was worth the trouble. "It's a two-way street, you know," thought

Frank. "I'm not willing to keep giving and giving without something in return." He shuddered at the thought of getting stuck in Al's team for the long haul. Al wasn't all that close to retirement. "Well," Frank mused, "I'm hedging my bets by playing the angles with several key players. I'm not about to put all my eggs in Al's basket!"

□ □ □

Frank was studying a report when he heard a knock on the door. He looked up to see Ross Cunningham, a new employee, enter the room. Ross was a real asset to Frank. He had made significant contributions since his arrival to the department.

"Hi, Ross. What's up?" Frank asked.

"Do you have a minute?" Ross replied. Frank nodded and Ross continued. "I wanted to talk about that assignment you gave me. It would be a much easier process if I set it up on the computer. I've written a program that could cut the work in half."

Frank listened intently. He had a lot to do but there might be something here of potential benefit. He motioned for Ross to proceed.

Just then the phone rang. "Ed Jackson is on the line for you," signalled the secretary.

Frank looked at Ross and said, "Could you wait in reception just a moment. I need to take this call, but I want to continue our discussion." Ross quickly rose and exited, closing the door behind him.

Frank picked up the phone. "Yes, Ed. . .Yeah . . .Absolutely . . . That's terrific, Ed. Say, about this morning. . .Let me explain . . .No, no, that's not right. You know how Ben reads things into a situation. I can't even remember discussing the matter with him, much less stating it in that manner. Don't get me wrong. I'm not calling him a liar or anything. He just misunderstood what I was saying. Don't worry, I'll meet with him and set him straight. Say, why don't you and I have lunch this week. Friday would be great. . .Okay, Ed, you're a real pal. I'll see you. Thanks for calling." Frank called the secretary and told her to send Ross back in.

"Okay," Frank smiled. "Now where were we?"

Ross laid out the general plan and Frank asked a number of pointed questions. Finally, Frank said, "On paper it looks good. I'm anxious to see how it works. How long do you anticipate it will take for you to get it up and running?"

"I can do a test run by this afternoon. Then you can review the data before I proceed any further," replied Ross. "It'll probably take a week to get all the bugs out but I don't foresee any major problems."

"Okay, get right on it. I'll be looking for you later," Frank said. Ross hurried to his feet and was about to leave when Frank interjected a final statement. "Oh, Ross. I want you to know that I appreciate your coming to me with this idea. I like it when my people check their thinking against my own before launching off in new directions. We're a team, you know, and you're one of my key players. Your initiative will be rewarded. Just be patient. Keep up the good work and bring me the test data as soon as it's ready." Ross nodded gratefully and made his departure.

Frank sat for a moment thinking about what Ross had told him, then picked up the phone and buzzed Al.

"Yeah, Al, this is Frank. My people are working on a novel idea that should cut our work in half. It's a program for generating those cumbersome reports we have struggled with for years. Besides saving expense, it should approach error-free results. That in itself would be a major step . . . Oh, yes, you'll love it! . . . What's that? . . . Tell you what, I'll let you know when we get it worked out. I want something concrete to show you . . . . Yeah, okay. Bye."

Frank thought about giving Ben a call. "A few good words could serve to mend that relationship," he mused. "I can't afford to have him as an enemy. Still, maybe I should just drop it. I don't want to get into another argument with Ben. Sometimes the best strategy is to just dodge the situation." He pondered further. "I know what I'll do! Next time I run into Ben I'll just pretend like the whole thing never happened. But if he brings it up I'll do whatever is necessary to make it up to him. Ben's a reasonable fellow."

□ □ □

Thinking about Ben brought Frank back to the present. He knew Ben had gotten a promotion. "Probably got that task force job I was aiming at," Frank thought morosely. He had been unable to get anything out of Al after Joe and Harriet left. "Well, I'll find out later. Maybe I'll give Joe a call. Better yet, I'll get Liz to do some scouting for me. Yeah, that's the ticket. I helped her on that Perkins deal. She owes me one. Besides, all I have to do is hint that change is in the air and she'll be on top of it in a minute." He turned back to the work on his desk, feeling confident that things would look up.

□ □ □

Opportunism, shown in Figure 8-1, is a Grid theory best understood by answering the question, "Who is the other person with whom the opportunist is dealing?" This is significant because the quality of a relationship is gauged in terms of how it impacts the future of the opportunist. An opportunist uses a combination of other Grid styles based on what is likely to get him or her ahead. The question to be answered is, "What interaction style works best with this other person to get them to do what I want?" Therefore, Frank may appear to be one way when dealing with Al, another when dealing with Ed, and yet a third when dealing with Ross. In other words, "who" is being dealt with is all important.

Opportunistic Management

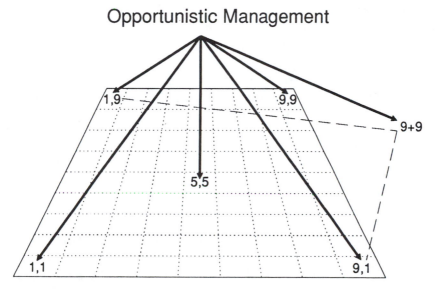

Figure 8-1. Opportunism is a combination of any or all Grid styles, depending on what is needed to advance the individual's gain.

Secondly, Frank operates off the basic assumption that "You never get something for nothing," so he determines in advance if the other party owes him a favor. If not, he must answer the question, "What do I have to offer that this other person wants?" Because Frank has connections up, down, and sideways in the organization hierarchy, there's usually something in his bag of tricks that another person needs.

Motivations

Personal motivation is critical in understanding how an opportunist like Frank relates to other people. The plus (+) pole is "desire to be on top," and is shown in Figure 8-2.

The opportunist studies relationships for their utility in terms of enhancing personal career success. That is, "What's in it for me?" If there's a lot of potential gain, then the opportunist makes every effort to play it to maximum advantage. If not, little effort is expended in that behalf. Frank seldom overlooks an opportunity. Even if he can't see its immediate payout, he knows that well-placed influence in the here-and-now can often be capitalized on at some point in the future.

The minus (−) side of opportunism, also illustrated in Figure 8-2, is "fear of exposure." It's important to the opportunist to "look good." The opportunist wants to be seen as a positive element, and this is why he or she exudes charm and enthusiasm. People like this are on a constant "high"; they like living life in the fast lane. When things get too serious, they are in jeopardy of having their true colors show. The opportunist has little tolerance for negativity. When the going gets tough, this individual is the first to jump ship.

The motivation "to be on top" may—or may not—result in action that contributes to organization needs. Either way, action is dictated by "What's in it for me?" rather than "How will this serve corporate objectives?" The latter is of secondary concern. If pursuit of personal gain is contrary to what the organization needs, whether this be of a detrimental nature or simply an ineffective use of resources, the

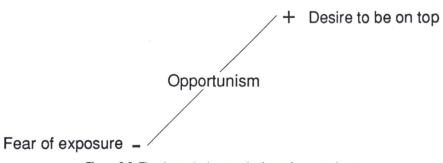

Figure 8-2. The plus and minus motivations of opportunism.

opportunist pays it little mind unless it places him or her in danger of exposure. Such an individual is often the reason that many organizations find it necessary to institute a "Code of Ethics." Even then, this does little to stop wheeler-dealers like Frank. They just get better at covering their tracks.

A further distinction can be drawn that clearly separates opportunism from any other Grid style. It can be seen in reference to "seizing an opportunity." It is healthy and widely understood that commercial life presents many opportunities. These often are "there," waiting for someone to take hold of them and do something with them. "Seizing an opportunity" and doing it in a fair and square way reflects something of the entrepreneurial spirit. When done in an open and forthright manner, the organization benefits from the initiative exercised in moving forward. The individual may also benefit as a fair and equitable reward for the contribution made.

Opportunism, however, is motivated in quite a different way. Opportunities are seized but in ways that are neither fair nor square, nor open and forthright. The opportunist gains self-advantage by taking unfair advantage, playing the situation close to his (or her) chest, playing Individual X against Individual Y, and trying not to get caught at this fast-paced game of intrigue and deception.

The opportunist makes a "total study" of others, ascertaining their Grid style, seeing what they have of potential value and what he or she has to offer in return, their preferences and biases, and their sphere of influence upon which the opportunist can build in making his or her way to the top. This Grid style gives prominence to the adage, "The end justifies the means." It is utilitarian and selfish and in the final analysis not driven by corporate interests, though this is not immediately apparent to the casual observer.

Something that compounds this "hiddenness" feature is that the opportunist compartmentalizes relationships based on the Grid style of the party with whom he or she is interacting. Therefore, to the degree possible, the opportunist seeks to keep people separated from one another. This is how Frank deals with Al, Ed, and Ben. Unfortunately for Frank, Ben and Ed got together and compared notes, discovered a discrepancy, and turned the tables on Frank.

Generally, though, the idea is to promote oneself by creating a favorable image with others. It means selling charisma and charm, not problem-solving ability, particularly with those over which one lacks any power or authority. The way to get what you want in an organization (to get to the top) is to sell influence, to work out a deal that is mutually beneficial to you and another party. On the surface, reciprocity of this nature sounds harmless and potentially quite satisfying to both sides. But it's a trade-off rather than seeking the soundest solution. Furthermore, when you get right down to it, it is not pro-organizational; it's pro-"me." It's individualism at its height. It's saying that sometimes it's better to deal with people in a 1,9 way; other people are best handled in a 9,1 way; and so on. It's reading another person's Grid style and fitting yourself to it. It's shifting behavior based on circumstance. It's creating in the eye of the beholder what that beholder wishes to see, although there are no sound principles of human interaction to back this up.

The problem with this approach is that it catches up with you. People begin to see your behavior as inconsistent. At some point in time the opportunist gets caught in a crunch and the true thoughts and feelings emerge for everyone to see. Remember, Ben saw through Frank's game, chiding him in a joking manner about his "slippery and evasive" behavior. The result was that Ben felt wary about placing any trust in what Frank said. Contrast this "shifty" approach with Ben's straightforward approach to dealing with people from whatever walk of life. Frank, who may initially cultivate trusting relationships with others, soon becomes viewed with suspicion as people begin to question his underlying motives. It doesn't take long for others to see that Frank is out for himself and, while it's inherent in human motivation to try to better our own positions, an opportunist has no qualms about doing it at another's expense. When it comes down to "them" or "me," the answer is apparent.

Different people are "used" or exploited in different ways. Whereas the opportunist practices ingratiation with some, a combination of affection and intimidation is used with others. If people are seen as inconsequential in the move to the top, they are paid little heed; rather, their contribution is taken for granted. All these behaviors are subtle, however, so as not to alienate members of any group. As Frank implied in the story, it doesn't pay to make enemies.

The selfish motivation that propels the opportunist forward is therefore kept undercover.

Conflict Solving

The opportunist avoids conflict whenever possible because it is seen as something that can lead to adverse consequences. Conflict implies winners and losers and the opportunist obviously doesn't want to lose. On the other hand, winning can create an enemy in terms of the one who doesn't win. "Far better," says the opportunist, "if we can both succeed in this little endeavor." Therefore, mutual benefit is sought but the scale often tips in the opportunist's direction.

Preventing Conflict

The main way an opportunist prevents conflict is to avoid it. You just don't bring up issues with those who are likely to disagree. You work around them. You develop a supportive contingent by lobbying those who are more apt to embrace your ideas.

The opportunist is always reading the situation to determine probable consequences. When dealing with other people, the opportunist does his or her homework. To get what is desired, the opportunist operates according to a system of exchanges and balances. Such an individual is keenly aware of what others need. This "what" may be tangible or intangible, but the opportunist decides whether he or she is in a position to supply it. If so, the game of "Let's make a deal" is in full swing. If not, this person is then viewed as a possible roadblock and the most effective strategy is one of circumventing the individual.

Adversaries, both potential and real, are kept at a distance. Rather than trying to engage their support, the opportunist tries to cut them out of the picture. He or she seeks to anticipate probable reactions when they eventually figure out what is going on in order to be prepared with a strategy to mollify them. The idea is to avoid antagonizing others as this could end up in conflict and cause bigger problems in the future.

When an adversary is promoting an idea, the opportunist cleverly "plants" seeds of doubt among key people. In this way the opponent is frustrated, meeting a wall of reservation and doubt, until he or she questions the validity of the idea. "Maybe I was way off base. Other people seem to think so. I'd better go back and study this problem some more." The opportunist sits back and smiles. The other person is suspect before any action has ever transpired. The opportunist is able to justify thwarting this individual's effort because "it's not in the best interest," that is, it doesn't meet with the opportunist's specifications for how things should be done.

Handling Conflict When It Appears

When conflict arises, the opportunistic approach is to circumvent it. This is done by supporting the positive and backing off from the negative. The desire is for reciprocity. "We'll work something out to our mutual advantage," says the opportunist. Generally, whatever is worked out is in the opportunist's favor. If not, it doesn't mean the opportunist has accepted the other point of view. It just means this individual is biding the time until another opportunity comes along to get what he or she wants. This is shown in Figure 8-3.

An opportunist doesn't want to lose because this is damaging to his or her plus (+) motivation to be on top. Losing is the same as being upstaged. It is losing face in front of those you have sought to influence. How can you hope to influence others without their respect? Therefore, the opportunist's goal in any discussion is to

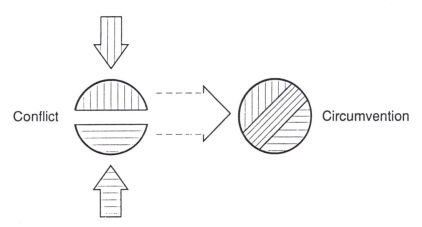

Figure 8-3. An opportunistic individual works around conflict, operating in such a manner as to avoid being defeated but equally to avoid causing others to experience defeat, thus maintaining their favor.

stay loose, to keep the options open, to explore preferences, and to defer decisions that might result in an unfavorable conclusion. In other words, the opportunist operates in such a manner as to avoid the price of being defeated but equally to avoid causing others to experience defeat. The idea is to keep the attitudes of others towards the opportunist favorable. There is less friction in moving toward the goal of personal gain among allies than among enemies.

If you are an opportunist, your desire is to keep negotiations open and never to burn any bridges behind you. You need to know you can count on support from others when you need it. You've got your eye focused on the long term and the scene envisioned has you sitting on the throne. For example, here is an illustration of Frank's negotiation with an outside contractor. The fellow was unreasonable and unwilling to settle for standard terms, asking for double the normal pay. As a non-organization member, he didn't have to play by the rules. He was exempt. As a stranger, Frank had no particular influence with him. Ed looked at this situation and said, "Just forget him! We'll find someone else." But Frank saw his usefulness at the present moment and said, "No, he's the only one who can help us. It doesn't matter if he gets away with murder on this one because we'll pay him back later in kind." This is using a person to accomplish what you want, the idea being that no deed goes unpaid. In this case we're talking negative reciprocity, an eye for an eye—in other words, revenge.

Of course, when you get right down to it, there's got to be a winner and a loser in a situation of polarized conflict—you either get what you want or you don't. The only middle ground is compromise and that means you only got part of what you wanted. As a result, the ideal for an opportunist is to win but without any negative side effects. And, if an opportunist plays the cards right, it's possible to create what appears to be a win/win situation. Then, people with opposing viewpoints don't feel like they have lost; nor do they feel taken advantage of and they don't leave with a bad taste in their mouths. The opportunist has a clear aim in mind and seeks to manipulate the discussion in such a way that others are brought to an accommodation where compromise becomes a possibility. It sets up the circumstance of trade-off. "You give me what I need on this one, and I'll support you on that." "I know I'm asking a lot and that it'll mean some overtime and weekends on your part, but I promise to make it up to you. So how about it? Can I count on you?'' The name of the game is reciprocity. ''You scratch my back and I'll scratch yours.''

There are a lot of ways to look at winning. For example, I might let you win this battle provided I win the war. By letting you ''think'' you've won this hand and gotten what you were after, I create an obligation with you. Because I have obliged you on this occasion, you'll feel like you owe me one and you can bet that I'll be around to collect. ''Remember that deal last month. I put my neck on the line in support of you. You owe me one, buddy, and I expect you to be behind me 100% on the next deal.''

An opportunist creates needs in other people as well, so that a previously nonexistent basis of exchange is formed. In situations of conflict, where the opportunist wants something from someone else and that someone else refuses to give it, there is a useful little tactic of putting the pressure on. All you have to do is to make life so unpleasant for other people that finally they are glad to change their minds and give you what you desire to make you stop. This may include talking behind their backs and damaging their reputations, embarrassing them in front of colleagues and subordinates by questioning their actions, and any number of tactics designed to damage reputation or thwart effort.

Colleagues of the opportunist are viewed as contenders for the ''top.'' They are competitors for what the opportunist is striving to achieve and must therefore be outsmarted or eliminated. At the same time, though, the opportunist sees colleagues as instruments that can be put to good use in his or her behalf. In other words, if manipulated just right, they can become a cheering squad for the opportunist in order to promote his or her personal interests, because cheerleaders are not contenders. Think about it this way. If you are an opportunist, what could be better that allying yourself with a 9,1-oriented individual or a paternalist? Then they fight the battles for you; you never need to tarnish your own image.

When Conflict Remains

In an extreme situation of conflict, the opportunist may take quite the opposite tack, *appearing* to give up and essentially saying, "Okay, you take it. I can see how much you want it and you seem to know what you're doing. Because you're so committed to this approach, I'd be the last one to stand in your way." It's almost a martyr role, with the opportunist gracefully stepping down, not in defeat, but in deference to another person. The ball is in the other person's court now, either to react to this "gracious ultimatum" by accepting the challenge or by coming off the polarized position and seeking a middle ground that both parties can live with. It's a sham on the part of the opportunist. The intent is not really to give up but rather to force the other person to be "more reasonable."

What are the motivations underlying this Grid style when it comes to conflict? The expression characterizing the positive (+) end of the motivational scale is, "I seek to bypass conflict because it impedes my progress in getting to the top." For an opportunist, conflict drains energy away from more important activity. It can lead to situations of antagonism where people end up enemies. Frank hoped his "conflict" with Ed and Ben would quickly blow over. Realizing it was a delicate situation, he sought to make amends with Ed and decided to just let Ben cool off. The point is that in neither case did he want to confront the conflict because this might create an adversary. An opportunist is dependent on having other people on his or her "team." The more people you have behind you, the more influence you wield.

The negative side of the conflict-solving motivation is, "I avoid situations of conflict because they may expose my own self-interest." This is what Frank is afraid of in the Ben/Ed situation. If the conflict persists, both colleagues may put two and two together, coming up with a realization that Frank plants seeds of doubt with third parties and plays up to the one he is with. This would certainly not be favorable to Frank's reputation. As a result, he is twisting and turning to alleviate the tension. He determines how best to deal with the matter, what approach and relationship style best serves his own ends.

Initiative

Opportunistic initiative is self-serving in every sense of the word. When the opportunist identifies a desired end, all the key players to its accomplishment are targeted. Then the question becomes, "What can I give them to get what I want?" The expressed objective is that we both get our needs satisfied while at the same time benefiting the organization. This, of course, is the best of all possible worlds. But when you get right down to it, the opportunist is certain that he or she gets what is desired, regardless of how the others and the corporation come out.

An opportunist exercises caution when taking initiative. The first step is to determine another person's Grid style and then to decide what style of relating achieves the goal. If you have an aggressive or strong Grid style, the opportunist may initiate in an indirect way so that an idea is planted in your mind only to emerge at a later time. In this way the opportunist achieves the desired objective, but the idea "seems" to originate with you. At some level you may be aware that the opportunist was instrumental in your arrival at this conclusion. In this case you may consider the opportunist a good sounding board and a worthy confidant, because you certainly haven't been "told" what to do. On the other hand, if your Grid style is weaker, the opportunist is more open to exercising forceful initiative. There is little hesitation in being demanding with you. Don't worry, though, the opportunist is behind you all the way!

Sometimes the approach taken is to sit back and take a wait-and-see attitude. In this way, other people's positions can be ascertained and counterpositions prepared for possible use. Certain reservations may be expressed so as to create doubts in the minds of others. At a point when frustrations are high and people seem about to give up, the opportunist can interject his or her own idea, which people embrace simply to get resolution; something is better than nothing and so people go along.

An opportunist also appreciates the value of doing his or her homework before making an initiative public. A key way to overpower competitors is to know something they don't and to pose this as a challenge in front of others. This puts competitors on the spot; essentially they are subject to ridicule and the opportunist comes out on top. When an opportunist initiates a new idea, those who don't immediately agree are flooded with evidence of the opportunist's vast knowledge. Any further questions are countered with challenges to offer a better idea, behind which lurks an unspoken threat of "You'd better not go against me on this one!"

Another way to seek a successful outcome is to form a coalition of supporters in advance of a public meeting. This can ensure a majority following to counter any minority resistance that may arise. This cheering section can take on the "dirty work," fighting for the opportunist's cause while he or she sits back and watches. If it doesn't pan out, the opportunist is less likely to be viewed as the culprit. If it does, all is well and good.

Generally, an opportunist only launches out on a winning cause; the prospect of losing is avoided. It is viewed as better to take an initiative in a one-alone manner if possible and allow others to question its validity once it's underway. The rationalization in such an instance is that "The proof is in the results achieved. Just be patient; wait and see!" Skeptics are told to hold their reservations until the initiative demonstrates its own soundness. Regardless of the outcome, good or bad, the hope is that resistance has dissipated by this time, thus decreasing the possibility of negative fallout.

The plus end of the motivational scale for initiative is revealed in the statement, "I exert effort in directions that put me on top." The minus end is, "I avoid initiatives that might expose my true intentions."

Inquiry

Opportunists, more than people of other Grid styles, have a profound need to know everything that is going on. This is not the same need a paternalist has in his or her effort to gain veneration. Rather, it is for the sake of leverage; it provides another basis for exchange. The need to know includes "who is in," "who is out," and particularly "who is on the move." Such inquiry not only focuses on people, it spotlights things, procedures, technology, new products and those still in development, what is obsolete, new proposals, new bids, and costing of all of the above. This information is essential to determine exchanges to be made with others in order to accomplish opportunistic ends. For opportunists who have achieved high rank in the organization, inquiry extends to knowing as much as possible about competitors, global markets, corporate tax law, both domestic and international, and any and all other considerations about company operation. It means being fully apprised of broad corporate planning and strategy especially as this impacts the opportunist.

The opportunist is hungry for information, and inquiry is pursued in ways that highlight the opportunist's diligence on behalf of the corporation. However, keep in mind that the underlying motivations are self-serving; corporate benefit is secondary.

Information acquired is tested for soundness and validity. The opportunist doesn't want to get caught with facts that may later prove inaccurate or incorrect. Therefore, the opportunist engages in constant verification, validation, and reassessment of his or her current knowledge and communicates information only to the extent that it has undergone vigorous examination.

Much inquiry, particularly as it relates to people, is garnered from third parties by being thoroughly plugged into the informal system of communication. The opportunist puts him or herself in a position to learn from third parties about second parties and uses this to cross-check, verify, and spot contradictions.

The positive and negative motivations for the opportunist when it comes to inquiry reflect the desire to be on top and the fear of exposure. The plus (+) motivation is, "I need to know everything that is going on in the organization so I can play the angles on behalf of *me*." On the minus side (−), the statement is, "I avoid asking questions that might indicate I am only interested in self-gain; rather, I use questions to demonstrate my concern for our mutual advantage."

Advocacy

One of the greater risks an opportunist confronts comes from the possibility that his or her true thinking may slip out where others can observe it. Because of this, an opportunist avoids spontaneous interaction. It could reveal underlying motivations. The opportunist prefers to diagnose a situation in advance. This permits an assessment of the style of behavior most likely to achieve the desired end. With a plan in mind, the opportunist can enter the scene with enthusiasm and charm. This invites attitudes of responsiveness and cooperation.

Once again, how an opportunist exercises advocacy depends completely on the situation. With some, the opportunist defers to the other party, resonating to the other's convictions, preferences, and biases. Such an approach can win favor and appreciation and endear the other to the opportunist for life. An opportunist might act in such a manner with a senior or boss. It usually occurs when this person has a strong and dominant Grid style. The only exception is when the individual is headed for a fall. An opportunist is careful not to jump on a sinking ship.

The tactics of advocacy with peers also reveals the motivation, "What's in it for me?" If little personal gain is to be had, it is unlikely for the opportunist to become involved. On the other hand, if a lot is at stake, relationships are cultivated to their maximum payout.

When the opportunist has an idea to promote, the typical approach is to ascertain its proponents and its adversaries. Then proponents are courted and their support gained prior to making it public. The doors of those who are seen as unsupportive are not entered.

There is little hesitation to express convictions on issues that have no immediate pertinence to the opportunist. Credibility is earned in doing so without any significant risk. Even under the most neutral conditions, however, advocacy reflects "fear of being exposed." An opportunist is cautious when it comes to making true motivations known. If it is recognized that others have a superior capacity to think or express themselves or have greater knowledge of the deeper ideological issues that are embedded within the situation, then the opportunist is more likely to listen and offer agreement, sometimes through rephrasing, in order to appear to be in harmony without simply embracing the other person's point of view.

When the other party is perceived to be "weak," the opportunist puts it on the line. You can afford to be tough with someone who fears conflict and is unlikely to resist. Why hold back when you can have the moon for the asking? However, all the while it is important to make the other person think they are getting something out of the deal as well. For an opportunist, it is always in the back of his or her mind to maintain the relationship for future exploitation.

Generally, the plus (+) motivation behind advocacy is, "I market my convictions to those I know will support my point of view because in this way I establish a loyal coalition that helps me get to the top." The minus (−) side is, "I avoid expressing my point of view with those who are unlikely to give me support because they might take advantage of such knowledge to undermine my effort."

Decision Making

When it comes to decision making, the opportunist really does his or her homework. The situation has been evaluated in advance to assess the level of agreement and support. The opportunist starts off in an open and inviting stance, receptive to all points of view. However, the stage is already set for what occurs next because the opportunist knows what needs to happen to further his or her own ends. The opportunist manipulates the situation to keep people hopping from point to point, but the manipulation is so subtle that participants are never quite sure where the group stands on an issue at any one moment. Suddenly the decision is made and, lo and behold, it is in the direction that the opportunist initially proposed. In the event that the opportunist cannot pull this off, doubts and reservations may be heard. Then the rationalizing starts, "Let's defer this decision until we have more information," or "It would be better if we consulted further resources or data," or "Perhaps we need a cooling off or sorting out period," or "Why don't we sleep on it." All of these are reasons that justify postponement, and postponement means time to exert influence.

This is not to say that an opportunist is reluctant or slow-moving. Quite the opposite. An opportunist is fast of foot and first in line to offer support through agreement—when this serves his or her own end. The arena of decision making is seen as a key area in which exchange occurs. "I'll support you now if you'll support me later." Or vice versa. The goal is not the quality of the decision made but rather the gain in terms of support offered. Politicking occurs behind closed doors—on the outside. In the situation of blocking a decision, the opportunist may withhold comment in public but doubts and reservations are made known privately and one on one.

The motivational underpinnings are reflected in the following statements. On the plus end, an opportunist might say, "I make decisions that are likely to get me what I want." The minus pole is, "I avoid making decisions that might be countermanded or subject to criticism; instead I defer taking action."

Critique

An opportunist vacillates when it comes to critique. It all depends on what is to be gained from the effort. There's no use critiquing what you already know. That would be a waste of time. On the other hand, critique can be very useful in overcoming obstacles, and it is here that the opportunist puts it to good use (for the opportunist). If you're an opportunist and you encounter resistance to some idea, rather than viewing this roadblock with irritation, it stimulates you to further investigation. Think of this source of resistance as a potential ally—if you can dig up enough information to convince this person of your point of view, you have gained a valuable friend. You are on top of the issues; with thorough critique under your belt, you know how to address the other person's concerns to bring him or her over to your side of the fence. Of course, this method isn't foolproof but at least you've played all the angles. This is using critique to "neutralize" disagreement and conflict.

As viewed from the opportunist perspective, critique is a tricky business. It can explode in your face. In situations where the stakes are low, an opportunist sticks to positive critique and shies away from the negative. If you look at it in a motivational way, the opportunist plays up to another person's "plus," that is, what this person strives for in life; and backs off from the person's "minus," that which is feared or avoided. An opportunist is hesitant to engage in spontaneous critique because it may alienate potential alliances. It is a much better strategy as far as the opportunist is concerned to keep people on your side. Self-critique is fine but it tends to be loaded with self-deception because it is based on rationalization and justification. We tend to see ourselves as we would like to see ourselves, not necessarily as we are perceived by those with whom we work. This is particularly true of the opportunist. Critique by an opportunist is done only by him- or herself as a means of finding out how to interact with another individual on some future occasion in a way that promises to be more successful than a prior attempt. Thus the goal is, "How do I get better at making people do what I want them to do?" not "How do I change things about me that could make me a more effective manager?" Opportunism is a somewhat conceited approach to life; there is not much thought given to self-improvement.

The plus motivation for critique is expressed in the statement, "I use critique when it furthers my knowledge about how to deal with other people." The negative statement is, "I avoid giving feedback to those who may be offended by what I have to say. It's better to keep quiet and maintain the relationship."

Variations of Opportunism

Opportunism can be expressed in numerous ways. Two special cases are outlined here.

Three-Way Opportunism

In this special case opportunism is played out according to a pattern, the particular features determined by the rank of the person being dealt with. A person higher in the hierarchy than the opportunist is almost always treated deferentially and in a supportive manner. A person of the same rank is dealt with following the precepts of exchange theory: "What can I get in exchange for what I have to give?" A person of lesser rank is dealt with more directly; i.e., little or no deference or support, and disregard for mutuality. The latter follows the master/slave model, with compliance from the subordinate anticipated as a right of "ownership."

This relatively static and fixed version of opportunistic leadership is more structured, less fluid, and more easily distinguished when seen but it is less common than the broader description of opportunism offered in this chapter.

Facade: The Extreme of Opportunism

At the extreme of the opportunistic Grid style lies facade. This concept is useful for distinguishing manipulative managerial practices from other Grid styles that have a more authentic quality. As used in architecture, the word *facade* refers to the face or front of a building as distinguished from the parts lying behind it. Sometimes the front is false—it obscures what actually exists in the interior.

A managerial facade is similar. It refers to a front, a cover, for the real approach lying behind. The face obscures the true intentions. They remain undercover. Hence, a managerial facade is deceptive. Facade is an extension of opportunism where the goal is to achieve by indirect or roundabout ways something that otherwise is unavailable or believed to be unattainable. Hence the thrill of risk and gamble. The approach is a manipulative one with the negative side being the fear of exposure or of "getting caught."

A facadist is an opportunist for whom the game has become an end in itself rather than just a means to an end. This prompts manipulative tactics, deception, distortion, denial, lying, cheating— in short, whatever is necessary to win. We denote this variation as "facade" because often the individual in an opportunistic way takes on the characteristics of another Grid style to deceive in order to achieve his or her purpose.

The general feature of all facades is that the person avoids revealing the contents of his or her own mind yet gives the impression of doing so. At a deeper level, then, this person is closed and hidden but gives the appearance of being open and aboveboard. Why? If one were, in reality, open and aboveboard, others would understand true intentions and the deceptive facade would be apparent. Neither can the "facadist" afford to be seen as closed and hidden because that raises suspicions and doubts, or at least it alerts curiosity.

One factor that makes it difficult to recognize a facadist is that the facadist qualities may not be present in all aspects of leadership. Sometimes a sound action can be expected to gain the endorsement of those who just implement it and there is no need for manipulation, deception, or hiding of true intentions. Facadist actions come into play when what the facadist wants cannot be accomplished through open leadership.

The facade maintained by a given individual may or may not be internally consistent. Stratagems may shift from time to time depending on what is workable or legitimate in the context of organizational requirements. The surface often appears as 9,9 or 5,5 and less frequently as 1,9 or 1,1, and almost never as 9,1.

The pleasure derived from playing this game stimulates the need for greater risk. A consequence of this version of opportunism that verges on recklessness is the continual need for more. Nothing satisfies; there is never enough of whatever is achieved. This results in taking even more risk, which magnifies the need for intrigue and trickery in an effort to avoid getting caught.

Subordinate Interaction with an Opportunistic Boss

Subordinate reactions to an opportunistic boss tend to be positive. This is because the opportunist views everyone as a potential ally and exerts considerable effort to stay on the good side of people, regardless of where they stand in the organization hierarchy. The opportunist may not pay a lot of attention to those who seem to have little to offer, but if another person seeks the opportunist's audience, the opportunist entertains the individual. The idea is that "friends" can always serve a useful purpose whereas enemies continue to be a thorn in your side.

9,1 Reactions to Opportunism

A 9,1-oriented subordinate gets along reasonably well with an opportunistic boss. The boss, noting the subordinate's "strong" style, takes a more easy-going approach and doesn't push. When the subordinate counters a directive, the boss promises to "check it out." This is accomplished and the boss returns with an arsenal of information to show the subordinate why this is the right way to go. As a result of the boss's thoroughness in this situation, the subordinate tends to accept what the boss is saying. The boss isn't a pushover so he or she commands some level of respect from the 9,1-oriented subordinate. At the same time such a boss resists getting caught in a polarized situation of conflict. This boss is evasive and hard to pin down, and a 9,1-oriented subordinate has difficulty trying to start a fight.

This boss/subordinate combination brings the reciprocity concept into play. The two of them bargain until they can find the right match. If the subordinate wants to accomplish certain results, he or she probably needs the boss's assistance or support in doing so. The opportunist is glad to supply it—provided there is an even exchange, and that means the subordinate has to do something in return for the boss. It's pure business and how well you make out on the deal is measured in tangible results.

1,9 Reactions to Opportunism

This is the "sucker" subordinate, subject to gross manipulation by an opportunistic boss. However, the subordinate probably likes the boss and is unaware of being twisted to the opportunist's will. Once again, it involves an exchange. The boss is playing up to the subordinate's "plus," that is, the desire for affection and approval. In exchange, the subordinate does whatever is required.

This is the individual that an opportunist may employ to handle unpleasant matters, things that might tarnish the boss's reputation. Although the subordinate doesn't like situations that might promote ill will, he or she would never say no. As a result the subordinate unwittingly colludes, completely trusting the boss's wisdom and absolute concern. This is the subordinate that an opportunist can entrust with a secret. "Let's keep this between you and me. No one else needs to know." If things don't turn out right, the subordinate serves as a scapegoat. After all, it's the boss's word against the subordinate's, and the boss has surrounded him or herself with a following of support. Who would you believe?

Paternalistic (9 + 9) Reactions to Opportunism

Here is another person that can be manipulated. This is the subordinate who is more likely to do the "really dirty" work, serving as a "hatchet man" to the opportunistic boss. This is how the subordinate fulfills his or her "plus," acquiring a sense of importance by announcing the bad news but conditioning it with "sympathy and understanding." Yet there are times when this subordinate questions what is going on because of the boss's "shiftiness" and lack of principled behavior. However, the boss is proficient at calming any fears the subordinate may reveal. Never are these misgivings shown publicly; generally they remain silent in the subordinate's own mind, with the paternalist exercising inward moralistic judgments in terms of should's and shouldn't's of the boss's behavior.

The paternalistic subordinate readily protects the boss from him- or herself and appeases those whom the opportunist has hurt through manipulative tactics. In this way, the paternalistic subordinate sees him- or herself as a savior and a pillar of strength. The subordinate aspires to be the trustworthy confidant(e) of the boss, in other words, the boss's right hand. This also fulfills the plus motivation to feel admired and respected by the boss.

1,1 Reactions to Opportunism

This subordinate gets along with the opportunistic boss provided the subordinate is invisible. If it is thought that the subordinate can serve a useful purpose, however, this boss is kind, considerate, and patient because then the person is another instrument that can be manipulated to do the boss's bidding. If unresponsive, the boss may have to motivate the subordinate, but that's okay. This boss is persistent and won't take no for an answer.

If friendly gestures don't work, the boss turns to threats—posed in a positive way, of course. "I thought you liked working for this organization . . . " This sets off the "minus" buzzer of a 1,1-oriented subordinate like no other statement can. The subordinate wants the security and safety of his or her job and will do anything not to lose this assurance. It's another negative exchange. To gain compliance from the subordinate, the boss puts the pressure on, either by yelling and screaming, or threatening to take something away that the subordinate doesn't want to do without, and so on; with compliance, peace and order are restored and everyone has what he or she desires. It's out and out manipulation to get another person to do what you want and it's negative because it's creating an adverse consequence that you will remove if, *and only if*, compliance is gained.

5,5 Reactions to Opportunism

Because the opportunistic boss is so adaptable, he or she has no difficulty dealing with a 5,5-oriented subordinate. There are lots of ways to get what you want with a 5,5-oriented person; such an individual is always willing to compromise. The only real difference between the two is that a 5,5-oriented subordinate is anchored to principles of tradition, precedent, and past practice; to organization norms and standards; to "what everyone else is doing." The opportunist, on the other hand, has broken free of such constraints, using them only as they serve his or her own needs.

The 5,5-oriented subordinate may be shocked by raw opportunism but at the same time somewhat envious. The subordinate would never dare take such a risk. This makes the boss somewhat of a hero in the subordinate's eyes. The subordinate is proud to work for such an influential character. This appeals to his or her "plus."

Opportunistic Reactions to Opportunism

This is the dangerous combination—for the organization, that is. When an opportunist deals with another opportunist, together they constitute a duet that can lead to unethical actions. After all, the only sense of ethics is that the end justifies the means, and this is based on personal interpretation. It's a game of high stakes and high risk because there's no check on what they are up to. Together they are playing the angles for self-gain, each reinforcing the other. There's an even exchange so they both feel satisfied with the nature of the relationship. For others, though, and the organization itself, it's a vicious cycle because nothing stands in their way. The likelihood is that they take the gamble, no holds barred, with no sense of self-doubt and with no thought of the consequences. It is the pairing of "schemers." They are twisty and slippery and likely to sneak up on your blind side.

9,9 Reactions to Opportunism

This is where the jig is up. The 9,9-oriented individual isn't fooled, quickly sensing the lack of principles in the opportunistic boss's behavior and finding it appalling. The subordinate tries to pin the boss down on convictions, but a good opportunist can manage to rationalize anything. You can talk until you're blue in the face but the boss, in an amiable manner, continues to shift the topic until no one knows what's going on. If you seek to inject an ounce of objectivity, out comes a pound of opportunistic rationale. Often, this takes the form of a story that parallels the situation, concluding with the opportunist drawing some connection with the present issue. Such tactics tend to throw a person off course. You end up confused rather than enlightened.

The 9,9-oriented subordinate, however, is just as persistent as the opportunistic boss and continues to press for principled behavior. The best that this boss can do is to find a reason to promote the subordinate out of his or her little domain. It's difficult to fire a 9,9-oriented person because they tend to be exemplary employees, but it is this factor that permits the opportunist to pass them on to someone else. They are in high demand. The alternative is to evade the subordinate and to work around him or her. In this case the subordinate often ends up so frustrated that he or she does anything to escape the situation, applying for a transfer or exiting the organization completely.

Recognizing Opportunistic Behavior

Figure 8-4 illustrates the words and phrases that characterize opportunistic behavior.

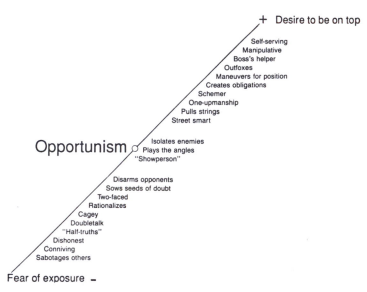

Figure 8-4. Words and phrases that characterize opportunistic behavior.

Summary

The opportunist operates according to the Grid style of the other party. It all depends on what is deemed to be most effective in getting what you want when operating with another person. The approach has its roots in self-interest; if others or the organization benefit, it's just a by-product of the opportunist satisfying his or her own ends.

The opportunist's plus (+) motivations are self-serving, to be on top, with focus on "what's in it for me." Corporate well-being is considered only when congruent with self-interest. Otherwise, the goals and objectives of the organization are of little or no importance to an opportunist. If a better opportunity presents itself elsewhere, there's no hesitation to throw the current one out the window and move on down the road.

The negative motivation (−), fear of exposure, causes the opportunist to exercise caution in what is revealed to others. Negativity is avoided. It's better to stick with the positive. There are several reasons for this. Your enthusiasm gets others to talk and to tell you things you may need to know. Furthermore, a positive attitude is a way to win friends and influence people. That's how you get an edge on the competition. Negativity, even when it's on target, brings people down. Most people would much rather jump on the bandwagon of enthusiasm than take a serious look at their problems. If the wagon is headed for a cliff, the opportunist simply hops off.

Chapter 9

9,9: "All for One and One for All"

Dan and Liz strolled toward the parking garage.

"That was a real tear jerker," said Dan. "It's hard to see someone who has invested his whole being into the team say good-bye. I've had my ups and downs with Al but, to tell you the truth, I'm going to miss him."

"Me, too," said Liz. "He was like a father to me, especially when I first got here. I remember how nervous I was and he really took me under his wing and made me feel like part of the family. I've always appreciated that. But why are we so sad? We should be happy for him. He's moved up and that proves to me that the system works—it rewards those who serve it well."

"You're right," said Dan. "I guess I'm a little worried about Ben taking over, not that I don't like him, but I just don't know what to expect. Ben's always talking about getting results. I'm not against results but I hate working in a pressure cooker. You know, Ben could turn into another Ed. That's what I'm afraid of."

Liz laughed. "I think they broke the mold when they made Ed. He's one of a kind! Seriously, I have a lot of respect for Ben. He's willing to take the risks that I would sometimes like to take but don't feel sure enough of myself to do. He's got guts but at the same time he's not a loner and not a gambler either. I've seen him include his people in activities; he gets their involvement and participation. Sometimes I think he gets better solutions to the problems. On the other hand, there are times when he could have made the decision easier by himself, but instead he takes the extra time to involve the team. I wonder why. But then I see what an incredible job his unit does. Do you know the answer? Quite simply, his people are motivated. They understand what they're trying to do and they're committed to succeeding. It's because they know that their input has been considered in coming to the final determination. Wouldn't it be something if our team could operate that way?"

"I guess so," said Dan. "I'm just cautious. I've been here a while and I've seen a lot of people let power go to their heads. My main concern is Ben's attitude toward conflict. Most people shy away from it but he always wants to get it out in the open. I don't know if that's such a good idea. Conflict can disrupt relationships, and how can people work effectively when they don't feel good about one another?"

"Whatever he does," replied Liz, "it seems to work. For myself, I've always thought that the best way to handle conflict is to find a reasonable balance. But I'm finding that's not so effective. I seem to keep dealing with the same conflict over and over again. Just when I think I've gotten it fixed in one spot, it flares up somewhere else. Ben may be right by handling it once and for all when it first arises. Then it's out of the way and you can move forward; at least that's how it's supposed to work."

They arrived at Liz's car. "Well, here you are," said Dan. "There's nothing more we can do with this one tonight so I'll see you in the morning, okay?"

"Okay, you take care," said Liz. "Good night."

□ □ □

Ben sat at his desk studying some notes. The phone rang on his direct line and he immediately responded. "This is Ben Thomas. May I help you?"

"Ben, this is Harriet," the caller responded. "I wanted to touch base with you on a few things. Do you have a minute?"

"Sure, go ahead," replied Ben.

"Joe and I are delighted you've moved into Al's old position. We only had a brief opportunity to talk the other day but there are a number of concerns I need to discuss with you. I don't know whether we should try to do it now or if you prefer to get together at a later time."

"Well," said Ben, "right now is okay with me. I have a few items I'd like to bounce off you as well."

"Good," said Harriet. "When Joe and I called on you, we were primarily there to see how you'd respond to the idea of assuming the leadership role in Al's team. We hoped you would, of course, but we didn't want to move forward without checking certain details out in advance. We felt it was a matter of some urgency, which I think we let you know, but we didn't provide you with the whole background rationale for this decision."

"Please go on," said Ben.

Harriet considered the matter but then proceeded. She knew it needed to be confronted directly. "We know the team is feeling very enthusiastic after its latest victory, however we have some real reservations about this." She paused before going on.

Ben took the moment of silence to raise his point of view. "I think that several of us had concerns over that 'pseudo-victory.' It might better be referred to as a near miss."

"Yes," answered Harriet. "I'm relieved you know what I'm talking about. Did you come to any conclusions as to what might have happened?"

Ben began, "I think the issue only became apparent to us a few weeks ago when Frank and I were having lunch. According to Frank, he had spoken with Joe who alluded to the end of the month deadline on the bid. Frank raised this issue with me because he found it confusing. No wonder. All of us had been operating on the premise that we had until the 15th of next month. Frank and I went straight to Al and, after some digging, were able to put together the chain of events and locate the missing piece of information. Without that clue from Joe, we would have been history. Obviously, it shouldn't have happened in the first place and I'm committed to critiquing the problem with the team to institute a system of cross-checks to avoid such a mishap in the future."

"It sounds like you're on track," Harriet responded.

"There's more," laughed Ben. "We might find a need to draw you into the process at a later time because it's been my impression, although this is from the perspective of two levels down, that communications aren't as fine-tuned between our department and headquarters as they could be. Most of the information flow has been between Joe and Frank. If information came to Al, it didn't always get to us in the same form and sometimes not at all. I think we could find a more effective way to operate."

"I couldn't agree more," Harriet replied. She felt better and better about the decision to put Ben in the leadership slot.

"Harriet, I have a question for you, okay?" asked Ben.

"Yes. Go ahead," Harriet said.

"I've been thinking, just in the short time since you and Joe talked with me, that I'd like to do some development work in this team. I haven't talked with others yet and I suppose there might be resistance. Still I'd like to raise the issue. Just what is the company's policy on developing its human resources?"

"Well," responded Harriet, "you know as well as I do that this company keeps a close watch on how the money is spent, but we've always believed that people are our greatest resource, and that's reflected in our stated policy. It doesn't matter what we have in the way of technology, financial backing, information sources, and so on if we don't have the human resources to put those things to good use. And, I think you'll agree, we're living in a new age where interdependence is crucial. It's a lot more than you doing your part of the work and me doing mine. We no longer have the luxury of *not* working together. Competition will wipe us out if we stay in the dark ages of the traditional organization. We're living in a high tech society and that takes high tech leadership skills."

"That's right!" Ben answered with enthusiasm. "I've never heard it put so well but that's where I stand, too. That's the extra step we need to take. I'd like to lead this team in that kind of effort."

"You're right on target. Talk it over with the team and get back to me when you have a more concrete idea on how you'd like to proceed. I'll help you submit a proposal for budgeting the effort."

"Thanks, Harriet," said Ben. "I'll get back to you soon."

□ □ □

It was Monday morning. Ben felt awkward, never having met with this team before as its leader. Still he was enthusiastic because he envisioned a new future of which he wanted to be a part. The opportunities were virtually unlimited.

Ben smiled as people came in and felt a little more at ease because everyone seemed open and receptive. Even Gil had perked up a bit and seemed to be taking interest.

Ben got the meeting underway. "As often as not, a changeover in leadership is ushered in by the new boss saying something like, 'I want us to move forward as though nothing has changed. As far as we're concerned, it's business as usual.' I'm not going to do that."

Ben paused. He had their attention. "What I'm going to do instead is to skip those kinds of reassurances and get to what I see as the key issue of this team. It's teamwork. I know you've heard me say it before but I want to see us operate more effectively as a team. How can we go about doing that? I have several ideas but I want to hear from you.''

No one said a word. This team was accustomed to being told what to do, although Al had certainly entertained their questions. Liz looked at Dan, and Dan looked at Frank. Ed shook his head and cleared his throat.

''Ben, you and I have been full circle on this one, haven't we? And you know where I stand. Just what is it you want to propose this time?'' Ed sat back and crossed his arms.

No one else spoke so Ben proceeded. ''Okay, Ed, I'll just mention what's been on my mind, so you can all give it some thought. It's an approach called the Grid. Have you heard of it?''

''I have,'' said Dan. ''Everybody knows about the Grid from college or some management course they've taken.''

''I'm talking about a lot more than just a book,'' said Ben. ''It's a whole approach to organization development. When I first came on with Celarmco, my boss decided to send me to a Grid Seminar. It's an experience I've never forgotten. But I've gone farther than I intended. This is the topic of another meeting. All I'll add at this point is that I think if we operated from this framework of thinking, we'd be able to 'talk' to each other in a better way, particularly in situations where we don't agree. That's a key piece of learning in the Grid—how different styles of management deal with conflict. And conflict is anything from silent doubts and reservations to an out-and-out fist fight. Conflict, in a word, is disagreement.''

Ed looked skeptical. ''So, in our spare time, you want us to do a little training, is that it?''

Ben looked agitated but he held his temper. ''I think the time invested in such an undertaking will more than pay for itself in better results. That's been my experience.''

Ed still looked dubious.

Liz spoke up, ''I'd be interested. From what you said, I take it that it would help us work through conflict more effectively?''

''Yes,'' said Ben. ''But let's just hold this thought. I have another proposal for right now to help us get started as a brand new team.''

Ben took a deep breath and went on. ''Let me start by outlining my idea. I want to be sure we get off to a good start and to do that I think each of us needs to know what's going on. For example, right now I have no clear idea as to all of the projects Al had underway with each of you. I asked him before he left but he indicated that it would be better to check with each of you. Rather than doing that on a one-to-one basis, I have another proposal. I want to suggest several agenda topics for consideration, and my idea is that each of us does individual study of these items and then we can get back together next week for the sake of clarification.

"The first item is to define your current list of activities. Then I'd like you to ask yourself three questions. The first relates to your team, that is, you and your subordinates. As a boss, what are the distinctive problems you are currently dealing with in working with your subordinates? The second question relates to this team, each of you, and myself. What do you think the barriers are at present that impede our progress? The final question is 'What do you think we should do to improve our team effectiveness?'

"I'd like you to be prepared to discuss these items next week. Furthermore, we won't be able to do this in an hour. To do a good job, we'll probably need to devote a full day to this discussion. Is it possible for everyone to arrange their schedules to permit this to happen?" Ben waited for their reply.

The team was silent for a moment; then Ed spoke up. "Most of this has little relevance to the whole team. I can see that you need to know everything that's going on but why not meet with each of us individually? I really don't care to sit in on your discussion with Liz or Gil or Dan or Frank. And, to be quite candid—I think that's one of your pet words—I don't really care to have them sit in on my discussion with you. Why in the world should I be forced to listen to problems that have nothing to do with me?"

"That's a good point," said Ben, "but I don't think it's completely true. Let me ask Liz a question. Liz, are there matters that would make it possible for you to accomplish your objectives with your subordinates or as a member of this team in a more effective way if you were more aware of what Ed was doing and if you had more input into how Ed was running his own team or operating within this group?"

"There's no doubt about it," said Liz. "I can think of all kinds of difficulties between Ed and myself that could be overcome with greater cooperation on both our parts. A big difficulty I grapple with is the communication gap. I could use my resources much more effectively if I knew what he was doing and if he and I could coordinate effort in a more systematic way."

"What do you think, Ed?" Ben queried.

"Well, that might be true. But, then, why don't you and me and Liz get together? Why do you want to bring the 'whole team' into this?"

"A problem for any individual in this team constitutes a team problem in my view," said Ben. "The reason is that if we are hampered in giving one another full cooperation, the whole team is bound to suffer effectiveness in some way."

"Well," said Ed, "maybe so and maybe not. Look, Ben, you're the boss so I'll do what you say this time. But I'm sure going to want to see some payout for myself. My time is valuable, you know. I don't want to sit around listening to what I already know."

"I appreciate your tentative support, Ed." Ben smiled.

"Do we need to prepare a written report?" asked Gil.

"That might be helpful," Ben replied, "but not anything formal. Just be able to outline the issues to the team and to answer any questions. This is informal. Think of it as a workshop."

"How in the world are we going to digest all this data?" Dan asked. "I won't be able to remember what everyone says without taking copious notes. I hate to say it but I'm not sure I can write and think at the same time. What exactly are you proposing?"

"I hadn't really thought of that. Do you have any thoughts on how to solve the 'data problem,' Dan? I agree that it could become overwhelming." Ben paused and waited for Dan to reply.

Suddenly Dan lit up. "Yes, I just thought of something. I've seen other human resource people conduct sessions that are not totally different from what you're describing. They use stand-up blackboards, flipcharts, or newsprints, and they keep a running account of what's being discussed. Why don't I get something along these lines for us to use? Then we can all be working and thinking together because we'll all be looking at the same thing?"

"Sounds like an excellent idea to me," Liz chimed in. "Furthermore, if we want to keep any of the notes for later, we can just have them transcribed and distributed. That also solves the problem of you writing down something different from me because we understood what was said in a different way. We'll all have identical copies of what we agree on as a team."

"Okay," Ben continued. "I think we're on track with this. There's only one final matter I want to mention. This is for all of us, not just for me. It's not a public progress check where each of you takes turns on the hot seat. The point of the whole thing is to see how we can operate more *interdependently* as a team. I think each one of us has a lot to gain by listening to others on this team, because what we do *does* impact what someone else on our team has to do. I feel enthusiastic about this commitment to take a full and comprehensive look at ourselves next week. Is there anything else we need to deal with right now?" Everyone shook their heads. Ben finished by saying, "If you have any problems with this, don't hesitate to give me a call. Or, you may want to meet with your own teams and have a similar discussion to look at the present activities. Get their input. Okay?"

Everyone nodded their agreement.

Ben smiled and said, "It seems to me that if we can do this as I've outlined it that it might mean an end to the 'do-your-own-thing' era and put us on a new path of interdependent teamwork. Anyway, that's my hope. I'll see you all later."

□ □ □

The one-day review session the following week proved productive for everyone involved. The team was off and running, working more efficiently than ever before. Several weeks had passed and the team was now meeting for its weekly session. Ben returned to the issue of "Grid." As usual, Ed was resisting but others on the team were becoming more receptive to the idea.

"If it's already in a book," stated Ed defiantly, "then why go to a seminar?"

Ben said, "It's hard to explain but I can tell you that I had the same reaction. All I can say at this point is that it has to do with getting an objective look at yourself—and, for me, that took other people. The power of Grid was a self-convincing experience for me."

Liz was talking. "I'm interested in anything that will help me be more effective as a manager, especially in the area of conflict resolution."

The wheels were turning in Frank's head. He began to see how this might work for him. "Better managers get promoted," he thought to himself. Suddenly, he spoke up, "Well, I'm game. I'd be willing to give it a try."

Ed broke into the conversation. "Since I seem to be the group skeptic, why don't you let me go and evaluate this 'Grid thing.' If I come back convinced, then you know it works."

Everyone laughed but Ed continued, "However . . . if I find out it's a waste of time," and he looked Ben in the eye, "are you willing to drop this stuff and get back to business?"

"I won't make any promises," Ben responded. "What I want you to do is to go with an open mind and then come back and tell us what you think. I do want your input."

"Fair enough," Ed said respectfully.

"Wait a minute," interrupted Gil. "I think a better idea is for two of us to go. That way we can compare notes and really assess the potential of such an undertaking."

Everyone turned in surprise and looked at Gil.

"Congratulations, Gil, you finally joined the team!" Liz interjected into the silence. Everyone laughed with new enthusiasm.

"I like that idea," said Ed. "What do you think, Ben?"

"I second the motion. Gil and Ed, come by my office later and we'll get the ball rolling. Liz, you and Frank are welcome to sign up as well. We just need to coordinate our schedules. But, as far as I'm concerned, each one of you that goes is just another point on the curve because I believe you're going to like this thing called Grid."

Ben felt they were moving in the right direction. He began to feel confident that his vision for this group of talented people could come to fruition. It would take a lot of hard work but these people were committed to doing a good job. "One step at a time, though," Ben thought. "First we get Ed and Gil to a Grid; maybe Frank, too. Then we'll see what happens next."

□ □ □

Ben is oriented in the 9,9 direction. Although we haven't had as close a look at Harriet, she, too, is characterized by the 9,9 Grid style. Each of these individuals has high commitment for getting results through motivated people who feel a sense of fulfillment from what they are doing.

In the story it is evident that Ben sees the potential for synergistic action made possible by involving people in decision making. He places high value on full use of R_1 resources—getting input from those who must work on an activity to make it a success. By seeking out the best thinking available prior to decision making, Ben doesn't diminish his authority and leadership capability. Rather, he becomes stronger because all effort is meshed toward the achievement of a single end. At the same time, however, others are becoming stronger by virtue of their involvement. As a result all members are able to make a greater contribution to corporate effort.

Specifically, here are some of the 9,9 features of Ben's leadership as he launched a "new team" effort:

1. Ben wants to get out of the formal, rules-oriented mode into one of more spontaneous interaction characterized by feedback and critique and conflict resolution.

2. He sees the severe limitations of trying to manage one-on-one and the lack of coordination and poor communication that result.
3. He wants to create an environment of shared responsibility to replace the culture of competitive "do your own thing."
4. He advocates discussions that are carried out in an open and candid manner rather than people waiting for him to give orders or feeling they must keep quiet to protect vested interests.
5. The goal is to solve problems in the soundest manner rather than simply to define them and leave it at that; the effort is toward maximum utilization of resources.

The 9,9 leadership style, shown in Figure 9-1, integrates high concern for production, 9, with high concern for people, 9, as indicated in the upper right corner of the Grid. Unlike other leadership approaches, the 9,9 orientation assumes no inherent contradiction between organization purpose and the needs of people to be productive. As a result, it becomes possible to effectively integrate the two by involving people in determining the strategies of work and achievement. This doesn't mean getting everyone together all the time to obtain their points of view. Nor does it imply that everyone agrees with the final decision. What it does mean, however, is that, when possible, those who are involved in a work activity have had the opportunity to voice their concerns, whether positive or negative, prior to a decision being made. Not only does this ensure that they have a better understanding of what is to be done and the underlying rationale for decisions, but it also increases the probability that decisions reflect the best available thinking of

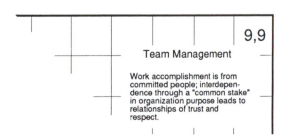

Figure 9-1. The 9,9 Grid style is located in the upper right corner of the Grid.

organization members. This is making the most of R_2 relationships—by maximizing the R_1 resources available to achieve desired R_3 results.

Thorough integration of the concern for results and the concern for people, such as is characterized by the 9,9 Grid style, is only possible through leadership that encourages organization members to fully commit themselves to corporate objectives by making extraordinary contributions. This is accomplished by establishing sound and mature relationships between members to achieve corporate goals. The aim of a 9,9 orientation, then, is to promote participation, involvement, and commitment to team effort directed at accomplishing organization purpose as fully as possible.

Motivations

The 9,9 theory of managing presumes an inherent connection between organizational needs for production and the needs of people for full and rewarding work experiences. The plus and minus sides of the 9,9 Grid style are shown in Figure 9-2.

The plus (+) motivation is "desire for fulfillment through contribution." This means knowing you have made a difference; that your effort has had a positive impact on the organization and those who work in it. A leader like Ben has a desire to contribute to corporate success by involving others so that they too can contribute. This enthusiasm and "can-do" spirit are contagious; they inspire a "win" attitude among others and promote feelings of spontaneity and openness. This positive motivation includes a genuine desire to help others reach their fullest potential. It is basic to creativity, commitment, and cohesion in a 9,9-oriented culture.

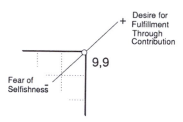

Figure 9-2. The plus and minus motivations of the 9,9 Grid style.

Ben has a development goal for his team. It boils down to better R_2 to get a full helping of R_3. This means mobilizing human resources to enable team members to work more productively together. Ben understands his role is to create such effort, but he must get acceptance from team members themselves. He needs their involvement and commitment for the effort to succeed. Ben is seeking to build such commitment through exposure to sound principles of leadership that will permit team members to operate from a common framework of thinking. Ed has doubts about the undertaking, but Ben is encouraging him to open his mind enough to entertain the possibility that there might be a better way. Only by seeing options to what we are doing are we then in a position to change.

The 9,9+ motivation is characterized by a high-spirited sense of gratification, enjoyment from work, and excitement for making a corporate contribution. The closer one comes to success in advancing corporate goals, the greater the sense of personal fulfillment. When the organization culture is characterized by and operated according to 9,9 principles of leadership, its members can expect to enjoy the benefits, both emotional and financial, made possible by corporate success. We will take a closer look at these principles in Chapter 10.

The minus ($-$) side of the 9,9 orientation is "fear of selfishness." This means losing perspective, becoming more identified with our own way of doing something and losing sight of input from others. It means a subtle shift away from "What's right?" towards "Who's right?" It is when your goal as a manager is no longer so much aimed at achieving an organization objective as it is on doing it your way. You may even have "reinterpreted" the objective in your own mind to justify how you are going about it. These are the actions a 9,9-oriented manager seeks to avoid because best thinking and best effort cannot be had when selfish motivations come into play.

Managers like Ben and Harriet avoid advancing their own selfish interests at the expense of others or the corporation because to do so invites suspicion and distrust and ultimately reduces the level of candor. Relationships characterized by low trust stand in the way of progress—they impede the flow of R_1 resources into R_3 results. Rather, poor relationships in the area of R_2 are at the root of adverse conditions that permeate many otherwise productive organizations, showing up in political maneuvering, stepping on others, withholding information, and the many ways in which we can block the efforts of our bosses, colleagues, and subordinates toward what could and should be our common goal.

Conflict Solving

We examined how managers dealt with conflict in each of the preceding Grid style chapters. In every case, an attempt is made to avoid it. This is true even of the 9,1 Grid style in a sense because a 9,1-oriented manager sees conflict as a barrier or delay to getting results; therefore, it is squelched and eliminated through force. Only in the 9,9 Grid style is there recognition of the missed opportunity that can be capitalized on by confronting conflict and facing up to it in a sound way. How does a leader use power and authority when the aim of conflict resolution is to achieve a sound result from an organization achievement perspective?

The aim is to find the best answer when power and authority are exercised in a dynamic way. Disagreement is valued as an inevitable result of the fact that strong-minded people have convictions about what is right. A person may say, "Nothing in our scenario is to be taken for granted. What are the facts, what are the causes, and what are the conclusions?" Emotions are confronted through direct discussion of them with the person involved in the disagreement. Resolution is possible but involves maturity and real human insight. It is something we are all capable of although we may lack the necessary insights as to what it entails or the skills for doing it.

This is the case when you're the boss operating with subordinates. But what about those times when you don't have power and authority over those with whom you must work—bosses, peers, those in other departments, or vendors and contractors on the "outside"? The principles of 9,9 still hold true as the most effective way of achieving sound results through people in a way that is aimed at solving problems—not pushing them under the rug. The straightforward and open nature of the 9,9 Grid style is valued as the soundest approach for human interaction worldwide[17].

The 9,9+ statement for conflict solving is, "I see conflict as an opportunity to gain a better understanding of 'What's right?' Its sound resolution leads to committed people who understand what we are trying to achieve." During their victory meeting, several of

Al's people expressed their frustration with how the team was operating. Ben was especially keen to solve this problem and sought to focus it for others on the team. When Al tried to divert the discussion as a means of smoothing over the conflict, Ben redirected attention back to the issue at hand, seeing it as a key problem to be resolved. When Al finally terminated the meeting, Ben sought to extract a promise from the team that they would revisit the issue at the next team meeting. He wanted to find out "What's right?"

The 9,9− side of conflict solving is, "I try to move people away from polarized positions that focus on 'Who is right?' and get them to focus on the soundest way to proceed."

Preventing Conflict

Before we turn to how a 9,9-oriented manager deals with conflict, let's examine some strategies for "bypassing" or preventing the emergence of disruptive conflict. These are not mechanisms aimed at avoiding conflict or smoothing it over but rather qualities inherent in the 9,9 style itself that promote problem-solving behavior rather than vested interests, polarized points of view, or disgruntled submission.

Getting early involvement from those affected by a problem lets them know that resolution is being sought and that their input is valued. This ensures the best effort in fact gathering, identifying alternatives, and evaluating the soundest way to proceed. It may even permit trial runs or experimental tests to provide further data for decision analysis.

Another quality of 9,9 leadership that obviates the need for conflict is the exchange of rationale and perspectives. Getting different points of view out into the open and thinking them through allows each person to assess the logic of each other person's convictions. It permits faulty reasoning and distorted thinking to be identified and dealt with, thus aiding to eliminate invalid information. This open approach to problem solving decreases the likelihood of disruptive conflict emerging.

Full self-disclosure is another way of avoiding misunderstanding. It means withholding nothing that might be pertinent to problem solving. This runs the full length of the spectrum from data and logic to attitudes, feelings, hunch, and intuition—anything that adds to greater insight. It may include personal or private information if these have a direct bearing on organization performance. A 9,9-oriented person seeks to be judicious in what he or she reveals to others, but if it increases understanding among people, the self-disclosure is provided with openness and candor. By doing so, others find themselves more in position to take a similar risk and to respond in kind.

A goal of 9,9-oriented management is to communicate in a clear and unpretentious manner. Some words and phrases are vague and difficult to understand whereas others are precise and descriptive; some neutral; others inflammatory. Some are valid in one context and yet have quite a different meaning in another. The words you use when speaking to another person can significantly affect what they hear. Certain words are "red flags" that trigger an emotional response; objectivity is lost; misunderstanding and misinterpretation result. Compliments can be equally confusing, because they may be so pleasing to hear that a person is thrown off guard.

We can illustrate this difference with Joe and Harriet. If Joe takes an idea to the president and is told, "Maybe we should hold off on that for now," Joe may return dejected, thinking the president turned him down. He tells Harriet, "We need to drop this. The president doesn't approve." On the other hand, if Harriet experiences the same thing, she explores the underlying rationale for the president's reluctance and discovers that it has nothing to do with disapproval or misgivings on his part. He embraces the idea but, because he is preoccupied with other matters, he fails to provide a full understanding to Joe. When Harriet digs deeper, she finds that the president only wants to defer action in the short term due to bigger picture fiscal matters. Three months down the road he says he can support her in this endeavor. All it took on Harriet's part was the persistence to explore the matter thoroughly rather than drawing an erroneous inference from the president's initial refusal.

A 9,9-oriented manager develops criteria for what constitutes a sound solution before going in search of one. By operating within pre-established and agreed-upon criteria, conflict is often avoided because there is an objective measure shared among those involved rather than the decision being based on individual subjective judgments. As a result, better solutions are achieved.

We need to examine one more point and that is the presence of personal needs and expectations. Violation of expectations is probably one of the major sources of conflict in interpersonal relations. If we could all be mind readers, this might not be the case. However, given our limitations as human beings, the answer to this dilemma lies once again in the principles of openness and candor. What usually happens is that we think everyone understands a situation just as we do. If not, that's their problem. It is right here that it can become our problem, too. If you carry through on an action in a way different than what I thought you were going to do, we have a conflict, and it is made bigger by the fact that it is over and done with and I may have no alternative but to live with it. When expectations are violated, the first reaction a person feels is surprise, then a sense of betrayal, and finally anger. Not only do we have a disagreement about the way a situation was handled, but now emotions have escalated and conflict of the disruptive sort is imminent. It seems rather simple to say that all this could be avoided by making sure everyone has the same expectation of an outcome in advance, but all too often this step is avoided. A 9,9-oriented leader recognizes this fact and that is why he or she sees it as essential to get the input of others; this includes their doubts and reservations, and it involves setting expectations for what is going to happen. This one step can defuse many situations of conflict before they ever happen.

Other kinds of conflicts can be prevented by making your needs known to those with whom you work. For example, Dan has a difficult time telling others what he would like, and it may be that he prefers for colleagues and subordinates to knock before entering his office. By not saying anything, he scores another resentment every time someone like Frank or Ed bolts in unannounced. However, unless Dan clearly expresses this preference to others, there is no way they can know how he feels. Frank and Ed can't begin to cooperate until Dan stands up for what he wants.

By getting expectations out into the open, we are relieved of the need to tiptoe around one another. If the requests that others make of us are reasonable, we can do our best to honor them. On the other hand, if the expectations others hold inhibit productivity, we can confront them and seek a sounder basis of operation.

Handling Conflict When It Appears

Even in an atmosphere of openness and candor (perhaps we should say, especially in an atmosphere of openness and candor), conflict is likely to emerge. When we say "conflict," we mean different points of view, two ideas about how to do the same thing, tensions related to a lack of shared values about how to achieve results with and through the efforts of others.

The 9,9 approach permits people to disagree, to work out their disagreements in the light of facts, and ultimately to understand one another. Such problem-solving constructiveness in conflict situations promotes candor among people so essential for both personal and corporate success.

Several outcomes may result from 9,9 conflict solving. In the first example, shown in Figure 9-3, the 9,9-oriented boss has a vertical point of view and the subordinate has a horizontal point of view. The boss may discover thinking of which he or she was unaware, finding that the subordinate does in fact have a better idea about how to proceed with a given task. In this case the boss accepts the subordinate's view because the boss is *convinced*. This is not yielding

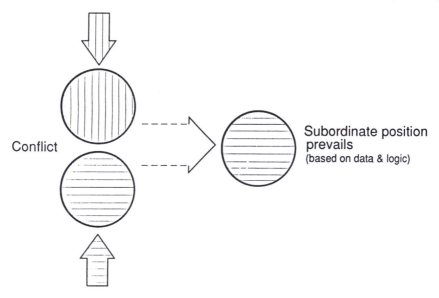

Figure 9-3. A 9,9 boss is convinced of a subordinate's viewpoint based on a new understanding of the facts.

in the 1,9 sense. This is the boss saying, "My approach was limited. You have a better way to go and I agree with you."

The reverse situation is also possible as shown in Figure 9-4. The boss may have the better answer. In this case, the subordinate can change his or her point of view, not based on compliance or compromise, but rather on an understanding of the boss's rationale and the soundness of that approach.

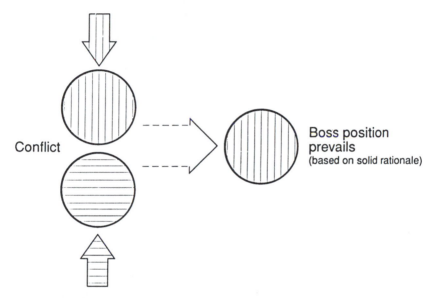

Figure 9-4. A 9,9 subordinate is able to accept the boss's position based on the conviction that the rationale is sound.

There is one more possibility. A solution not seen by boss nor subordinate emerges, as shown in Figure 9-5 by a solid circle of larger size. The new solution is bigger and better; it is preferable and sounder than the position initially held by either boss or subordinate. When this kind of teamwork happens, members have achieved *synergy*—the emergence of a solution that may or may not incorporate something of both positions but also adds unique or more inclusive elements that make it superior to any of the prior formulations. Synergy is an indicator of teamwork characterized by excellence; it means people working together in an interdependent way to achieve what no individual was capable of doing alone.

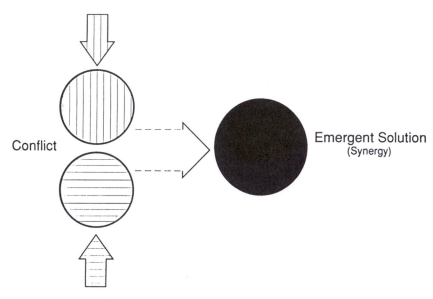

Figure 9-5. A superior solution is produced through effective interaction, which spurs creativity.

Synergy is a goal of 9,9 problem solving and is made possible by facing up to conflict and confronting it rather than trying to suppress it or run from it. Conflict causes people to withhold information, misread one another's motivations, and sometimes even deny its very presence, keeping tensions and antagonistic feelings "under cover."

There are two kinds of "confrontation" and it is useful to distinguish between them. One type of confrontation polarizes points of view to bring them into sharp focus. This confrontation tests the strength of one against another. The underlying assumption is that the stronger point of view will prevail. We call this "confrontation for combat." This is how Ed deals with conflict.

"Confrontation to compare and contrast" has quite a different meaning. It means solving conflict by bringing it out into the open so that differences can be resolved. Emotions that usually accompany conflict—anger, hostility, fear, anxiety, doubt, and disappointment—can also be explored. This is 9,9 confrontation, as used by Ben, who seeks to bring his differences with others, such as Ed, out into the open where the soundness of underlying thinking can be examined. In this way discrepancies are reviewed and removed by creating greater understanding of the opposing viewpoints. Ben cannot argue the merits of teamwork with Ed until Ed has an opportunity to expose himself to the same thinking that Ben has entertained. Once Ed has done so, they will both be in a position to examine the validity of such an effort. Ed may bring new thinking to light that Ben has not considered. Or, Ed may become aware of sounder approaches to doing things that he was previously unwilling to try. In either case, the possibility of a sound decision being reached that all parties can embrace is increased.

Confrontation for combat and confrontation to compare and contrast may look the same on the surface. There is, however, an important underlying difference, often recognized only by those involved in the confrontation itself. In the case of confrontation for combat, there is an unmistakable contest of wills; the holder of one view feels threatened by the holder of the other. To yield in this situation means losing, no matter how you look at it. The 9,9 kind of confrontation implies a condition of mutual trust among those who are seeking to resolve the difference. Such a climate is characterized by goodwill and respect for the other point of view. To prevail over the other person is not the ultimate aim; to find a sound solution is key.

There's not a winner and a loser in 9,9 confrontation. Everyone comes out ahead by virtue of finding a sounder solution. If your solution is not the one embraced, it means no loss of face. Nor is it capitulation or weakness. Rather, it is a demonstration of your commitment to a better solution achieved through logic and reason and the removal of reservations and doubts. We have worked together as a team to discover "What's right?" rather than try to solve the age-old question of "Who's right?" Now we can proceed with accomplishing our goal, each of us with a shared understanding of what we are trying to do.

When Conflict Remains

What happens when conflict doesn't find resolution? Several additional steps can be taken to end the conflict or to manage it in the soundest manner possible.

The first is ventilation, where one or both parties seek to relieve the tensions in their relationship by discussing the issue of contention with a third party. Each party may meet separately with the "outsider" to vent frustrations, which serves to bring emotions back under control. With the issue more clearly in perspective, the two parties may resume deliberation of the facts.

Another possibility is to engage a third party to meet with those in conflict and to provide review and feedback from a "neutral" perspective. Because the disagreeing parties have become so enmeshed in the problem, it is likely they have lost objectivity. The addition of a neutral element can provide an unbiased reaction and, because there is no vested interest in the outcome, the two contending parties may be willing to consider this new perspective. The neutral participant-observer can be another manager, a staff person, or an internal or external consultant—anyone removed from the conflict itself. *This person is not an arbitrator* but rather serves to lend objectivity to the situation. Responsibility for resolving the conflict remains with the contending parties.

When conflict persists but action is required, it may be necessary to defer the disagreement in the interest of a superordinate goal of team accomplishment. For the 9,9-oriented manager, the conflict is only put on hold but not permanently. A later critique can be used to explore the deeper issues underlying the conflict to establish a sounder basis for working together. Conflicts that "don't go away" are usually indicative of a deeper underlying problem. A 9,9-oriented manager sees it as critical to get to the bottom of such matters.

Initiative

In the 9,9 orientation, initiative is exercised in a strong, pro-organizational manner. A 9,9-oriented leader like Ben is eager, vigorous, and thrives on productive effort. Personal energy is focused on exercising initiative in an enthusiastic and spontaneous way that arouses the involvement and commitment of others.

Not all initiatives have equal priority in mobilizing effort, and so the 9,9-oriented manager plans, prioritizes, and then follows through, retesting along the way to ensure soundness. When faced with two problems of equal importance, the one offering the largest payout gets priority, although critical features like urgency might get factored into the equation. If two options offer equal payout, items such as expense and optimum use of resources are considered.

Initiative does not rely solely on the 9,9-oriented leader and proposals may arise externally to the team or from any of its members. This norm for widespread and spontaneous initiative taking ensures that no one can say, "That's not my problem. Let someone else handle it."

The 9,9+ side of initiative can be summed up as, "I introduce new activities aimed at stimulating productivity, creativity, or satisfaction from work." Ben's development proposal is one aimed at making the team more productive in its efforts. His goal is to give others the same experience of fulfillment through contribution as he finds in his own work. His enthusiasm is contagious and others begin to pick up on his ideas—including Gil who for the first time in our story shows an interest in team activity.

The 9,9− statement is, "I avoid initiating new activities that divert attention from primary objectives even though I might find them personally interesting." Because a 9,9-oriented person is open to a large range of interests, many opportunities appear on the horizon that offer potential. However, this leader makes sure that team effort is directed towards those activities that offer the greatest pay-out rather than engaging in those that hold some degree of fascination from a personal perspective. One way to do this is to seek input from other team members who are in a good position to evaluate their relevance against the shared objectives of the team.

Inquiry

9,9 inquiry is comprehensive and in depth. The objective is to ensure that all sides of a question are evaluated in a thorough and analytical manner, thus increasing the likelihood that real problems are fully understood by those who must grapple with them. Managers like Ben and Harriet "know the score." They understand what they're talking about. A premium is placed on developing facts and data and digging out contradictory as well as supporting evidence on an issue. Clear separation is maintained between fact and opinion. This enthusiasm for thoroughness is reinforced by a natural curiosity.

Questions, of course, are basic to inquiry, but 9,9-oriented questions have the unique quality of being open-ended to promote further input. It is a two-way process with subordinates as free to initiate queries of the boss as the boss is of subordinates. Questions may take the form of, "How would you evaluate the situation?" "Can you make any sense of this?" or "Can you describe to me your understanding of the problem?" All elicit much more than a "yes"/"no" response from the targeted audience. The nature of the questions is such that one question serves to generate another. The purpose of the questions is to produce further data and facts to assist in a sound decision-making effort. This establishes a common framework of understanding and aids team members to assemble isolated bits of information into a coherent whole.

Listening can be characterized as open and active. Even so, the 9,9-oriented listener is aware that his or her own assumptions can distort interpretation of the message. Therefore, the 9,9-oriented person seeks to paraphrase what others say in an effort to see if understanding has been conveyed as intended. If not, misunderstandings can then be clarified.

Sound inquiry also involves investigating any sources pertinent to grasping the full complexity of a problem. Written documents are studied in a proactive manner. The 9,9-oriented reader is alert to every detail, taking nothing as given. The reader seeks to understand the underlying rationale of a writer: "Why did she state the problem in these terms. Are there any exceptions to what has been said? Are there alternative ways of looking at this problem? Is there bias in her approach?" It is important to double-check and test information in order to authenticate its source. The 9,9-oriented leader might approach a subordinate and say, "I have studied this material but will you check it against your own understanding to confirm the conclusions if valid or to offer alternative thinking if not?"

A final consideration is unique to 9,9-oriented inquiry. The optimal approach to understanding is of an interdependent nature, carried out on a team-wide basis with all who have something to contribute simultaneously engaged in digging out and testing facts, data, and evidence. This process enriches the quality of inquiry because it permits each participant to examine facts and see the problem from more perspectives than when thinking is undertaken in a solo manner.

Thoroughness and depth of inquiry are at the heart of 9,9-oriented management. "Prework is a prerequisite for participation" is another way of saying that problem solving can be no better than the thinking that leads to the conclusion, and thinking is limited by the available input of information. Additionally, every team member has access to the thinking and understanding of every other team member as the basis for exercising sound initiative and decision making.

The plus motivation (+) of 9,9 inquiry is, "I try to gain full understanding of what is going on and I stimulate others to do the same; that puts us in the best position for directing team effort and evaluating the cause-and-effect relationship of what we do." Ben wants his colleagues to explore team development further. He has offered one possibility but it is necessary to get others involved in the process to accurately determine the best way to proceed. Already he has gained their commitment to explore next steps and once team members have more data on the different options available to them, they can evaluate the soundest course of action.

The minus (−) side is, "I avoid asking questions that merely serve to further my own ends and keep me locked within a limited perspective." To do so would only be for the purpose of furthering one's own selfish ends. That is why a 9,9-oriented person like Ben or Harriet tries to ask questions in a way that is open to another's perspective rather than leading a person to reply favorably to a predetermined point of view.

Advocacy

Information and ideas are presented clearly and without hesitation. Reservations are put forth in an aboveboard manner. Advocacy in the 9,9 orientation means to "tell it like it is." Such an approach earns the wide respect of other team members whether or not they agree with what is said. Furthermore, the strength with which these convictions are held is admired. Yet, if information contradicting the validity of convictions is offered, the 9,9-oriented person is ready to move off a position towards the sounder solution. Others see a

9,9-oriented leader as assertive and self-assured but also open to alternative points of view and therefore not rigid or arbitrary.

Strong advocacy increases the likelihood that every viewpoint receives the attention it merits. This means that Ben must convince the team that there is a better way to operate than has characterized them in the past. If they are not convinced that improvement is a possibility, it is unlikely that they will shift to another position. Part of Ben's purpose in exposing Ed and others to the concepts of Grid is to build their convictions for engaging in a development effort.

The plus side of 9,9 advocacy is, "I feel convinced about the right way to go unless others can show me that there is a sounder approach. I offer my underlying rationale to others so they can understand my thinking and I seek to discover the reasons for their positions as well."

The minus side of 9,9 advocacy is, "I avoid taking strong positions that block input from others or that lead to issues being seen from a limited or narrow perspective." Ben is enthusiastic about his own Grid experience but he remains open to different possibilities. In fact, he is open to the possibility that this is not the way to go. However, he wants each team member to explore the matter in greater depth before discussing the validity of his idea. He would rather have Ed skeptical than noncommittal, because he sees this as the best way to test the soundness of such an undertaking. If Ed becomes convinced that such an effort is worthwhile, Ben has gained a strong advocate.

Decision Making

Most decisions are almost self-evident before they are ever made in a 9,9 team. The reason is that members have been involved in the whole process from initiation of an idea, its testing through inquiry and anticipatory critique, the deliberation through advocacy of various positions, to the final decision itself. While decision-making responsibility is usually vested in the leader, a decision is not seen to be the leader's sole possession. Rather, because everyone has been involved by virtue of having had the opportunity to provide input, the whole team feels ownership of the ultimate product.

Decision making by a 9,9-oriented leader is aimed at achieving understanding and agreement among those who are impacted by the decision itself. This describes the optimum condition because it means all doubts and reservations have been worked through and consensus has been established toward a specified end. The linking of the words *understanding* and *agreement* is important because action without understanding can be little more than obedience or compliance. That's why providing rationale to those involved in implementing a decision along with seeking their input and involvement is key. In this way people are enabled to understand why a decision has been made. Even if full agreement is not possible, team members have a sense of commitment to the ultimate decision because they know they have had an opportunity to present their best thinking and to express doubts and reservations.

Does 9,9 decision making mean that everyone on the team is involved in making all decisions? Obviously, no. It would not be a productive use of resources to engage those who have nothing to contribute to solving a problem. The idea is to look at "Who can contribute?" and "Who is impacted by this decision?" These are the people who need to be involved—if that is possible under the conditions of any given situation. There are several variables involved in determining participation and we will explore these further in Chapter 10.

Before we leave 9,9 decision making, a closer look at delegation is in order. From the 9,9 perspective, delegation provides a major development opportunity. The boss aids a subordinate to gain experience in a new area that enhances the subordinate's sense of autonomy and personal achievement. Although it may require time initially to help the subordinate get started, in the long term it frees the boss to concentrate on other activities.

This example describes how Ben delegates an activity to a new subordinate:

"With new and inexperienced subordinates I identify the problem and discuss it thoroughly. I ask them how they might solve it. Then I review their thinking to explore points they may have overlooked before leaving them to complete the task. I ask them to check their progress with me so that we can jointly critique the activity along the way to completion."

"When a subordinate with more experience comes to me for advice, I ask if the issue has been explored with colleagues. I try to instill a solution-seeking perspective rather than a wait-for-the-boss-to-tell-me perspective. Getting help and support from colleagues and interdependent teamwork is critical to successful delegation and development."

Turning to the motivational side of decision making, the 9,9+ statement is, "I make decisions that reflect the best available thinking and I seek to involve those whose understanding and commitment is critical to a successful outcome." The 9,9− side is, "I avoid making decisions that divert attention from the main game or that exclude essential resources." In Ben's effort to develop the team, he could have made an arbitrary decision about what he wanted the team to do, but it is unlikely that he would gain the necessary commitment to make the effort a success. Rather, he saw it as important to involve people in the decision-making process itself so they would understand and gain commitment to the endeavor.

Critique

All Grid styles incorporate some form of feedback, although it may only be message passing as in 1,1 or positive remarks as in 1,9. However, the 9,9 Grid style is the only style that goes a step beyond and includes the larger concept of critique. Critique refers to the continuous examination and reexamination of activity. It deals not only with the "what" and "who" of decision making but also with the "how" and the "why." Sound critique permits an objective analysis of how well things are going or how ineffective they are. Often we forget to stop and look at how success was achieved when things go well. Rather, we praise ourselves and race ahead with no idea of what we did right and, as a result, no way of repeating the effort on some future occasion except by chance. Continuous examination of what we are doing ensures that the process is as effective as possible at all points from start to completion.

Sometimes we encounter barriers to effectiveness. Regardless of the source, one thing is evident—they impede productive effort. Barriers to effectiveness range from faulty logic, vested interest, hidden agendas, jealousies, favoritism, blindness to alternative courses of action, fear-provoking remarks, poor timing, unwitting collusion to mediocre goals, and the failure to recognize potential resources. 9,9 critique can eliminate many of these impediments by offering an opportunity for reflection and evaluation. It can be a steering mechanism that helps us to avoid less-than-sound decisions.

Critique is not restricted to telling others what is being done well or what is being done poorly. As is true for everyone, leaders like Ben or Al or Harriet or Joe are likely to have limited understanding of a complex situation. Seldom do we find ourselves in the unique position of being able to make a completely solo contribution. The 9,9-oriented leader is self-critical and receptive to feedback from other team members. When critique is done effectively, the potential for strengthened decisions is increased. This double-loop approach to feedback permits learning from experience to occur. Learning in and of itself is just another source of 9,9 gratification.

Effectiveness of critique is characterized by several properties, including:

☐ A climate of openness and candor as this fosters "best" decisions.
☐ Critique throughout an activity or task, not just at the beginning or at the end.
☐ An understanding of what is happening and the consequences that result; this reinforces the idea that critique should be undertaken as soon as possible after an event so that cause-and-effect can clearly be seen.
☐ The idea that critique is nonjudgmental, i.e., it doesn't label things as "good" or "bad."
☐ A focus on topics that relate to the task at hand, not observations that have no relevance to a person's productivity.
☐ Highlighting consequences of behavior in terms of how that behavior impacts the productivity of others on the team; this aids each individual to learn how to operate in a sounder and more interdependent way on future activities.

Now we can turn to the motivations underlying the 9,9 exercise of critique. The 9,9+ statement is, "I strive for synergistic action and interdependence among team members. Critique permits me and others to learn from our experience." Think about how Ben conducted his first meeting as a leader. He proposed that they do an in-depth critique of team action and current activities, taking a full day the following week after each member had an opportunity to study the situation. This was instead of "business as usual," moving right along to the next activity without paying attention to the one just completed. How many of us operate with thorough and deliberate critique on a daily basis? This may be the greatest missed opportunity in management, either because it's forgotten or written off as too time consuming or seen as threatening to harmonious relationships. Critique saves time in the long run, gets people operating at their peak performance in a synergistic way, and bonds people together in relationships characterized by mutual trust and respect. There is no greater tool for building sound team interaction.

The 9,9− statement is, "I avoid critique that is subjective and aimed at furthering my own ends; I try to keep the focus on learning from what we have done so that we can do better in the future."

Subordinate Interaction with a 9,9-Oriented Boss

A 9,9 leadership style has the greatest likelihood of achieving positive consequences with and through other people regardless of their Grid style. This is because dealing with people in a 9,9 way has the effect of bringing them up to a problem-solving level. How does a 9,1-oriented person fight strong convictions that are presented with openness and candor and grounded in facts and logic? The 5,5-oriented person can't get away with being non-committal; nor is the 1,1-oriented individual allowed to stay "invisible." The same is true with the other styles. Plain and simply, it's easier to deal with a 9,9-oriented person in a 9,9 way than to resist, evade, or avoid from some other Grid style. This doesn't mean that if you act in a 9,9 way that everyone around you will turn into 9,9-oriented people, but it does mean that people are likely to work together in a more productive manner when you approach them from a 9,9 stance. 9,9 tends to bring out the best in people because 9,9 principles are core values of every human being. Sometimes we just lose sight of them.

9,1 Reactions to 9,9

A high concern for results appeals to the 9,1-oriented subordinate's production orientation. Because the 9,9-oriented boss is open and aboveboard, the subordinate is less likely to feel suspicious. Nor does the subordinate feel exploited because the boss demonstrates a willingness to jump in and help. Generally, a 9,1-oriented subordinate starts out skeptical about the 9,9-oriented approach, seeing it as "weak" because it involves concern for people. Thus, the first point of entry for a 9,9-oriented manager is to develop trust, which is accomplished by engaging the subordinate in a problem-solving discussion. It soon becomes apparent to the subordinate that this boss *knows* what he or she is talking about. At the same time, however, it is not a contest of wills because it is obvious that the boss values the subordinate's thinking and input. Questions and misgivings are responded to openly and forthrightly. The boss doesn't mince words but instead goes right to the heart of the matter. At the beginning of our story it was clear that Ben and Ed didn't see eye to eye on things; perhaps they never will. Nevertheless, there is little doubt that they have established a basis for mutual trust and respect. They can work together in a sound and productive way.

1,9 Reactions to 9,9

The 1,9-oriented subordinate immediately senses the boss's concern for people. Because the subordinate wants to please the boss, he or she is likely to say "yes" to any request made. The boss soon ascertains the need to supplement the subordinate's knowledge base and to establish clear expectations for performance. To the extent possible, the subordinate is encouraged to contribute ideas for how to accomplish a task. Open-ended questions on the part of the boss help to elicit new thinking from the subordinate.

The benefit for a 1,9-oriented subordinate is that he or she is in a better position to act given the rational/dynamic approach that characterizes a 9,9 orientation. The boss strives for excellence and promotes this value to others as well and, while goals and objectives are high, they are still tuned to reality. The boss works with this subordinate to ensure that expectations match what the subordinate is realistically able to do. The goal is to get the subordinate to stretch and grow but not to break.

The boss doesn't criticize this subordinate for the lack of thoroughness but does offer constructive critique and opportunities to expand. A problem for the 9,9-oriented manager is that this subordinate is unlikely to challenge anything said and therefore provides little insight as to the validity of the proposed approach. We talk about people getting pushed into the 1,1 corner but this may be true of 1,9 as well. Somewhere early in life these individuals learned that the way to get what you want, i.e., happy feelings, is to be nice to people. In the real world, that philosophy alone is unlikely to be successful. These people get stepped on and end up resenting those who don't appreciate their kindness. Then they just try harder to be nicer the next time around. A 9,9-oriented manager can help this individual by drawing a connection between this person's behavior and the consequences of that behavior. People want to feel a sense of purpose and the 9,9-oriented boss can help the subordinate to claim this through productive effort. If you never try, you don't know what you're missing, so the 9,9-oriented boss helps the subordinate experience a sense of fulfillment through contribution. Once the subordinate gains an understanding of how productive effort can be meshed with concern for people, he or she is on the way to becoming a more valuable member of the organization.

Paternalistic Reactions to 9,9

A paternalistic subordinate tries to impress the 9,9-oriented manager with his or her knowledge and expertise. "You can depend on me!" The idea is to become the boss's favorite and in this way to be in a position to exert control over the rest of the team. The 9,9-oriented boss is unlikely to accept this power play. The 9,9 need for self-convincing evidence becomes an insulation against the efforts of a paternalist to usurp control or to influence the exercise of authority in his or her own direction. An expectation of openness and candor is established early in the relationship. This has the effect of blocking the paternalist from any exercise of indirect or subtle influence.

The dilemma for a 9,9-oriented person in managing a paternalistic subordinate is that it can be like dealing with a child. This is because the subordinate only gives with an expectation of getting something in return. This subordinate is likely to act in a disapproving manner or even go so far as to give the boss the silent treatment when things are not being done the way he or she expects them to be. The boss's premise is that this subordinate can "graduate" to a higher plane of interaction, moving out of the realm of conditional give-and-take to a position of unconditional and mutual support. It takes two to play the paternalist's game and, when the boss fails to respond, the likelihood is that the subordinate will move toward a problem-solving basis.

1,1 Reactions to 9,9

The 9,9 leadership style has the potential of activating a different backup style in a dominant 1,1-oriented subordinate and stimulating an interest in work activity that might otherwise remain dormant. Efforts to overcome 1,1 apathy are manifest in the way the boss works with knowledge and enthusiasm to discover what might create a spark of interest. Open-ended questions may serve to stimulate thinking. The 9,9 way of relating to people on the basis of mutual trust and respect may get this subordinate to take another look at him- or herself. Through delegation of activities and the use of critique and feedback to monitor progress, the subordinate is likely to gain a sense of accomplishment and an enhanced feeling of self-esteem, which can draw the individual out of 1,1 and back into a previously-held, stronger Grid style. The key point is that 9,9 leadership doesn't let 1,1-oriented people get away with apathy and non-involvement. The 9,9-oriented leader continues to push for contribution and to search for creative ways to get the 1,1-oriented person involved in team activity. For the 1,1-oriented person, it is easier to give in and do what the boss wants than to continue to dodge the invitation to participate.

5,5 Reactions to 9,9

The 5,5-oriented subordinate is responsive to a 9,9-oriented boss because protocol dictates that you act in such a manner with your boss. The subordinate likes the idea of togetherness and therefore is quite receptive to teamwork based on involvement and participation. The boss exerts an effort to steer the subordinate's thinking into problem solving. Once again, this is accomplished through the exercise of inquiry and advocacy, confrontation of differences, feedback and critique, strong initiative, and sound decision making. The 9,9 approach is to convert the subordinate's customary reliance on tradition, precedent, and past practice into a greater readiness to consider innovative and creative solutions. Furthermore, the boss pushes the subordinate to stretch beyond mediocrity, to envision what can be rather than what is. Encouragement from the boss to take more risks based on thorough problem-solving effort can help this subordinate to grow into a stronger, more contributing organization member.

Opportunistic Reactions to 9,9

The opportunistic subordinate is careful in relating to a 9,9-oriented boss. This subordinate can't afford direct or open engagements and at the same time satisfy opportunistic needs. The opportunist is compelled to play the angles on the sidelines but to keep his or her nose clean with respect to the boss. The subordinate seeks to keep opportunistic actions hidden because bringing these to light would be devastating in a performance review. This subordinate is slippery and tries to stay out of the 9,9-oriented boss's way.

Because it is impossible to play it any way but in a straightforward manner with the 9,9-oriented boss, the likelihood is that this person will seek a transfer or change of position. The only other alternative is a change in behavior because the 9,9-oriented leader will continue to confront the opportunist's lack of principled behavior.

9,9 Reactions to 9,9

The greatest personal reward for any 9,9-oriented leader or 9,9-oriented subordinate lies in dealing with another person of the 9,9 ilk. They immediately click; they are on the same wavelength. Not only is discussion geared to solving the problem or capitalizing on an opportunity, but it is conducted on the basis of facts, data, and logical reasoning. Critique of the ongoing process is spontaneous. Efforts on both sides are made to ensure that expectations are realistic and valid. In essence they are consultants to one another as to the soundness of any action under consideration. The boss's approach is one of creating the conditions for subordinate involvement and participation in problem solving with a successful outcome being the most likely result.

The 9,9-oriented boss commands great respect from the subordinate for the logical use of in-depth knowledge in conjunction with solution-seeking behavior. Spontaneity is the word that captures the essence of this relationship. There is no holding back, no tentativeness, only attitudes of mutual trust and respect. This makes participation and involvement a natural process of give-and-take, not of the reciprocation sort but one of unconditional and proactive support. It is easy for the boss or subordinate to discuss doubts and reservations openly and without fear of negative reactions. There is a sense of gratification for both parties from the learning to be gained by critique and feedback of activity. This is a combination likely to be characterized by interdependence and synergistic action.

Recognizing 9,9 Behavior

Figure 9-6 illustrates the words and phrases that characterize 9,9-oriented behavior.

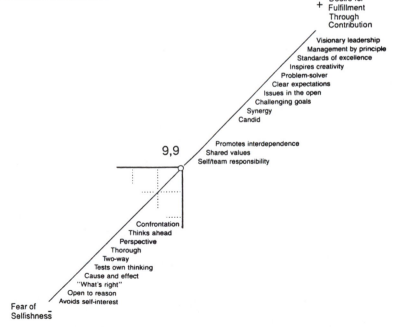

Figure 9-6. Words and phrases that characterize the 9,9 Grid style.

Summary

The 9,9 Grid style offers the greatest benefit in terms of payout for the individual who acts with some consistency in this manner. There is a strong desire to achieve organization results because this generates a sense of fulfillment through contribution. People who are oriented in a 9,9 way know that their presence in the organization has made a difference. They have impacted the company in an excellent manner. They have left their mark and they have helped other people to do the same.

Furthermore, the 9,9 Grid style is the best way of achieving results with and through other people, and that's what management is about. A 9,1-oriented manager is also after results but not in a way that brings out the best people have to offer. As a result a large part of the potential contribution is lost.

Are we describing a fictitious person? Would anyone really do this? Is it altruism with no thought of personal gain? Not really. We all want payoff from our effort, and the 9,9 Grid style is not without tangible rewards to accompany the intrinsic gain derived from a feeling of having made a contribution. Research confirms that managers who conduct themselves in a 9,9 way tend to enjoy the greatest gain as measured by career advancement and financial earnings. Furthermore, when the corporate capacity to compete is strengthened through seeking full cooperation, personal security is greater than when corporate strength is retarded by actions that weaken competitive position. Everyone in the organization stands to benefit.

But, is it possible, and is it practical? We believe it is and we have seen it operate from the top of an organization down to the lowest position. The key to 9,9 success is that operating from this mode, according to sound principles of behavioral science and values that lie at the core of human motivation, engenders a like response. That is, people stop fighting, resisting, dodging, evading, accommodating, and manipulating. They open up in a receptive way; they are drawn to the problem-solving orientation of a 9,9-oriented leader. Although their personal Grid style may not change, the quality of their interaction tends to shift toward a 9,9 way of operating, and this is in the best interest of everyone concerned.

This is the model Ben holds in his mind as the objective to be achieved by his team. The first step is to get them to buy into the effort. It appears they are on their way.

Perhaps the ultimate credibility and utility for this value is that the 9,9 Grid style is characterized by the highest stage of ethical reasoning as demonstrated in its integrity and consideration for basic human principles of justice, honesty, health, etc. This is a boon not only for the organization in terms of reputation and perpetuity but also for all those who work and interact with a 9,9-oriented individual.

Chapter 10

9,9 Principles and Tactics in Action

The 9,9 orientation can be distinguished from other styles by the connection with basic values or principles of human interaction inherent within this approach. We've seen the 9,9 Grid style in action as Ben has operated as a subordinate in Al's team, a colleague to others on the team, and now as the new leader, determined to move the team toward a goal of excellence. Although we have not had as close a look at Harriet, she also displays the qualities of the 9,9 approach in her interaction with Ben and Joe.

This chapter explores the principles that undergird a 9,9 orientation and some of the specific skills that 9,9-oriented managers like Ben and Harriet employ in exercising leadership.

Let's start by taking a closer look at Ben's team. As you will recall, Ben asked his colleagues to do some homework by critiquing efforts currently underway for the purpose of reconvening in a week for a team review of the findings. Here's what happened when they got back together.

Ben's Team Review

The review served several useful purposes. First, some projects were revealed that had not been known by all but needed to be because of ultimate impact on the whole team's operations. Second, by listing each team member's activities, it was then possible to rank order them in terms of priority to the team and to eliminate as many as half from future consideration. Many were found to be redundant—a result of the do-your-own-thing era where everyone protected his or her piece of the action. Finally, the review established a common theme for how this team had been operating, which laid the groundwork for deciding what changes were needed to operate in a sounder manner.

Ben concluded the discussion of specifics by saying, "That provides a good inventory of the obligations facing this team. We've managed to get rid of many that no longer merit our attention as a team. For those we still consider important but that don't require everyone's involvement, I think the best approach is for me to meet with each individual, couple, or trio to determine next steps. Does that make sense?"

Everyone concurred.

Ben continued, "Far more important is what has been revealed about the culture of this team. We've looked at our historical action, taking each of our activities and piecing them together, and as a result a pattern has emerged. We've disclosed many of the dynamics by which we operate. These are our norms and standards, which is just a fancy way of saying 'how we're used to doing things.' Some are effective and support our efforts; some are not. Speaking for myself, I was unaware of many of the deeper aspects, and I presume that a number of you share this feeling of surprise with me.

"There are several key characteristics I see as impediments to our achieving what could be characterized as excellence. Number one is what I might call deadline-controlled team effort. I think I heard you say, and I certainly agree, that we have become passive, waiting for the next deadline to tell us what to do. We also agreed that we don't have to continue to operate that way. We have a measure of control, that is, some free choice over what we decide to do or not do. We can take a more proactive stance than we have in the past. However, as a team we can't do this without a shared value system that tells us what's important. Only with agreement on the values that guide team action can we be versatile in responding to opportunities in a deliberate and thoughtful way, rather than reacting to things as they appear on the horizon. Would you agree with what I've said? Or, would you add or delete anything?"

"I agree with you one hundred percent," exclaimed Ed, crowding out Liz to express his point of view. "I think we all see that as the 'big' issue."

"What else?" asked Ben.

"Well, I agree, too," said Liz. "But I wanted to focus on a second concern I heard expressed. I think it's just as central to our problems. It involves conflict—the avoidance of it, that is. The difficulty as I see it is that we make the unacceptable acceptable. We accommodate individual differences even when they hold us back and act as barriers to progress."

"We keep the peace rather than dare to confront conflict," smiled Ben.

"What do you mean?" inquired Dan.

"Let me explain," Liz continued, "because this was at the center of many concerns we've talked about. Like Ben said, we tolerate, rather than confront, different ways of doing things. I know we are all unique individuals, each with our own resources to contribute to the problem-solving process. The differences I'm talking about are barriers to team action, our inability to mesh effort that stands in the way of getting excellent results. The biggest obstacle is our discomfort with conflict; we'll go to any lengths to avoid it. We go along to get along; we back off in the interest of progress; or we play politics to see if we can work out a satisfactory compromise. In other words, we will do anything to be a congenial group, even though we know it's hurting us as a team."

"And as career-oriented individuals," added Frank.

"Right," said Liz.

"I certainly agree," said Frank. "In a way, we are all somewhat adept at practicing dishonesty in the interest of social grace, harmony, and personal career efforts. I'm not excluding myself, but I'm also not alone. And do you know why we continue to do it? Because it lets us 'do our own thing.' We never have to be accountable to each other. It is pretty insidious when you take a close look at it."

"Yes," said Ben, "and this falls within the scope of management responsibility to fix. It's a problem we own and that lies within our jurisdiction to change. I'd like to say that it happens rarely but I'm afraid that's not true."

A silence came over the team as they reflected on what had been said.

"Well, perhaps this is enough for the moment," said Ben. "Our goal for now is not to be exhaustive, producing a laundry list of our sins, but to try to identify opportunities for increased effectiveness that we can capitalize on as soon as possible. I can resolve the special projects by meeting with each of you, one-on-one. However, these teamwide problems are a different matter. They are, and continue to be, problems because all of us have become 'unwitting co-conspirators' in perpetuating them. The only way to solve these problems is through a shared, explicit commitment to do so. They won't just go away. They'll take interdependent effort to keep from slipping back into old ways of doing things."

Everybody nodded their agreement. Ed asked, "What's the next step?"

Ben replied, "Well, to start with, I'd like to ask each of you to come to terms with what we've discussed today. If we do have the shared commitment to move forward, the next thing we need to know is 'how' to do it. My proposal would be for Dan and me to talk with Harriet Turner at headquarters to explore her experience with solving these kinds of teamwork dilemmas. Then we could report back to you to determine what action to take next."

Dan smiled. "That sounds like an excellent proposal to me."

"I'll be anxious to hear what you learn," said Gil. "Believe it or not, I want us to find a new and better way to work."

"I'm glad to hear that," said Ben. "By the way, Gil, have you and Ed thought any further about going to a Grid?"

"We're already signed up!" exclaimed Gil.

"Well, that's another next step. We'll all be interested in your report," replied Ben. "Anything to add before we close?"

"I think this has been a productive discussion," said Ed. "It's brought some new information to light for me. We've proved to ourselves that we have a few problems. I guess that's self-evident. But no one is standing in the way of our doing things in a more effective manner so I say let's go!"

Everyone clapped to acknowledge their endorsement of what Ed had said. The day's work concluded, people lingered, not seeming to want to leave. With all its rough spots, it had been an invaluable first step for changing the way this team looked at itself.

□ □ □

The proof in any approach to management lies in how it works. The 9,9 Grid style is the only way of working with and through others that brings all parties to a problem-solving level. As you can see in the story, team members may not have changed their basic orientation, at least not yet, but they do begin to respond to Ben's open and confronting leadership style with new ideas and new initiatives. As a result, a level of 9,9 team action has been established even though all members of the team do not have a 9,9 orientation. This is important for a leader to remember because too often rationalizations are made to put off doing things in an effective manner "until we can get everyone on board." It is always time for 9,9.

Interdependence or Independence: Are They Mutually Exclusive?

Interdependence is key to 9,9 team interaction. While its primary purpose is to strengthen the outcomes in terms of results achieved, it is also a condition that proves to be fulfilling in and of itself. Interdependence, however, is not bought at the expense of stifling individual initiative—just the opposite. Effective teamwork makes possible the achievement of synergistic results where the results are greater than the sum of all individual resources initially present. But what about individual initiative, creativity and innovation, the entrepreneurial spirit? Aren't these qualities of independence inconsistent with the very aims we seek to achieve through a team approach? Must we sacrifice one for the other? Are they mutually exclusive? Actually, they are congruent. When individual initiative is meshed with interdependent action, the potential exists for achieving even greater results.

Earlier we introduced resources, relationships, and results—R_1, R_2, and R_3. The corporate concern is with what you do with the resources you start out with in order to achieve the results you are ultimately after. Given available individual resources, in other words, what happens in the interactive sphere of R_2 is all important. That's what determines outcomes.

For example, a 9,1-oriented manager suppresses subordinates into compliance and shuts out input; this translates to the loss of potential resources. A 1,9-oriented manager excludes him- or herself from the feedback loop, preferring instead to go along with whatever others want to do, whether or not that is the soundest approach. The paternalist (9+9) already has the solution and it is simply a matter of selling it to others—for their own good. A 5,5-oriented boss is looking for something everyone can accept in a live-and-let-live way. Such a manager is willing to compromise and accommodate, shift values, avoid thorough inquiry and critique, all in the name of finding a decision that lets everybody have what they want in a "do your own thing" way. Then we all "win"—at least a little bit. The 1,1-oriented boss is noncommittal and goes whichever way the wind blows. An opportunist tries to orchestrate events in a manner that will lead to him or her ending up on top.

Only in the 9,9 approach is the effort put forth to find the best solution, not just to maximize the status quo, but to examine all possibilities, to see barriers to achievement, not as constraints and limitations, but as challenges to be overcome. A 9,9 orientation values interdependence and individual initiative alike, provided they go hand in hand, with each building upon the strength of the other, rather than dividing and compartmentalizing in the name of false individuality, individuality that has become a means for avoiding the confrontation of conflict and the development of shared values as to the best manner in which to operate.

A closer look at this issue of teamwork vs. individuality is important because the argument is often raised that you can't have one if you have the other. However, it's a false premise that teamwork must necessarily diminish individuality, although this is certainly true of a paternalistically-led team and a 5,5-oriented team. But in the proper sense of the word, what teamwork does is to enable a person to make the best contribution of resources through effective relationships. An individual can thwart or enhance the dynamics occurring in R_2. Individuality in disregard of teamwork can be a thrilling but dangerous business. Another name for it might be reckless entrepreneurialism. In the hands of those few who are capable, it has led to great achievements; but in the hands of those who are less adept, it has resulted in many more failures.

Entrepreneurialism in the absence of sound teamwork is perilous because people who are single-minded often start out on a commercial venture with a dedicated blindness that, while good in itself, is too often not reinforced by critically needed business acumen outside the particular line of competence with which the entrepreneur is concerned. As a result, many entrepreneurs meet with failure, not because their ideas were poor or off base, but rather because the supporting knowledge essential for fostering and bringing key ideas to constructive ends was not sought out for application.

Teamwork can supply what is needed to avoid such deficiency and is the highly desirable, if not indispensable, factor that can increase the likelihood of success by supplying the concepts and skills not in an entrepreneur's immediate possession.

Given the whole conceptual base of 9,9 Grid theory, contribution by individuals to greater team achievement becomes a reality: getting greatest results through maximizing the effectiveness of individual people. This contribution is related to the R_2 activity where technical resources often get flushed. Such a loss has nothing to do with the presence or absence of the technical resources themselves but rather with the ineffective use of those resources, that is, the inability of team members to operate in an effective way in the domain of R_2.

When individuals take the step of meshing independent action with interdependent teamwork, their contribution toward moving the team forward merits individual reward and acknowledgment. Far too often we reward team effort because that's what we're after; we want people to move from a competitive stance to a collaborative one. If the team does well we credit the achievement to effective collaboration—only. That's okay except that it overlooks the relative contributions of members. Think about it this way. How motivated would you be, as a person in a seven-member team, if you and one or two other members consistently carried the weight of responsibility for seeing that things got done on time with high quality but then you gained no more in terms of reward than the least contributing member? This is a common practice in many organizations because bosses don't like to evaluate individual effort. They're reluctant to tackle this problem unless someone can provide a mechanical "numbers" system by which to make the assessment. Otherwise, it puts their judgment on the line. Most of all, it creates the likelihood of conflict. This is probably the key reason why individual initiative is often incongruent with good teamwork. In actuality, the problem lies in weak leadership.

Remember what Liz said about the team. The way they had operated in the past had tolerated individual team member behavior and actions that were nonproductive because no one wanted to confront the problem. It was seen as easier to live with this kind of mediocre teamwork, letting everyone do his or her own thing, than to challenge it and replace it with a sounder team culture. The idea is not to forfeit individual creativity but to create a system of shared values whereby talent can be meshed.

Team members should celebrate effort aimed at propelling the team forward to accomplish its goals. Different people have different resources to contribute to different tasks; team members with greater experience have a responsibility—to the team—to help develop those with less experience and to build their strength for greater future contribution. To deny individual contribution is to squelch motivation and to create mediocrity. A meaningful illustration of this is conformity pressures that exist in any organized setting. These subtle forces serve not only to bring underachievers up to par, but also to drag the overachievers down. When we accept the status quo as the best we can achieve, we may be accepting unnecessary limitations. Only when we open ourselves up to new and challenging possibilities, saying, "What if we could . . . ?" and then really examine what it might take to get there, are we then in a position to maximize interdependent effort aimed at synergistic outcomes. That is the true meaning of excellent teamwork.

Principles of Effective Human Interaction

9,9 management has its roots in sound principles of behavior that underlie effective human interaction. When applied on a consistent basis in working with others, these principles can lead to the development of relationships based on mutual trust and respect. The evidence of their soundness can be seen in enhanced productivity, creativity, satisfaction, and health.

9,9 versatility is the capacity to use these principles on a day-to-day basis. It is important to distinguish between a 9,9 principles-based *strategy* and the *tactics* used in applying these principles. Tactics dictate how a principle is applied across a variety of different situations. Most of us would agree that 9,9 represents the best way to go, but sometimes we fall back to another Grid style in order to accomplish our objectives. Why?

We have already said that 9,9 principles underpin effective behavior. They are constant just like the laws of physics; they apply in all situations. Unfortunately, we as managers sometimes lack the essential skills to apply them. That's okay because we can learn from critique how to do it better the next time around. But we must be aware of what we are doing. We have to realize when we shift to a backup style so that we can shift back to a 9,9 orientation as soon as the opportunity permits.

Let's examine a versatile leader. How does this individual view conflict? A versatile leader recognizes that the soundest way to resolve conflict is to confront differences so that their causes can be identified and eliminated. There are two reasons why this is so. One is that disagreements are relieved by insight, and the other is that the tensions are relieved. Eliminating tensions arising from conflict means that energy remains available for dealing with production problems. Resolving tensions is healthier than living with them.

Does this mean, then, that a versatile manager rigidly applies a principle without regard for the particulars of the situation to which it is applied? Not at all. A versatile leader is concerned with applying a sound principle in a way that is appropriate to the particular situation. In dealing with a new employee, for example, discrepancies in opinion that might lead to conflict are dealt with differently from conflict that arises with an employee of longer standing. With the newly hired subordinate, this leader might first examine the events leading to their disagreement. In this way causes of conflict can be identified that both boss and subordinate might otherwise fail to recognize. In contrast, the long-term employee understands quite well the activity being undertaken, and it would be wasteful to engage in the same procedure as that taken with a new person. In the latter case, it is possible to identify key differences more quickly and to explore the underlying causes. Confrontation is relied on in both situations as the basis for finding a meeting of minds. The principle remains constant, but the application varies with the circumstances.

The principles that form a foundation for 9,9 management are as follows:

☐ *Fulfillment through contribution is the motivation that gives character to human activity and supports productivity, creativity, satisfaction, and health.* When people are committed to the success of the organization, they are motivated to take the actions essential for making it happen. Fulfillment through contribution means gaining personal satisfaction by taking action that is useful, making a

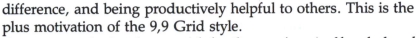

difference, and being productively helpful to others. This is the plus motivation of the 9,9 Grid style.

☐ *Open communication is essential for the exercise of self and shared responsibility.* When communication is free and open, organization members have access to the information that is pertinent to their interests and responsibilities. Organization members can make maximum contributions only when the information requisite for sound thinking is available to them.

☐ *Conflicts are solved by confrontation, with understanding and agreement as the bases of cooperative effort.* Differences are bound to arise when people share their ideas. This is well and good because it enables us to test the soundness of our thinking against the best thinking of others. Choices must be narrowed and a single selection made. However, when poorly handled, intense conflict leads to the erosion of mutual trust and respect, distorted communication, and diminished feelings of personal efficacy.

Confrontation means taking a problem-solving approach to these inevitable human differences and identifying the underlying facts, logic, or emotions (prejudices, preconceptions, or antagonisms) that account for them. When conflicts are resolved through confronting and understanding their causes, people feel responsible for finding sound solutions.

Decisions that result in understanding and agreement are possible when members participate openly in resolving conflict. This in turn generates conviction and commitment to outcomes and stimulates the effort essential for realizing them.

☐ *Being responsible for one's own actions represents the highest level of maturity and is only possible through widespread delegation of power and authority.* The ability to make a maximum contribution depends on one voluntarily and spontaneously exercising initiative. This is possible only when self-responsible action flows down through the organization. Then, opportunities to be more productive and creative can be acted on by those in direct contact with the situations needing resolution.

☐ *Shared participation in problem solving and decision making stimulates active involvement in productive and creative thinking.* Viewed from one perspective, participation is a human right, something to be honored as a condition of freedom, autonomy, and self-responsibility. It involves full involvement and commitment of one's resources. Participants feel they have a stake in the outcome of a decision or an action, leading to the notion that people support what they help create. When team-wide understanding and agreement have been reached, a consensus is present, which is supported without reservation. Such shared participation stimulates the kind of creative thinking that produces optimal solutions.

☐ *Management is by objectives.* Productivity and creativity are enhanced when individuals engage in achieving goals to which they feel committed. Management-by-objectives is the operational way of bringing a goals orientation into widespread use. Managers identify and agree on goals and set in motion concrete activities for achieving them. When commitment is attached to a goal, then one is drawn to it, wants to achieve it, studies and evaluates how this can be accomplished, and then puts forth the necessary effort to attain it. When management-by-objectives through goal setting is done in a sound manner, the goals of individuals and the goals of the organization are integrated and congruent.

☐ *Merit is the basis of reward.* When rewarding individual contribution, two criteria are paramount: (1) Does the contribution further the organization's prospects of success? (2) Does the contribution lead to the individual becoming a stronger leader? When these conditions prevail, organization members experience the system of promotion and pay as fair and equitable. This is the meaning of reward based on merit. Only when reward acknowledges personal contribution in this way is the readiness to make contributions reinforced.

☐ *Norms and standards support personal and organization excellence.* Much of our behavior is regulated by norms and standards to which each of us conforms. When norms and standards are set at high levels, this stimulates the pursuit of excellence and contributes to the satisfaction people derive from work. Alternatively, mediocre norms and standards lead to just that—mediocrity.

☐ *Learning from work experience is through feedback and critique.* Feedback and critique is a process of stepping away from or interrupting an activity to study and assess what is going on, to see options for improvement, and to anticipate and avoid activities with adverse consequences. Critique is a more or less "natural" way of reflecting on what is happening or what has happened. When organization members have widespread understanding of and skill in using critique, it becomes possible to accelerate the rate at which they learn and in this way to progress.

An organization can maximize its members' contributions by applying these principles daily, which in turn helps to ensure relationships among members are based on mutual trust and respect. This is using principles of 9,9 to ensure good R_2—maximizing R_1 resources that lie in *people* in order to get the best R_3 possible. Then, and only then, does it become possible to make full use of other organization resources: financial, technical, natural, etc.

Tactics of 9,9 Teamwork

Effective teamwork is a significant aspect of an individual's leadership behavior. The 9,9 orientation embraces a concern for integrating the needs and views of people into the requirement to get work done. When problem solving and decision making are conducted in a 9,9 way, they are characterized by thorough inquiry and strong advocacy on the part of everyone involved.

Guidelines for Participation

As stated in the last chapter, 9,9 decision making *does not* mean getting everyone together before a decision can be made. Some people get the mistaken notion that 9,9 means sitting in meetings day-in and day-out. If that were the case, when would people ever get their work done? Obviously, 9,9 leadership means people meet when they need to meet. There are several criteria that determine when others are to be included in the decision-making process. Let's go back and look at Al's team for the different possibilities.

Some "team" problems involve Al making a decision by himself. Others involve Ben or Ed or Liz working by themselves. In other words, one-alone (1/0) decisions are those involving Al working alone or, alternatively, those activities that Al has delegated to one of his subordinates. They are one-alone because a single team member has the responsibility and the necessary resources to solve the problem. R_2 can contribute nothing further—to bring in anyone else would be a waste of time. Furthermore, these are situations with little or no impact on other team members. It's in the interest of teamwork to solve the problem by yourself and avoid duplication of effort.

A special case of solo initiative occurs whenever one team member substitutes him- or herself on behalf of another team member. An example of this kind of supportive teamwork between Dan and Liz clarifies what we mean:

> "Dan, I know you are planning to visit Harriet Turner next week to get her to review and sign some paperwork. I need to talk to her about some matters concerning my marketing group. If you want me to get that signature for you, it might save you a trip. What do you think?"
>
> "That would be great," replied Dan. "I've got my hands full right now. Why don't I drop the papers by your office today and explain what's involved."

Another example of substitutional teamwork occurs when Liz covers for Dan while he is away on a business trip:

> "Dan is out of the office this week at a development program, but he left me with instructions on this matter. How can I help you?"

This kind of team action calls for a high degree of trust because, while the initiative has shifted to a substitute, ultimate responsibility for the outcome remains with the original party. In other words, Liz may take an action in Dan's behalf, but he is still accountable for the outcome.

A second kind of decision making occurs on a one-to-one (1/1) basis. These are problems that involve two team members, for example, Ed and Al, Ben and Gil, or Frank and Liz. In other words the resources of two people are required, but it would be superfluous to involve others in the process. These may be delegated activities that involve a boss/subordinate pair. However, one-to-one activities also occur between any two colleagues.

A variation on this is one-to-one-to-one (1/1/1) where the first member takes a certain action that makes it possible for the second member to take an action, and so on until everyone has contributed in sequence to the end result. Each team member plays a key role in the outcome. For example, smooth coordination from a salesperson who writes up the initial order to those who receive and fill it, to those who prepare the invoice, and to those who package and ship the product constitutes a complex sequence of interdependent operations. Done well, they satisfy the customer and build repeat business. Though there may be no face-to-face interaction between those who work together in this effort, what they do links them together as a team. This is called sequential teamwork.

One-to-some (1/some) involves more than two people but not the whole team. These decisions fall somewhere between one-to-one and one-to-all. It's a situation where Ben, Ed, Al, and Gil need to be involved but not Liz, Frank, and Dan. Such interactions represent interdependent action but not by all team members.

One-to-all (1/all) decisions involve those problems that can only be solved by the whole team working together. That means Al, Ben, Dan, Gil, Liz, Ed, and Frank all have a part in the action. This is simultaneous teamwork. A 9,9-oriented leader relies on one-to-all decision making when:

1. No one has all the information to formulate the best answer, but together they have the potential of reaching it.
2. Coordination is essential for successful task achievement; therefore, each member's committed participation is significant to the outcome.
3. All must understand what is going on so that each can fit the effort required into other ongoing activities.

Guidelines that clarify when to use 1/0, 1/1, or 1/all are provided in Table 10-1. These guidelines answer the question, "Under what conditions are each of these arrangements for participation most likely to be effective?" Disregard Grid style because the issue at this point is only, "Who participates?" not the quality of the relationship. The left column of Table 10-1 identifies criteria that help a manager decide which approach provides the soundest basis of action.

Table 10-1
Decision-Making Criteria:
When Should Action Be Based on 1/0, 1/1, or 1/All?

Criteria	Approach		
	1/0	1/1	1/All
1. Who owns the problem?	Only one person	Two people	All of us
2. Do I have time to involve others?	No time to involve others	Some time but not much	Enough time to involve potentially valuable resources
3. Do I have the competency to make the decision alone?	Yes, I'm fully competent	My competence is only marginal	My competence is insufficient; I need more resources
4. Is synergy possible?	No synergistic possibilities	Synergy is probable	Synergy is highly probable
5. What is impact on rest of team?	Low	Low to moderate	Moderate to high
6. Do I need involvement and commitment of others?	No	Helpful and possibly essential	Necessary and essential
7. Is there development potential for others?	No	Possible	Yes

You may act without consulting others when the criteria for good decision making and problem solving match conditions in the 1/0 column. When conditions match entries in the 1/1 column, it is best to consult one other team member, and when the circumstances match conditions in the right column, 1/some or 1/all actions should be taken.

The first four criteria of Table 10-1 relate to maximizing decision-making quality by effectively using human resources.

1. *Who owns the problem?* If you can look at the problem and say, "That belongs to me and I can solve it by myself," then 1/0 action based on self-initiative is in order. However, if you lack

the full capacity for solving the problem or if it overlaps with another person's responsibility, then it represents a 1/1 situation. If the problem belongs to the whole team in that everyone owns some piece of it, then 1/all is the best strategy.

A second question for you as a boss is, "Can I delegate?" This serves a two-fold purpose of freeing up your time for more important activity and providing a development opportunity to subordinates. Sometimes bosses are reluctant to "let go" of activity that could prove to be a learning experience for others. Alternatively, in the case of the 1,1-oriented boss, responsibility is passed down to get rid of it. Whether or not to delegate depends on how the other variables for involvement weigh in. For example, if the situation offers the potential for teamwide synergy, it is best to handle it 1/all rather than 1/1.

A general rule can be stated. Other things equal, delegation is relied on when (1) subordinates can deal with a given problem as well as or better than the boss; (2) the subordinate's managerial effectiveness is enhanced; (3) delegation, not abdication, is the boss's motivation; (4) the boss has more time to focus on more important issues; and (5) conditions are such that the subordinate has a reasonable prospect of successfully completing the delegated task.

2. *Do I have time to involve others?* In an emergency situation, you may need to take one-alone action simply because there is no time to consult with others. Split-second decisions of this nature, however, are the exception rather than the rule. Usually time exists to pool available resources to get an accurate reading on the *real* problem and to determine the soundest solution. When you do have time to call in other resources and to do so would prove advantageous, a 1/1 or 1/some decision is best. If time exists to convene the entire team *and* their involvement is likely to produce a better decision, then 1/all is the sound approach.

3. *Do I have the competency to make the decision?* If you have the depth and experience to exercise sound judgment on a problem and no benefit is served by drawing in other people, the best approach is 1/0. If your experience is limited and a better decision can be made by using the expertise of another, the

situation is 1/1. If sound judgment is contingent upon the combined resources of all team members, the problem should be resolved in a 1/all way.

Other factors involved in answering this question include whether or not information is required from levels above, below, or from other departments in the organization. This may create or obviate the need for others' involvement in the decision-making process.

4. *Is synergy possible?* Synergy means that everyone working together produces a sounder outcome than what any one, two, or several members might have developed working alone. Sometimes 1/all teamwork is the best way to go, if time is available, because you can see the possibility of achieving synergy. Think about it this way: If you are the leader of a team, this provides the opportunity for you to hear the opinions and ideas of subordinates as they wrestle through a problem. In this way you gain a wealth of understanding and insight into the strengths and weaknesses of different approaches for dealing with a particular matter. Doubts and reservations and underlying rationale for different positions are fully developed with this kind of open leadership. However, if no synergy can be expected and no other need is served, it is best to take a 1/0 action; if only one other person's involvement can lead to a synergistic outcome, then 1/1 action is appropriate.

The next item relates to the readiness of team members to implement a decision once it has been made.

5. *What is the impact on rest of team?* If the action has implications for you alone, and you can implement the solution without the assistance of others, then it may be handled in a 1/0 way. On the other hand, if it has relevance to another team member or perhaps it involves one of your subordinates in its implementation, you would approach it in a 1/1 manner. Sometimes an action has far-reaching operational significance, such as setting up a matrix structure or shifting reporting relationships within an organization, and in these cases the entire membership of a team should be involved to understand all the issues.

Other factors to consider are whether it involves changing how the team operates, i.e., shifting team norms. This requires 1/all involvement. Alternatively, an action may have critique potential for one member only, for two or several, or for all. As a rule, the more likely an action is to affect team purpose, direction, character, or procedures, the more desirable the participation and involvement of all members.

6. *Do I need involvement and commitment of others?* Gaining an understanding of the problem and the decision-making process surrounding its resolution may be critical to successful implementation. Only when people understand the rationale for a decision are human resources fully being used. If you alone are responsible for carrying out the solution, there may be no need to get the commitment of others. However, if you are asking a colleague or subordinate to assist you in this action, their involvement in this process is necessary. Furthermore, when simultaneous teamwork is called for in resolving the matter, 1/all action is essential for success to ensure full understanding of the task.

   As a general rule, those whose future actions are affected by a decision need to be able to think through an issue and discuss its implications so that it is thoroughly understood and that they are committed to it. The larger the number of team members who have personal stakes in an action, the greater the need for them to discuss the decision.

The final criterion is concerned with using decision-making situations to develop and enhance the skills of team members.

7. *Is there development potential for others?* Sometimes it is useful to involve team members even though their contribution is small due to lack of experience. Their involvement, however, aids them to gain knowledge and to develop the judgment needed for dealing with such problems in the future. If the situation has no development potential, it should be dealt with 1/0; if it has management development implications for only one other, it should be dealt with 1/1; if it has management development

implications for all team members, it constitutes 1/all team action.

In the first item, "Who owns the problem?" we raised the question of delegation. Delegation represents the possibility of development for others on the team. This constitutes 1/1, 1/some, or 1/all interaction.

These seven criteria can help managers determine when to involve team members in giving input or helping to make decisions. The idea is that we are living in an age of input; it has become vital for bosses to solicit the best thinking available from those who carry out the actual work. This does not mean one-to-all consensus. The boss still has responsibility for decisions. However, to get *good* decisions, it is important to take full advantage of all resources available. Society is on the move; the rapidly advancing technology and accelerating change occurring in organizations today requires interdependent action.

Therefore, participation does not have to mean consensus but it does mean involving others in thinking through an issue, offering suggestions and counterproposals, expressing doubts and reservations, and working to gain shared commitment. All of these are helpful, useful, and essential to good management. These are the benefits to be derived from engaging the resources of those who can contribute in sharing and thinking through problem definition and solution.

Conflict Solving

In the story Liz made it clear that conflict was an area in which they lacked the necessary skills (R_1) to get better results (R_3) because they didn't know how to resolve conflicts that emerged in team interaction (R_2). Rather, they avoided conflict, skirted it, circumvented it, accommodated each other rather than take the risk of confronting ineffective behavior.

If 9,9 is the most effective way to manage, why don't most of us do it? Usually the answer is that we just lack the skills; we don't know how. Sometimes we see people who display many characteristics of 9,9 management but when confronted with conflict, they revert to a 9,1 backup or a 5,5 backup. A 9,9-oriented person may fall back on another style of management if the skills for dealing with a situation have not yet been acquired, but the person can still be aware that it's *not* 9,9 behavior. Call a spade a spade; then critique the situation, explore options, and discover a better way to do it. If you don't have the skills, make the effort to get them so that the next time a similar situation comes around you are in a position to deal with it in a more effective manner.

Conflict is inevitable in any team, no matter how good the resources. In fact, in a well functioning team, conflict has free expression and is welcomed as an opportunity to expand perspective. We can have excellent communication skills, shared values on how to accomplish our objectives, a high level of team spirit and cohesion, and strong commitment to working with and through people in a productive way; nevertheless we are bound to disagree on some points. That's because we have strong convictions if we truly believe in what we are doing; we are exercising strenuous inquiry and advocacy to make sure we have the best answer and that we are headed in the right direction. If we are a 9,9-oriented team, we relish conflict—not because we enjoy a good fight, but because it offers stimulation of creative thinking; it tests the strength of our thinking and keeps us from falling into complacency and mediocrity; it heightens our commitment to move forward.

There are several skills a 9,9-oriented manager uses in dealing with conflict in an open and confronting manner. These are examined more closely as they may occur in one-to-one or one-to-all situations with specific suggestions for how to resolve conflict in a constructive manner.

Resolving One-to-One Conflict

If you are a 9,9-oriented person and you find yourself in conflict with a colleague or subordinate, here are a number of concrete actions you can take to confront and relieve the differences between you:

☐ Tell the subordinate or colleague the reasons for your thinking, the rationale underlying your decision or action, in a way that does not cause the other party to feel personally attacked or belittled. Remember, it's "What's right," not "Who's right."

☐ Take nothing for granted while listening to the other person's ideas and feelings. Don't draw assumptions and don't mind-read—ask for clarification rather than leave a statement uncertain.

☐ When you answer questions, be forthright to avoid creating suspicion about your position. Don't withhold relevant information to avoid what you perceive might create an uncomfortable situation. Keeping facts undercover in the interest of harmony is more likely to create greater problems at a later time.

☐ Challenge the other person's thinking regarding different courses of action, but only after you have an understanding of the other person's basic values, needs, and assumptions. In other words, know where the other person is "coming from" and why he or she thinks that way.

☐ Probe for reasons, motives, and causes that give the other person a clear and possibly different perspective on an issue.

☐ Help the other person explore the operational consequences of his or her preferred solution.

☐ Get help from the other person to explore the consequences of your preferred solution. You may have overlooked something. Stay with the discussion in a persistent way to get agreement and only terminate it unilaterally (as a boss) when no avenue of resolution can be found.

☐ Make sure that the process of deliberation regarding the outcome is open and not predetermined. This allows the other person to know he or she can have an influence on the outcome. If the other person suspects you are simply acting in a condescending manner and that you have no intention of altering your point of view, the discussion is unlikely to be productive and only serves to heighten tensions.

☐ Constantly search for new definitions of the problem that make its sound solution self-evident. By meshing your best effort and thinking with that of another, together you may achieve synergy!

Resolving One-to-All Conflict

Sometimes the conflict is teamwide. This occurs when each person has a solution that no one else is prepared to accept. The situation becomes even more intense when one person feels that it constitutes personal defeat if another person's solution is accepted. This is a win/lose situation in which people are asked to choose sides. When such tension exists between team members, it is often assumed that the best that can be hoped for is compromise, and the worst is impasse. However, if conflict can be confronted in an open manner by the team, resolution becomes a possibility with advantages accruing from finding better solutions as well as retaining and strengthening the involvement of individual members.

Usually this only occurs when the boss brings it about. For example, Ben might start out by posing the dilemma: "Each of us has a different view of the solution. Probably none of us is completely objective. However, there is a sound solution to this problem; it's simply a matter of finding it. Our job is to step back and try to understand why we are locked in. Ed, how do you see the problem and how does this differ from what you've heard me and others say?"

Starting with Ed and continuing until all have aired their views and have demonstrated that they understand the different positions held is the first step toward cutting through subjective feelings and creating a greater readiness on the part of each team member to consider the problem in an objective way. Sometimes the blockage is caused by antagonisms that exist between one or more people. The "problem" becomes controversial, not because members are at a loss to deal with it, but because they need the controversy to feed their emotional antagonisms. It may have to do with something else entirely; the tensions may be residual resentments that are blocking current team action. When this is the case, the resolution is to get those who say "black" and the others who say "white" to recognize the antagonistic factor in their relationship; to examine openly what they are doing to foster it; and to bring it to an end.

Even when not directly involved in the controversy, Ben, as the boss, joins with the members of the team to help antagonistic elements work through their differences, challenging those in disagreement to explain their underlying rationale. Each person's reactions indicate whether the situation has been understood in the same way—or not. If not, Ben keeps asking questions that allow team members to confront differences and to present facts and counterarguments to test the level of objectivity. Once people come to understand their own values and underlying assumptions, Ben is in a position to challenge their thinking and logic regarding the different courses of action available; he can probe for reasons, motives, and causes to provide a clear and possibly different perspective.

Conflict can erupt among team members, not because of subjective attitudes or antagonisms, but because of a lack of team goals to which all members are committed. Under these circumstances each member pursues his or her distinctive version of the team goal as well as personal goals, and these often come into conflict. Once again, this is the "do-your-own-thing" dynamic and people are bound to collide. Now the solution is to get members committed to teamwide goals and to tailor their individual goals to be aligned to team goals in such a way that collaborative effort replaces disruptive competition.

A more structured approach to narrowing the areas of disagreement is by using the 4,3,2,1 method. In the event of perceived impasse, it often serves to move a team forward. This approach involves asking each participant to write out a position statement. These positions are exchanged and a four-point system is used to examine each of them. Any one of the following may apply:

4—"I agree with the statement as written."
3—"I agree with this statement as rewritten in the following way."
2—"I wish to ask the following questions for clarification of the meaning of this part of the statement."
1—"I disagree with this part of the statement for the following reasons."

The parties then exchange their findings. This activity is completed when as many of the 1's, 2's, and 3's as possible have been converted into 4's, reflecting mutual agreement.

When team members are working effectively together, it is often unnecessary to engage in more formal steps of conflict resolution. However, close examination of how people solve conflicts when they get sound results suggests that the approach approximates the 4,3,2,1 method. They break the overall problem into parts and then discuss how much agreement and disagreement is present for each component. These kinds of considerations make it possible to review complex issues and think in areas where disagreement persists, to supplement one another's factual information, to test and revise the logic, and to gain an understanding of personal feelings. Members are often heard to say, "Well, look, I can agree with that proposal if we'll reword it slightly," or, "I need more information about that aspect," or, "I disagree with the third part because of the following . . . The way I see it is . . ." All of these represent informal applications of the 4,3,2,1 model.

Though managers may realize that open confrontation is the most direct and valid approach to team and one-to-one conflict, they often avoid initiating such a discussion. There are several reasons, with the most important being the fear that the discussion may get out of hand; that conflict, openly acknowledged, might escalate out of control. Another is the worry that the boss who initiates such a discussion may look weak, or actually lose control and be unable to resolve differences in a quieter, more sophisticated, "private" way. The idea is it is better for the manager to mastermind the solution and base it on the premise that, "The matter has already been decided." Alternatively, there is persuasion where a manager "sells" an idea to those who must implement it.

A frequent reason for avoiding conflict is the belief that open confrontation of issues takes too much time. Certainly, while an individual is still learning to apply techniques of conflict resolution, it may take longer because the various facts, views, and alternatives are all being considered. However, because such a discussion involves "causes" rather than mere "symptoms," real solutions are identified to solve problems once and for all. And, with practice, sound solutions can be found faster because people work interdependently in their problem-solving efforts.

While all of the above are "real," they are not valid reasons for avoiding confrontation as a means of conflict resolution. Through the exercise of sound leadership, the discussion can be channeled and need not get out of hand. Once tensions are identified, the pressures and strains on those who feel them can be relieved. Bosses like Ben and Harriet who create such open discussion appear strong, not weak, because they show confidence and skill in using the resources of others in a problem-solving direction. Finally, by open discussion, rather than masterminding a solution, teamwide commitment is maintained and attention can be focused on consultation, exchange of viewpoints, and consensual resolution of differences.

Critique: The Hallmark of 9,9 Leadership

Human values of candor, conflict confrontation, and an experimental attitude make it possible for a 9,9-oriented team to constantly learn how to improve its effectiveness. Such values open up the realistic possibility of using feedback, which is the critical factor in permitting team members to learn from critique. Critique denotes a variety of useful ways to study and solve operational problems members face either singly or collectively as they seek to carry out their assignments. Ben's "review" was a critique of team action as it stood at the present time.

Participants in an experience frequently know that performance is below par and can often describe what happened, at least in mechanical terms. Liz might say, "We started at 10:00 a.m. We should have finished by 12:00 noon but we ran an hour late and concluded at 1:00." Or, Dan might report, "I needed to talk to Frank but he was unavailable so I tried to get the information from Liz but she didn't know. So I was operating in the dark. By the time I got to Frank, the project was well underway. Then I saw my mistake." Describing it is a mental reconstruction of the event, involving awareness of the way things occurred as they were happening. That is important, but it is only half the picture.

As a method of learning, critique usually occurs when two or more people exchange their own descriptions of an event both have directly experienced. If Dan, Liz, Frank, Ed, Ben and Gil had come together and answered the question, "Why is it that when the information gets to the last person, it's useless?" they would have been using critique to improve their situation. People also learn from critique when two or more people describe the actions of a third person and each pictures the meaning and intent of those actions as understood by each. By describing and discussing these similarities and differences with the third person, potential misunderstandings, errors of perception, or other unanticipated consequences of personal actions can be corrected.

When and How Critique Occurs

Critique can be used at the beginning of an activity, as it is taking place, or when it is over.

Before an Activity. Contradictory as it may seem, critique is an excellent approach to learning about problems even before the activity has occurred. Introduced before the beginning of an activity, critique helps team members think about the activity in which they are about to engage. Determining what each participant knows, what each expects to happen and how, and what each wants to see done, makes better use of human resources. In this way it is frequently possible to anticipate problems and thus to avoid them.

Concurrent Critique. Critique can also occur, spontaneously or according to plan, at any time during the activity. Feedback from one team member to another during a team meeting increases the likelihood of understanding between them and strengthens each team member's efforts. The likelihood is increased that both parties will examine their behavior and recognize how bad habits can block problem-solving effectiveness.

Postmortem Critique. When critique is introduced at the end of an activity, it permits participants to review and reconstruct the entire experience and to ascertain why the results were less than they could have accomplished. It enables them to trace interpersonal influences, to identify and to evaluate critical choice points, and to verify recurring patterns. Such insights are significant for deciding what is and what is not the best way to carry out a comparable activity in the future.

If a post critique is delayed too long after an activity is completed, recollections of what happened may be fragmentary. The possibility of making real use of the lessons learned is remote, i.e., changes needed, even though identified, are less likely to be put into action. Maximum benefit is possible when critique follows immediately on completion of the activity.

Many organizations lose much of the real benefit of postmortem critique because leaders rush headlong into the next activity, glad to be through with the last one. This is how Al's team operated. The justification for operating in this manner is, "Let's not look backward, That's history. You can't do anything about it. Let's look to the future and get on with the next project." This attitude rejects the notion that learning from experience is even a possibility.

The Role of Feedback in Critique

Sometimes critique is relied upon to discover what occurred to prevent it from occurring again, but the facts and data that have to be marshalled for the study have no human content. They are facts based upon the breakdown of machinery or equipment or a power failure, or any number of mechanical things; but people are not a significant component in the performance.

The primary use of critique from the standpoint of a 9,9 orientation occurs when the human factor is the critical ingredient; equipment and physical factors reflect human decisions rather than problems independent of them. This is critique to strengthen the R_1 resources of a team. When these conditions prevail, the primary means of data gathering relies upon the direct experience of the participants themselves. This means that the critique is likely to be successful only when those who are participating can feed back their observations, experiences, and feelings to one another in an open, problem-solving way.

Feedback that is motivated by or is seen as unconstructive criticism promotes defensiveness. In turn, that can generate counterattack, with those who started out to be helpful turning instead to recrimination, antipathy, etc. Thus, it is essential for those who are involved in a critique to be committed to carrying it out in a constructive way.

There are certain mechanical "rules" that can maximize the benefits from critique:

☐ *Feedback is received most appreciatively when it is descriptive, nonevaluative, and nonjudgmental.* Nonevaluative feedback is descriptive. It pictures, in an accurate and reconstructible way, what happened in the situation and what consequences occurred as a result of what did happen. This feedback is most valuable and is less likely to generate defensiveness and counterattack, and less likely to hurt, and/or cause subjective feelings of rejection. It is also less

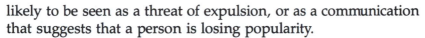

likely to be seen as a threat of expulsion, or as a communication that suggests that a person is losing popularity.

☐ *The closer the feedback to the event it describes, the better it is.* When an event and the critique of it occur in close connection with one another, it is easier for the person whose behavior is being described to reconstruct the actual event and the thoughts, feelings, and emotions surrounding it. This greater capacity for reconstruction enables the person to learn more fully because of the ability to "identify" with it and thereby understand one's own role in it.

☐ *Small units of feedback, but not trivia, are to be offered.* Feedback can be specific, concrete, and limited enough in magnitude to enable it to be thoroughly understood. This is better than a general assessment that is so lacking in specific detail that it is difficult to understand fully what it is attempting to convey.

On the other hand, trivia, or things of minor or no importance, have little bearing on the key aspects of individual effectiveness and so contribute very little to personal learning.

☐ *Concentrate on things a person can change.* Those things a person has a reasonable prospect of doing something about are far more worthy topics of feedback than are things a person is highly unlikely to be able to change. Because feedback is expected to form a basis for change, the more it relates to things that can be changed, the more useful the feedback will be. It might be more comfortable to concentrate on characteristics and conditions not in need of change, but this is not desirable in the context of learning to be more effective.

☐ *Be aware of the personal motivations for giving feedback.* An individual is most helpful to others when he or she knows the underlying motivations that stimulate feedback. One motivation is often a 9,9 orientation of concern for contributing to others through a caring attitude toward them. However, feedback opportunities can be used, for example, to score a point or to reap vengeance, and this characterizes what might be the extreme motivation of a 9,1-oriented person. By comparison, a 1,9-oriented person might give positive feedback to be endeared to the recipient. A 1,1-oriented person might do so to indicate a sense of being "with it," and to move things along even though the underlying attitude is "I couldn't care less." A 5,5-oriented person provides feedback to communicate that the recipient is a valued person, and in this way gains some popularity for him- or herself. An opportunist is vying for position. The paternalist gives you critique "for your own good."

In comparison with these, the 9,9-oriented person is motivated by the desire to make a contribution through caring for the effectiveness of others and to gain results.
   Critique is useful when:

☐ Work is bogged down and people are unclear of the causes of their lack of progress.
☐ Work practices have been relatively formal and there is a readiness to move toward informality and more spontaneous collaboration.
☐ A new procedure is being introduced.
☐ A group is embarking on an innovative activity.
☐ A group's membership is changed, particularly by the introduction of a new boss.
☐ 9,9 teamwork values are understood by team members who are motivated to learn how to increase their effectiveness.
☐ Results are less than what they can and should be.

   Critique is unlikely to be useful when:

☐ Two or more participants are overtly antagonistic to one another and would use the opportunity for destructive criticism.
☐ There is a crisis and the time needed for deliberation is unavailable.
☐ Activities are so mechanical and routine that few benefits are gained by examining them.
☐ Participants are inexperienced in face-to-face feedback methods, or fearful of open communication.

Limitations of Critique

The use of critique ensures that those whose participation is under study become their own students and teachers. Then it is most likely that the conclusions reached will be implemented because the implications of what has been learned are well understood. Yet, if it is so valuable, why is it so seldom used?

One limitation lies in the difficulty many people experience in being objective and in making sound observations when they are deeply involved in an activity itself. Their reactions to the activity, as well as to the people in it, may influence what they think and feel, and therefore, how they react. This is a strength as well as a limitation because the more points of view about an activity, the more likely people can learn from it.

Observation and feedback require effective and skillful communication. Participants must develop such skills if the full benefits of critique are to be realized.

The major limitation to using critique is that it is premised on 9,9 values of candor, conflict confrontation, and reliance on an experimental attitude. If these values are lacking, team members may go through the motions, but it is unlikely that the activity is worth the effort. It may be necessary to shift values before the benefits of critique can be realized. The good news is that these skills are available to be acquired by any manager willing to work for them and put them into use.

Summary

When tactics of 9,9 teamwork are applied to problem solving, there are numerous issues of how interaction occurs in a constructive way. One consideration is that those involved in problem solving often are not the "right" ones. There may be too many, too few, or the wrong people involved. Some problems are best solved one-alone, some one-to-one, some one-to-some, and still other problems on a one-to-all basis. Some may not be solved even on a one-to-all basis because of the need for external resources in finding and implementing a sound solution. Trying to solve a problem without mobilizing the necessary human resources is to risk failure.

Critique of problem solving both for operational results and for learning is stepping away from the entire cycle and exploring strengths and weaknesses of decisions made at each juncture along the way. In this way the members involved gain insight as to what should be retained and repeated—or identified and eliminated—in future problem-solving cycles.

And finally we come to the principles underlying the 9,9 orientation. An organization can maximize its members' contributions by applying these principles daily, which in turn helps ensure relationships among members based on mutual trust and respect. It then becomes possible to maximize the use of financial, technical, natural, and other resources.

In the next chapter we focus on personal change.

Chapter 11

Individual Change: "It's a Matter of A-B-C"

The theme throughout this book has been "change." We have described each Grid style in terms of its impact on productivity and the people with and through whom we must accomplish the required work. The evidence indicates that the 9,9 orientation offers the soundest way to achieve productivity, quality, service, etc. through increased involvement, commitment, and use of personal skills, and to do so in the most creativity-stimulating and at the same time most personally satisfying manner. The importance of change to this stronger way of operating is the challenge for anyone who wishes to further his or her own career while simultaneously advancing corporate well-being.

Change doesn't happen overnight, however. It takes more than a personal pledge or a private act of will. It cannot be had by edict or persuasion; nor can it be bought. Some or all of these may help but none are likely to be sufficient in and of themselves.

The missing link lies in acquiring personal insight into your own Grid style and the cause and effect nature of your behavior. Along with seeing in an objective manner *how you really operate*, you need to be able to determine that there is indeed a better way to do what you are doing. When these two conditions are met, the first step toward change has been taken because a gap has been created between where you currently are and where you would like to be. More is needed, however, before enduring change can be expected to occur. What is it, then, that can help us to make change a realizable possibility?

Part of the answer lies in the dynamics of the change process itself; that is, "How do we as adults learn?" We often take this for granted, but it is not such a simple matter to explain this process. We need to go back to our R_1-R_2-R_3 model to add a fourth "R," i.e., Reflection.

Reflection (R_4)—The Basis for Change

Numerous leadership dilemmas were revealed in the Al Jennings story. Another dilemma in the present context is, "How can one individual, apart from the help of others, increase his or her own effectiveness?" If Ed put his mind to it, what would he have to do to be in a position to strengthen his contribution to the team? The same question holds true for the other team members, and for each of us, too. Opportunities for individual change abound. Whether we do anything about these opportunities is partly a matter of personal desire but equally important is knowing what to do; this is contingent on being able to see what we're doing now that limits our effectiveness. Some of these limitations have been addressed in previous Grid style chapters. This chapter examines what we might do differently to operate more effectively.

Generally, all of us want to be effective in doing what we do. It's something that we've been stimulated to think about at home, through our schooling, and during our business careers. For some, the desire may remain dormant, but for many it's an active pursuit. Knowing what to do is a different matter; that's what the Grid is all about. The 9,9+ motivation and the six elements of leadership provide a roadmap of strong, effective behavior.

The main tool we have for seeing the discrepancy between how we behave and how we would conduct ourselves if operating according to a sound model like 9,9 lies in the fourth R—Reflection. Reflection, or R_4, allows us to observe ourselves in operational settings to ascertain why others react to us as they do and to diagnose how some ineffective action that we have taken might have been done in a more productive way. An illustration of how R_4 relates to $R_{1\text{-}2\text{-}3}$ appears in Figure 11-1.

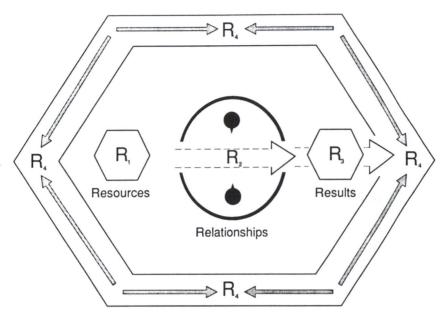

Figure 11-1. R_4, reflection, encompasses R_1, R_2, and R_3.

There are three special categories of R_4 that operate more or less simultaneously. Usually we pay them much less attention than they merit. The first category of R_4 is *introspection*. This is what happens when we study ourselves in a solo way. We may ponder why something we planned got off track or perhaps we inwardly celebrate a personal success. Sometimes we focus on repetition of the same activity between one time and another, saying, "It went better the second time around. I wonder why?" Sometimes introspection is more difficult to describe. For example, we may go to sleep deliberating a problem and wake up with its solution, or we may have one point of view on an issue and arise with a new perspective. This special category of introspection is called incubation. It can provide us with a new basis for understanding.

A second form of R_4 is the *informal feedback* we get from others when they tell us about ourselves. It may not always be offered in a constructive manner, but nevertheless it can cause us to reflect on why something we did or said elicited that particular reaction. In the Grid style chapters we looked at subordinate reactions to each of the leadership approaches depending on which Grid style subordinates (or other people) were coming from. This process of informal feedback can tell us much about ourselves that we didn't previously know. We just have to stop and pay attention.

The third category of R_4 is the more *formal process of critique,* though it may appear informal and spontaneous once you get to know it. Critique happens whenever we discuss with other people how something we have done together went and what might have been done to make it more productive. Critique can happen in advance when we anticipate what problems and obstacles may be encountered and how to overcome them. Best of all, critique can happen all along the way to keep us on track with our set objectives.

All three of these ways of learning more about ourselves are available for designing specific and concrete things we can do to increase our effectiveness. This can be undertaken with our own self-initiative and without asking others to change. R_4 is basic to bringing about individual change.

Why Do People Resist R₄?

How often do we hear as the rationalization for an unsuccessful change effort the reason, "People have an inherent resistance to change"? There is no doubt that sudden change can be threatening to our self-image, particularly when it seems overwhelming and out of our personal control. We may be frightened by excessive positive change as much as we fear excessive negative change. Change is stressful, whether it involves the loss of a loved one, getting married, buying a house, or promotion to a new position. This has been shown time and again.[18]

There is an alternative explanation for why people resist change. It is because the feedback may challenge a person's concept of his or her "plus" (+) motivation while validating the "minus" (−) motivation. There is another side to this, though. People *don't* resist feedback when it reinforces their plus or helps them to deny their minus motivation. Because of this, we sometimes see people exercising what might be called selective listening; they hear only what they want to hear.

Self-Deception

It might seem that the straightforward way to find out people's ways of working with and through others would be to just ask them. Who knows better than they what they want to accomplish? Contradictory to common sense, however, this turns out to be the worst way of getting the right answer. The reason is that people are prone to self-deception.

When the subject is a topic as serious as change towards greater effectiveness, why then do people kid themselves? Where does this process of denial begin? There are several explanations. One is that we simply take for granted what we do day in and day out. Our behavior becomes second nature to us. We think we know ourselves so well on the surface, while at a deeper level we don't know ourselves at all. Second, we do many things to provide ourselves false explanations for our actions to feel secure with ourselves. Managers who chew out subordinates never stop to listen to what others think about them. People who are easily offended or hurt give off signals that say, "Don't tell me anything unless it's nice." Those who have gone to sleep on the job aren't paying attention anyway and don't want to hear what is said that they might need to know. People who buy the status quo lock, stock, and barrel take offense from anyone who suggests something so risky as change. Paternalists draw around them those with worshipful attitudes that blind them of the flaws they might possess. Opportunists are masters at telling others what they want to hear while discounting any feedback that comes their way. All these behaviors can work hand-in-glove with one another and produce massive self-deception, with managers in the center of something they think they understand, but they do not.

For example, take as a case in point a week-long Grid Seminar. Before attendance, people read the Grid book so they have knowledge about the seven styles and then complete a self-assessment instrument that indicates their typical approach of working with others. At the beginning of the seminar, 65% of attendees see themselves as 9,9. They are already managing in the soundest way so there must not be much to change. A major purpose of the Grid Seminar is to reduce self-deception so that the participant gains a more penetrating and valid self-portrait of underlying assumptions and thinking. By the end of the week, when attendees do a second self-assessment in light of critique and feedback obtained from colleagues, the percentage of those seeing themselves as 9,9 has dropped to 17%. This shift from 65 to 17 is indicative of the large degree of self-deception people hold when looking at themselves. Part of the reason is that we tend to measure what we do by our intentions, rather than our actions. I may intend to operate in a sound way with subordinates, but what I say and do may not be perceived by others in the manner intended. All they have to judge me by is my actions; they can't read my mind.

Therefore, one way to get past self-deception is to rely on what others tell you in order to see yourself. When you begin to hear objective reality rather than depending on your own subjective internal reading, self-deception is being stripped away. You are now looking at how other people see you. This solution, based on concepts developed by Alfred Korzybski, can provide invaluable learning because it helps us see the consequences of our actions. That is a key and it is the topic we look at next.[19]

It's As Easy As A-B-C

In analyzing how people change, it is useful to consider Figure 11-2, in which "A" represents our underlying assumptions, that is, what we believe to be the best way for working with and through other people, and "B" represents our behavior. These are the actions

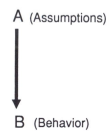

Figure 11-2. Our assumptions "drive" our behavior.

that other people see, and feel; appreciate or resent. Our behavior reflects the underlying assumptions we hold about how to do something. Our assumptions are an aspect of the R_1 resources we bring to bear on problem solving.

Take Ed as an example. Ed has 9,1 assumptions about how to manage. He believes that the easiest way to get results is to push people to do what he wants to see accomplished. Relationships (R_2) are based on authority/obedience. He doesn't see any particular advantage in consulting people or getting their input; in fact, he views this as a waste of time. Ed's way of dealing with relationships omits the possibility of R_4 self-learning.

Figure 11-3 is a diagram representing Ed, whose 9,1 assumptions lead to 9,1 behavior as it is experienced by others.

What is the missing piece in this equation for Ed to even consider changing? It is "C," or the results (R_3) that are the consequences of Ed's 9,1 behavior. Consequences are a direct measure of the actions we take, yet seldom do we stop to make this connection. When something doesn't work out the way we would like it to, we place the blame somewhere else rather than look back to our own assumptions (A_1) and behavior (B_1). We can begin to gain an awareness of these R_3 consequences through feedback and critique from others—R_4, which permits us to "see" the connection between our underlying assumptions, the resulting behavior, and the results (R_3) we achieve, particularly the consequences on others that limit or liberate their ability to contribute. This is shown in Figure 11-4.

If Ed sits down with his subordinates to talk about these matters at this point, however, he is still unlikely to get an honest or clear

Figure 11-3. 9,1 assumptions lead to 9,1 behavior.

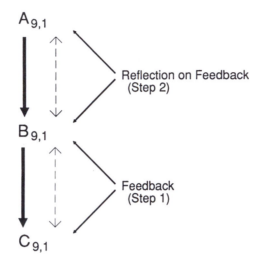

Figure 11-4. Feedback and critique allow us to see the connection between our assumptions, behavior, and achievements.

message because he is not open enough to hear what they are saying and furthermore, it is unlikely they would give him a straight answer. Ed has a reputation as a bully and no one wants to get beat up. So in the absence of any straightforward feedback and with self-deception in full swing, why would Ed change? He already thinks he's doing the best job possible based on his underlying assumptions and belief systems. Subordinates won't take the risk to tell him differently. If he sees himself at the top, there's no where else to go. Sounds like that's the end of change.

This is where the Grid comes in. The Grid provides a "comparative model" for managers to see a wider range of options for working with and through people. Only when you can see several alternatives can you select the soundest way to proceed. As indicated earlier, most people, when they read through the different Grid style descriptions, identify themselves as 9,9. They are evaluating their intentions rather than their actions. They have picked how they would *like to be seen* rather than how they *are actually seen*. Through objective feedback from others, who see us working on a daily basis, or R_4, we begin to get an idea of the gap between "ideal" and "actual" behavior. Once we do that, we start to see the connections between consequences (R₃), behavior (R₂), and assumptions (R₁).

Through exposure to Grid concepts of management, people become aware of the assumptions underlying the different approaches and the consequences of each. This happens first by looking at other people. Ed can look at Liz and say, "She's 5,5," and then look at what she achieves in terms of results. Then he can look at Ben and maybe, by listening to what other members of the team have to say about him, Ed may decide that Ben is 9,9. Ben's record looks pretty good. He is rising rapidly in the organization and he seems to get results without all the "people problems" that Ed encounters in his own department. Ed now has a "discrepancy" that can motivate him to try something different. He begins to look at the consequences (R₃) of his leadership behavior approach (R₂) and to *make the connection* to his assumptions (R₁). What he sees, pictured in Figure 11-5, is that 9,1 assumptions lead to 9,1 behavior which leads to 9,1 consequences. The consequences are a direct result of how he thinks about managing people.

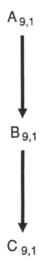

$A_{9,1}$

$B_{9,1}$

$C_{9,1}$

Figure 11-5. Ed's 9,1 assumptions lead to 9,1 behavior, which leads to 9,1 consequences.

$$B_{9,9}$$

$$\downarrow$$

$$C_{9,9}$$

Figure 11-6. Ben's 9,9 behavior leads to 9,9 consequences.

Ed might take a second look at Ben and see another connection, illustrated in Figure 11-6. Ben has a 9,9 management style (R_1), which shows itself in his behavior (R_2) and leads to 9,9 consequences (R_3). When Ed talks to Ben, he learns about how Ben thinks—his underlying R_1 assumptions—about working with and through people to accomplish organization purpose.

Ben is getting better results than Ed, but Ed would like to get good results, too. How does Ed get away from his 9,1 assumptions ($A_{9,1}$) about how to do things to get 9,9 consequences ($C_{9,9}$) for greater productivity through a motivated work force?

An easy answer is that Ed needs to "act in a $B_{9,9}$ way." This common sense approach is depicted in Figure 11-7. If Ed started acting in a $B_{9,9}$ way, he would get $C_{9,9}$ consequences, right?

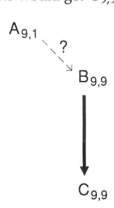

$$A_{9,1}$$

?

$$B_{9,9}$$

$$\downarrow$$

$$C_{9,9}$$

Figure 11-7. If Ed "acts" in a 9,9 way, but still has 9,1 assumptions, will he get 9,9 consequences? No.

Wrong! Unfortunately, it doesn't work that way, although many advocate such an approach in programs focused on behavior modeling, i.e., copy a model of good management and you will become a good manager. People attempt to do this for a period of time and it may work as long as the model is "visible." But when the model "disappears," the tendency is for people to slide back into their old ways of operating.

Why would this happen if people are aware of sounder approaches? The reason lies in the underlying A_1 assumptions. If *assumptions* don't change, *actions* don't change, and the *consequences* we get are based on our actual behavior and the underlying assumptions. That defines the big problem of individual change. How do people shift their underlying assumptions? How does Ed move away from $A_{9,1}$ to $A_{9,9}$? Take a look at Figure 11-8.

$$A_{9,1} \xrightarrow{\text{?}} A_{9,9}$$

Figure 11-8. How does a person move from 9,1 assumptions to 9,9 assumptions?

Needless to say, it's easier said than done. Individual change of this sort is possible but improbable, particularly if the system within which an individual operates is adverse to that change taking place. Changing your Grid style is not something that happens in isolation. It depends on your openness and the openness and candor of those with whom you interact. If Ed wants to change his Grid style, he needs help from his boss, his colleagues, and his subordinates. Others need to know and *understand* what he is trying to do. If he receives this support and maintains his commitment to change, then he might be successful.

Take a look at the conversation between Joe, Harriet, and Al to see the depth of the problem created by lack of openness and candor. Joe *misleads* Al, suggesting that his past performance is responsible for his present promotion. But the truth is that it is Al's *bad* past performance that causes him to be "kicked upstairs." Harriet points out the contradiction and the deception, but to no avail. As a result, Al is more likely to persist in his current ways of behaving than to see how he might increase his effectiveness in his new assignment. It is a problem of a less-than-sound organization culture in which these players operate. This will be examined in more detail in the next two chapters.

We said earlier that no one changes over night. Rather, change is a process that occurs over time. Ed has opened his mind enough to see that there might be a better way. As a result, he tests out some new assumptions and behaves consistently with 9,9 principles. He tells others what he is trying to do and they provide feedback and critique on how they perceive his behavior. Undoubtedly, Ed finds himself acting in old 9,1 ways as well but, now that he has a theory-based model for comparison, he can contrast the results or consequences of each. Figure 11-9 shows a picture of Ed in the phase of transition.

If Ed is persistent in his efforts, he can eventually become convinced that one way works better than the other. Based on our experience with managers—and subordinates—and what they report to be of value to them, we would bet on Ed moving over to a 9,9 style of management. Ed can move towards a 9,9 way of doing things based on self-convincing evidence of what is seen to be more

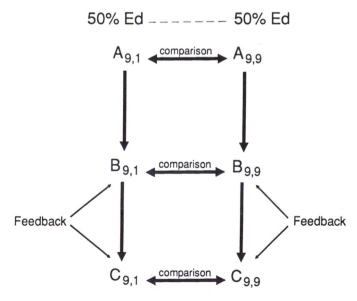

Figure 11-9. The transition to a 9,9 person.

effective. So now, based on feedback, Ed operates 75% of the time from a 9,9 style but in the other 25% he reverts to his old 9,1 style, shown in Figure 11-10. What is said of Ed is only for illustration. The same strategy of change is basic for Al, Liz, Dan, and the rest.

Why do people move to a backup style? This may be due to any number of reasons. Sometimes, people revert to a back-up style in situations of tension, conflict, or crisis because they do not have the skills to continue acting in their dominant style. Alternatively, it may have to do with how high the stakes are. We may be somewhat oblivious to our own behavior during routine activities. This is where it is especially easy to be fooled by self-deception. We may think we are acting more effectively than we actually are. In other words, it's easy to bypass input when you think you know the answer. Why bother to consult others? The converse argument, however, that we often fail to look at is, "How do we know we have the best answer if we don't take that extra step to test it against the thinking of others—if we fail to take advantage of the tremendous potential offered by input, feedback, and critique?" Once again, we are missing out on R_4.

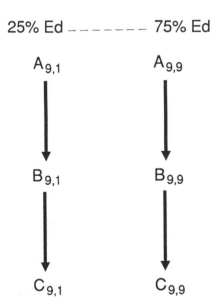

Figure 11-10. A back-up style, in this case 9,1, may still be a part of a person's behavior who is 9,9-oriented most of the time.

Change doesn't come easy. It takes persistent effort and the support of others to create it.

Conflict Provides a Clue

What does conflict have to do with it? How we approach conflict reveals how we deal with many situations in life, including how we manage work with and through others. It also provides further insight into why many people bypass R_4 and lose the potential advantage of feedback and critique to help them change.

Generally, people value openness and candor as basic human values and yet at the same time they are afraid, because they fear that openness and candor will result in conflict. And most people feel uncomfortable with conflict because they don't know how to deal with it effectively. That's why every Grid style is an attempt to avoid, circumvent, or suppress conflict. Conflict is automatically seen as "bad," and this value judgment immediately causes us to lose sight of the great gain that can be had by getting arguments out on the table where they can be jointly deliberated by those involved. It's a matter of underlying assumptions and attitudes—A_1.

Most Grid styles operate from a premise of "Who's right?": 9,1 says, "I'm right and don't you forget it!" 1,9 says, "You're right and please like me for saying so." Paternalism says, "I know best. Do it my way or suffer the loss of my approval." 1,1 says, "Who cares who's right? Not me!" 5,5 says, "We're both right if we compromise." Opportunism says, "I know what's right for me and I plan to get it, but I'll let you think whatever you want." Only 9,9 is after "What's right?" "What is the soundest solution to our problem?" That's the key difference.

All other styles tend to take critique and feedback "personally" and, by doing so, when you express doubts and reservations about my ideas, you are attacking me as a person. I close my mind in defense and, as a result, your thinking is lost. The 9,9 mind stays open to any possibility that there might be a better way to do "it" because 9,9 knows how to separate the "what" from the "who."

Let's examine another character in our story to see how this works. Consider Liz. At one level she's a friendly, easygoing person who is drawn into friendly interchange. She seems to enjoy relating to others; in fact, she seems uncomfortable when she is not. Looked at from a different angle, though, we can ask ourselves, "With whom is Liz most comfortable?" Certainly, Dan is a person with whom she can talk about things in a nondefensive and open manner. They are constant companions. She also likes Al when he has a favorable disposition, and she is supportive though cautious in her dealings with him. What about a person with a more abrasive personality, like Ed? Here we see little or no interaction initiated by Liz. She and Ed don't seem to be on the same wavelength, yet neither are they adversaries.

We can study these examples to learn something about the way Liz approaches conflict. Liz is drawn into relations with those people she perceives to be nonchallenging, who do not offer a threat to her self-image. She certainly stays out of harm's way in the Ben/Ed fracas. When the environment is positive, she is able to exert a stronger influence and to advocate her own definition of the team's problems and even to acknowledge her own sense of limitations when it involves dealing with conflict in a healthy way. We saw this in the last chapter as the team examined its mode of teamwork.

Prior to Ben's assuming leadership of the team, Liz's uneasiness about conflict seems to prevent her from asserting her ideas. As she comes to understand the Grid, though, she uses and diagnoses the team problem in managing conflict in an open and constructive way, as well as realizing that she must push to make her positions known. Only then are the high-quality results she has the potential to contribute likely to be made available.

Liz has begun to experiment with doing this—speaking out more forcefully—and she has made a significant new discovery. Others appreciate the point of view she expresses rather than being defensive or putting her down. This serves to reinforce her change effort and may be the key to helping Liz become a new person. It is also true that a person has to experiment by trying out the new behavior and measuring and testing its consequences. Often the central consequence or what was feared the most is not the outcome at all. Once you know the A-B-C connection, Grid style is a self-convincing experience. No longer can you be self-deceived that approaches other than 9,9 are the most effective. The consequences just aren't there to support that argument.

Taking the Plunge to 9,9

So what about you? How do you stack up on the Grid? Keeping in mind our inclination for self-deception as well as the possibility that others may be telling us what we want to hear (rather than what we need to know), take another look at the elements of leadership in Chapter 1. Transfer your self-evaluation rankings from pages 18–22 to Table 11-1. (Note that the Grid style options at the front of the book were scrambled, so place your answers by the corresponding letter in Table 11-1 to re-sort them by Grid style.) Add up the points in each column and the one with the highest sum is indicative of what you see as your dominant Grid style; the next highest indicates your backup Grid style, etc.

Table 11-1
Grid Style Self-Assessment

Elements	9,1	1,9	9+9	1,1	5,5	Opp.	9,9
Conflict Solving	F	G	A	B	D	C	E
Initiative	B	C	D	E	F	G	A
Inquiry	D	E	B	G	F	A	C
Advocacy	E	F	G	A	C	B	D
Decision Making	G	A	B	C	E	D	F
Critique	A	B	C	D	F	E	G
Total Points per Grid Style							
My Dominant Style is							
My Backup Style is							

The next step is to go back and review the "Subordinate Interactions" that appeared in each of the Grid style chapters. Pay close attention to the area of conflict and how you deal with it. Ask yourself, "Is this the way my subordinates react to me?" As you review the various people with and through whom you work, you may begin to see a pattern. In other words, you may find most of the subordinate reactions described toward you falling in the 1,1 chapter. This may lead you to conclude that a 1,1 way of working with and through others is characteristic of you. The same holds true for the other chapters. From a subordinate reaction point of view, which is the Grid style most characteristic of your behavior? What would your backup style be? Does this match your self-assessment, or is there a discrepancy?

By comparing these rankings, you may be able to draw conclusions about your own Grid style by contrasting these data. For example, if you came out with a dominant 9,1 based on your self-evaluation and you got a dominant 9,1 on your judgment of subordinate reactions, this suggests that your basic orientation of working with and through others in the organization lies in the 9,1 area. On the other hand, if you got a 1,1 in both, the probability is that your only motivation is to avoid losing your job and to be left alone.

Follow this same analysis with each of the other Grid styles. See if you can reach a conclusion as to your dominant Grid style and your backup Grid style. Is a consistent pattern revealed? If not, there may be a number of explanations for this. One is that your basic orientation may be opportunistic. In this case you work with and through others in whatever Grid style you think serves your own self-interest. Alternatively, it may be that you have not been as thorough as needed to recognize the systematic themes that characterize how you work with other people. Still a third possibility lies in the area of self-deception. You may be reading your intentions and not your actions. For example, if your self-evaluation reveals a dominant Grid style of 9,9 but subordinate data contradict this, it may be that you've read your good intentions while discounting your actual behavior, whereas subordinates read your actions and may never even be aware of the intent behind them. Actions are what count; they are the name of the effectiveness game. They are what cause subordinates to react to you as they do. They are what motivate or fail to motivate others to contribute resources they hold and that are important for achieving R_3 results.

Variations on a Theme

There are other useful ways of assessment that can be relied upon to complement your own self-analysis. For example, you might ask a friend or your spouse to engage in this same exercise. See how this person evaluates you and get an explanation for the ranking. Additionally, give this book to a subordinate or your boss. Tell them what you are up to so they will understand that their objectivity is important in your change effort. This may be the most powerful piece of information you can get because they are reporting how you come across to others and, no matter how much we try to strip away self-deception, seeing ourselves from an outside perspective is something we cannot do alone.

Taking this extra step serves as further reinforcement when combined with your own perspective. Underlying consistency indicates that your self-assessment is objective, whereas inconsistencies suggest that it might be worthwhile for you to take another look. Inconsistency suggests self-deception, or it may indicate opportunism. Go back and examine Frank and see if there is any of Frank in you. That may offer another clue. The utility of self-assessment is limited by the human tendency toward giving oneself the benefit of the doubt, confusion of intentions with actions, and convenient rationalizations that allow you to think one way and yet do the opposite. The degree of openness and candor that others are prepared to express toward you can be another limitation, so it is important to stress that their honesty with you is central while their efforts to make you feel good are not. This, however, does provide a good first step.

Imagine what might happen if Ed were to do this. Ed is in good touch with his own values. He values dominance, mastery, and control as positive features of strong management. By way of a self-assessment, he would be likely to see a 9,1 orientation in his own management style. It's difficult to believe he would behave in significantly different ways at home, so there's a good probability his wife would picture him as he has characterized himself. If he were to ask Ben or Liz or Al to provide rankings, the probability is that they also would arrive at the same conclusion. Then Ed would have three more or less independent sources of evidence that support his own assessment. With several points on the curve he now has something with which to work.

If you are a paternalist, like Al, and you ask subordinates for feedback, be aware that they are likely to tell you what they think you want to hear. In this case, reexamine your own rankings and see if you alternated between the 9,1 and 1,9 styles because both these ways of behaving may reveal your paternalism. Also, to get a sharper focus, go back to the 9,9 and the $9+9$ chapters and restudy the distinctions between what characterizes a 9,9 style and a paternalistic style.

Once you have a clear idea in mind as to your own orientation, the next step is *action*.

Suggestions for Change

This section provides suggestions as to how each member of Al's team might consider increasing his or her R_1 capacity for contributing in a more effective manner. You will find that it can serve as a useful model of change for you as well.

Ed: 9,1

Conflict Solving

1. Check your underlying motivations before striking out. Are you operating from a desire to control, or are you looking for the soundest solution?
2. Because you tend to be aggressive, let the other person begin. When you answer, repeat what you think was said before stating your own position.
3. Seek closure of the kind that results in shared understanding if not shared agreement. Don't cut conflict off or suppress it. Confront it and work it through.

Initiative

1. Allow others to take initiative rather than imposing your solution. Ask them how they would do it — before you tell them how you would do it.

2. Involve someone in your next effort and let them critique the process as you go along (keep an open mind!); then get involved in their next effort and do the same.
3. Ask other people for input on what you plan to do. If you don't, you may be shutting out valuable information.

Inquiry

1. Don't automatically discount the ideas of others. Ask them to provide their rationale instead.
2. When you ask questions, provide your rationale so people know where you're coming from.
3. Stop looking for "Who is guilty?" and start looking for "What is the solution?"

Advocacy

1. Get others to speak before stating your own position.
2. When advocating your own position, state it objectively; that includes strengths as well as weaknesses of the approach.
3. Look for the positive features in what others are saying rather than focusing on the negatives. Then look at how the negatives might be overcome. Advocate *solutions*, not *problems!*

Decision Making

1. Test possible decisions against the thinking of others before making them final.
2. Incorporate the sound ideas of others. Just because they're not yours doesn't mean they're wrong.
3. Involve those who are to implement the decision in the decision-making process itself.

Critique

1. Your previous style is to place blame, so for the time being, if you can't say something constructive, don't say anything at all.
2. Develop skills of active listening. That means don't talk while others are talking; your job is to listen.
3. Don't discount the suggestions of others. Give them a try (more than once) and compare consequences.

Dan: 1,9

Conflict Solving

1. Encourage others to disagree with you and when they do, restate your position and ask them for further clarification.
2. Seek to understand reservations and doubts about what you have formulated and be willing to air your own on what others have said.
3. If you think someone has a better solution than you, state specifically that you are changing your mind and then state the reasons why—*specifically*! Otherwise, you will be seen as indecisive and wishy-washy.

Initiative

1. Exercise initiative in situations where you tend to back off. Just open your mouth and go!
2. If you see a better way to do something, take the initiative to improve it.
3. Replace "I'd better not" with "I'll take a chance." Then, remember, actions speak louder than words.

Inquiry

1. Reexamine your own understanding of issues in advance of meetings. Be prepared!
2. Strengthen inquiry by asking questions in an open-ended way that invites explanations.
3. Keep questions specific and focused on turfing significant data. For the time being, avoid social niceties; you already know how to do that.

Advocacy

1. Examine your convictions on the issues in advance and rehearse them so you won't forget.
2. Be the first to speak when opinions are requested.
3. Be specific about what you think. Don't be wishy-washy and don't build yourself an escape hatch. Put it on the line!

Decision Making

1. Stop procrastinating even if you find decision making embarrassing or unpleasant.
2. Involve others only if they can make a contribution; stop consulting just to win permission, acceptance, or approval.
3. Make one-alone decisions when appropriate and communicate these to others along with your rationale.

Critique

1. Be open, candid, and straightforward when describing your observations of other people and how they impact you. Remember, being nice *is not* the same as being helpful.
2. Ask others for their help in being more assertive. Tell them to give you spontaneous feedback every time you back down.
3. Continue to look at the consequences of your behavior. Ask others how they have seen you at the end of each major action. Ask them to tell you how you could have done it differently and try that next time.

Al: Paternalism

Conflict Solving

1. Acknowledge that differences and disagreements are basic to clear thinking and learning. Stop taking conflict personally.
2. Stimulate the expression of different points of view to investigate alternative solutions and to derive new insights that may exist beneath the surface.
3. Accept contradictory opinions for what they are worth rather than by virtue of who speaks them.

Initiative

1. Before embarking on an activity, go to another person and ask how he or she would do it and try it that way instead.
2. Delegate activities to others and let them figure out how to do it without suggestions from you.
3. If it becomes necessary to change what you are doing later on, don't be reluctant; just do it.

Inquiry

1. Accept information given as the best available; go beyond it if necessary to clear up uncertainty or misunderstandings.
2. Get those who are silent to express their convictions.
3. Probe for the rationale behind "why"; more often than not it leads to sounder conclusions.

Advocacy

1. Let others express their opinions before expressing your own.
2. Stop giving others hints about what you would like them to say or do.
3. Avoid using should's and shouldn't's. Stop prefacing replies with "The way I would do it is . . ." and just ask others to explain how they think their approach will work. Give them the benefit of the doubt.

Decision Making

1. When you delegate an activity, let that person(s) make the decision without your interference.
2. At the conclusion of a decision-making discussion, ask others where they stand. Make the decision based on the weight of the evidence, not your personal preference.
3. Stop trying to persuade and coerce others into believing as you do and ask for their feedback to let you know when they feel this is happening.

Critique

1. Make yourself an equal in giving and receiving feedback and critique. In fact, consider yourself the student and others as your teachers.
2. Avoid judgmental reactions, even if you disagree with what is being said. Just express appreciation for the honesty and check it out with others later for its objectivity.
3. Once you have offered your point, drop it. Don't keep hammering it home. Enough already, okay?

Gil: 1,1

Conflict Solving

1. Because you have taken a neutral stance in the past, take a firm position on every issue. If you don't know the pros and cons, ask, and then make a judgment.
2. Avoid censuring your beliefs even though they may not prove popular.
3. Persist in pushing your points until others have convinced you of their limitations. Likewise, push them to provide their rationale for their positions. Don't buy in just to avoid a fight.

Initiative

1. Take action to solve problems within your area of responsibility and solicit the assistance (not initiative!) of a co-worker to do it.
2. Ask for more assignments, particularly joint assignments.
3. Offer help in solving problems you share with allied teams. Get involved with the whole organization. Become a volunteer!

Inquiry

1. Rebuild your knowledge base by asking questions of subordinates and peers. Don't be afraid to let others know that you don't know.
2. Pick up and digest pertinent literature, articles, and news reports. Become informed!
3. Do your homework on current work problems and be prepared to ask intelligent questions in group meetings. Have a written list ready!

Advocacy

1. When you state a position, pose it in such a straightforward way that its meaning cannot be missed.
2. If you are caught short on the facts, promise to follow up and then get back to the relevant parties. Tell them to come get you if you don't!
3. Commitment is demonstrated in actions, not words. Take actions as the real basis for your re-acceptance. You can regain the respect of others but only if it's deserved!

Decision Making

1. Ask yourself, "Have I delegated this task in a message-passing way?" Get subordinates to give you feedback when they feel this is happening.
2. Persist in pushing yourself into the arena of action. Stop standing on the outside looking in. Get involved!
3. Avoid capitulation simply to get yourself out of a difficulty. Take responsibility for yourself and your actions.

Critique

1. Take the initiative to start a critique. When a meeting is being concluded, stop and say you would like to critique the discussion before closing. Provide your assessment and then listen to what others have to say. Critique means how well you worked together (R_2!), not a rehash of what you did.
2. Ask for direct feedback from others on how they react to you. Ask them for improvement steps you can undertake to do better.
3. If people ignore you, persist until you get an answer. Remember, you were "invisible"; it takes a while for people to see you again.

Liz: 5,5

Conflict Solving

1. Evaluate different arguments without regard for who will gain points or who will lose face. Remember, "What's right," not "Who's right."
2. Be open and receptive to examining differences. It is unlikely that a situation will become polarized into a win-lose conflict with these attitudes.
3. Be proactive and provide rationale without being asked. Probe for the underlying thinking of others as well. If others are silent, get their input.

Initiative

1. Step out in front by getting needed actions underway. Take center stage and lead the effort.

2. Recognize that tradition, precedent, and past practices are without merit unless they point to the soundest actions to be taken. And, you never learn better ways to do something without taking a risk.
3. Avoid backing off from what you think is a good idea simply because you think others might not go along. Be willing to take a stand and don't deflate your position with uncertainties.

Inquiry

1. Be more thorough in data gathering. Develop an agenda prior to meetings for what you would like to see discussed.
2. Ask additional questions to ensure your understanding is complete. Take notes if necessary and keep them to refer to at a later time.
3. The broader and deeper your knowledge, the greater your security so be prepared and get other people to tell you what they know. Anticipate that others are going to ask you deep and probing questions. Position yourself so that you will have the answer.

Advocacy

1. State your point of view regardless of where other people stand. Then listen to the merit of every position and align yourself on the basis of sound thinking.
2. Say what you really think rather than editing or shaping convictions to make them acceptable. Persist in your own point of view unless convinced of its limitations.
3. Don't automatically go with the majority point of view. Pay particular attention to minority opinions and get sound rationale for why they are held.

Decision Making

1. You have a tendency towards one-to-one decision making. Reassess this and involve all who are impacted or all who can contribute thinking in the decision-making process. Reassess whether you are using resources in the soundest possible way.

2. Make decisions in a timely way. Don't stop and take a vote to see if you have majority support. Involve the resources you need and take a stand.
3. Ask others for their input, but not their agreement, in decisions that only you can make.

Critique

1. The best way to get sound feedback is to show you want it. Ask for it and then accept it as it is given. Period.
2. Feedback provides a check on what you may plan to do before you have to take action. Once again, this is not taking a vote on which way to go but asking the opinion of one or several whom you respect.
3. Feedback gives you an opportunity to express your reactions to the thinking of others. You provide them a disservice if you are not straightforward or if you try to hide the truth.

Frank: Opportunism

Conflict Solving

1. Voice your disagreements publicly. Don't imply agreement by hiding behind silence.
2. Avoid trying to circumvent conflict or to smooth it over. Keep it in perspective and seek to understand it. Provide your rationale slowly, point by point, and let others interject their arguments as you go.
3. Listen to what others are saying instead of preparing a strategy to distract them. Remember you are looking for "What is right," not "Who is right." Ask them to explain what they are saying.

Initiative

1. Prove to others the worthiness of your means, that is, how you plan to undertake an effort. See if they can offer a better approach.
2. Fight for principle, not expediency. That which is worthwhile in life is worth fighting for—so do it!
3. Risk losing. You can learn from your mistakes.

Inquiry

1. Tell others what's behind what you want to know. Stop being cagey.
2. Don't hide what you don't know. Just say, "I don't know. Please tell me."
3. Don't play games. Don't let others think you don't know something you do or that you do know something you don't. In other words, *be honest*.

Advocacy

1. Let what you usually hide become known. Play it straight.
2. Deal in a direct way with those who doubt your word. Confront them and put it on the line. Tell them you are as good as your word. *Then be as good as your word.*
3. Go ahead and state a position before you know where others stand. You have the right to change your mind if someone offers a better solution.

Decision Making

1. Put the organization first. Ask others if a decision is consistent with corporate objectives.
2. Challenge others to shoot your decisions down. Ask them to tell you how they would do it.
3. Don't change decisions just to please the political landscape. Stand by your decisions once you make them and be responsible for the consequences.

Critique

1. Put truth over politics, honesty over deception, principle over expediency, the soundest model over the practical approach. Ask others to watch you like a hawk and to let you know when you stray from this path.
2. Avoid expressing yourself in abstractions that are so high and lofty that they have no meaning. Be specific and concrete in what you say.

3. Express your negative thoughts as well as your positive thoughts. Stop being so nice and charming and just tell the truth.

Summary

Theory provides the basis for being able to identify and understand the differences between the seven Grid styles. This is the first step toward change. Throughout the book we have spoken of the assumptions underlying any Grid style. In the final analysis, Grid style is based on *assumptions* about how to achieve production with and through others. This leads to clearly recognizable patterns of *behavior*. It is this behavior that impacts others and leads to identifiable *consequences*. When we examine the consequences of acting in each of the seven Grid styles, the evidence available clearly points in the direction of the 9,9 Grid style as being the most effective from the standpoint of achieving production by whatever criterion: volume, quality, speed, safety, customer service, return on investment, etc. Furthermore, 9,9 seems to be the Grid style most capable of producing creativity that promotes individual satisfaction.

In this chapter we have examined change from the perspective of the individual, discussing how the Grid can be used for monitoring personal change. We discussed R_4, and some of the resistances to change that can limit a person's efforts at increased effectiveness. Several suggestions were offered for how a person operating in any Grid style might experiment with change toward a 9,9 style.

Now we want to take that a step further and look at the teams in which we work because these "teams" are groups of individuals, a collection of R_1 resources, and how they join together in an R_2 way is all important in what we achieve by way of R_3.

Chapter 12

Teamwork Development: "We've Only Just Begun"

Personal change can be an exciting achievement for an individual, but it's only part of a much larger story. In the last chapter we examined what each of us can do to start the process of personal change. For big change to occur, however, the process is more complicated. Consider Ben, for example. He persistently sought to get Al's group to address issues of team effectiveness but to little or no avail. As a new leader of the team, however, he is in position to wield greater impact. Others have now become involved in Grid learning, which enables the team to operate from a common frame of reference. Regardless of what Ed or Liz or Dan may seek to do in terms of personal effectiveness, it is unlikely to have great impact on the team's productivity due to the limitations and constraints contained in the situation in which they work. Something else is needed to strengthen the work setting in order to offer an environment that can enhance productive effort.

The most significant context of our work effort occurs within the work teams of which we are members. Almost everyone, except perhaps a solo scientist, works with and through others to accomplish task. The problem of change is as much in how people work together as it is in how each person exercises individual leadership skill. Al's team provides an excellent illustration of this. After they got rolling on the bid, they got complacent, thinking they had more than enough time. Nobody challenged whether or not they were doing okay as measured against some standard of excellence, that is, what they could really be doing if they put their minds to it. Complacency almost led to defeat. Only by chance did Ed and Frank discuss the issue and the error suddenly become evident. The team had simply been rocking along without much awareness of how casual they had become.

Revisiting Al's Team

One way to think about how we work together is found in a reexamination of Al's team. If the barriers to human effectiveness that these people confront can be understood, we then gain insight into how similar obstacles in our own work environments might be changed.

The members of Al's team have "relationship problems" that impede their effectiveness as a group. Fortunately, all, save possibly Gil, are motivated, but in distinctive ways, to serve Celarmco. However, each operates by his or her own personal agenda. Together they seem to lack the ability to mesh effort in pursuit of a single overriding goal, namely, getting there first by beating their competition to the punch. Unable to see beyond themselves even in a crisis, the most they could contribute was the best individual effort possible towards a solution, while trying at the same time not to block the efforts of other team members. It took an external input to shock them into recognizing the facts of life. This saved them from themselves; they were able to pull together for success.

- [ ] Al, the veneration-seeking leader, seeks to establish and maintain a supportive and loyal family. While that contributes to his security through satisfying his personal needs, it does not create a sense of urgency to get the real job done.
- [ ] Dan, the happiness-driven human resource manager, concerns himself primarily with cultivating good relationships among the team based on the dubious notion that happy people get the job

done. That results in his turning to "soft" people, rather than the more abrasive ones.

☐ Liz takes the reasonable approach. She is the "good" team player in the sense of balancing the needs of people for support and approval with the need to complete a task, unwittingly stifling her capacity for initiative and creativity.

☐ Frank is a mystery. You just don't know about him because he's operating according to his own hidden agenda; what you see on the surface may bear little or no resemblance to reality.

☐ Ben is promoting openness and candor while challenging the group to become more interdependent and focused to achieve synergistic results. He is tired of the status quo being accepted as good enough; he knows they are capable of bigger and better accomplishments. Initially he has little success because no one seems to understand what he's shooting at.

☐ Ed is pushing for a turnabout to tough-minded, boss-directed leadership and voices his readiness to dispose of anything resembling employee input or participation. That causes others to pull away from him.

☐ Gil is the invisible member, motivated mainly to hang on to his job in order to enjoy the benefits of retirement. As a result he is a non-entity, failing to carry his own weight but at the same time not directly standing in the way of others.

Each member has a personal Grid style and is doing his or her own thing, playing the game according to the dynamics of one of the seven Grid styles. Except for Ben, no one seems sufficiently oriented to think about the conditions necessary for success if the team is to accomplish its goals and objectives.

What is it that prevents Al's team from becoming a truly outstanding and productive team? Several factors are apparent:

1. No set of explicit and shared values exists among team members for how human resources might be mobilized in a sound and effective manner.

2. Though spoken of in "mechanical" terms, a common goal that is real in the sense of being felt and acted upon by each member is missing. They lack a shared understanding of team purpose.

3. Members are unaware of how to deal effectively on a team-wide basis with their internal conflicts and how to bring about sound conflict resolution as inevitable differences appear.
4. Team members are complacent and appear to lack any real desire to do better than "good enough."
5. A "live and let live" acceptance of each others' Grid styles as a matter of personal prerogative prevents them from offering constructive and helpful feedback to one another and setting standards of excellence.
6. The use of critique for monitoring effectiveness and learning to shift direction when necessary is absent.

Because these are the features of teamwork that are lacking, the question becomes, "How can team members implement needed changes for bringing about better action? Can they shift to a 9,9 basis of teamwork?"

Team Building

Team building offers a systematic approach for answering this question. It allows a team to study how it is operating relative to how it might be operating. There are six dimensions of team building that are subject to systematic study by the team members themselves. As a team pursues excellence, each of these six dimensions is shared in common by all team members. That is to say that team members are participants within the context of examining how each of these six dimensions is helping or hampering teamwork. If any one of these dimensions is less than sound, productivity of the team as a whole inevitably suffers. However, when action in all of these dimensions is sound, team members feel challenged to pursue and achieve high standards of excellence.

We return to our model of R_1-R_2-R_3, because teamwork, whether effective or ineffective, is what occurs within the arena of relationships—R_2. The effectiveness of teamwork is a function of how R_1 resources are used to achieve an R_3 result. R_1 is what "individuals" have to contribute—the knowledge, ability, and skill of each team member. R_3 is the results achieved from team interaction and problem solving, measured in productivity, profit, quality, creativity and innovation, sales and service. R_2 is "how well we do things" in the effort to get from R_1 to R_3.

Because how effectively resources are used and what kind of results we achieve depends upon what happens in the arena of R_2, this is where change can impact both quantity and quality of results. This is the arena of Grid Organization Development. Team building is the next step in this process. We examine the big picture in Chapter 13.

The six dimensions of team building viewed from the perspective of R_2 include power/authority, norms/standards, morale/cohesion, goals/objectives, structure/differentiation, and critique/feedback.

Power/Authority

When a leader exercises power/authority in a way that suppresses the resources that others have to offer, the result is that relationships suffer and results are sacrificed. People learn *not* to offer input to a boss who steps on them. Likewise, when an individual fails to exercise any kind of strong and directive leadership, resources are uncoordinated and people flounder and become frustrated. When power/authority is used to channel the full resources that organization members have to offer, they feel a sense of ownership and become involved in the achievement of productive outcomes. This exercise of sound leadership shows up in quantifiable R_3 results.

By way of illustration, power/authority as exercised in two of the Grid styles, "closed" 9,1 and "open" 9,9, are presented in Figure 12-1.

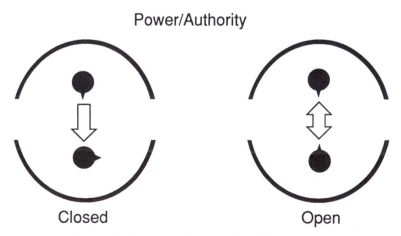

Power/Authority

Closed   Open

Figure 12-1. Power/authority viewed from 9,1 and 9,9 styles.

Norms/Standards

Another source of blockage that can work against R_2 lies in the area of norms and standards. These are the organization's and the team's traditions, precedents, and past practices. They guide people's behavior. They define the parameters within which we may operate and they also define what is "taboo." These are the conditions people have come to accept as the "rules of the game," to be followed without a second thought. Often the norms and standards that exist are outmoded and antiquated. They bind people to rigid forms of behavior that characterize an organization or team culture. The necessary flexibility for converting resources into results is lacking. Creativity and innovation are stifled. They pervade every area of relationship, characterizing the nature of interactions between pairs of individuals, within teams, between departments, and throughout an organization as a whole.

Two examples of "inhibiting" 9,1 and "enabling" 9,9 norms and standards are shown in Figure 12-2.

Norms/Standards

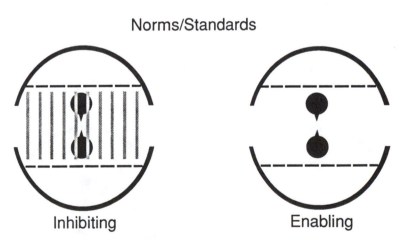

Inhibiting   Enabling

Figure 12-2. Norms/standards viewed from 9,1 and 9,9 styles.

Morale/Cohesion

Whether or not individuals in a team feel a sense of membership with one another and identification with the organization as a whole also can have a profound impact on productivity. Significant resources may be sacrificed when people feel unmotivated to work with one another. Even in a team that appears to be functioning well, synergistic opportunities may be lost because each member is off doing his or her own thing, rather than working interdependently with the others.

This may be one of the larger problems in organizations today. Managers have mastered rational techniques for running an organization but often the dynamics of teamwork seem foreign. As jobs have become more and more specialized and the pace in modern organizations has accelerated, it becomes imperative rather than just desirable to ensure collaboration and cooperation among team members toward a common goal. Successful work relationships of this nature are based on trust and respect and lead to people feeling responsible for one another's success. The work culture comes to be characterized by an atmosphere of interdependent entrepreneurialism where people feel motivated to succeed and to help one another in doing so.

Two illustrative perspectives on the relationship dimension, Morale/Cohesion, are shown in Figure 12-3.

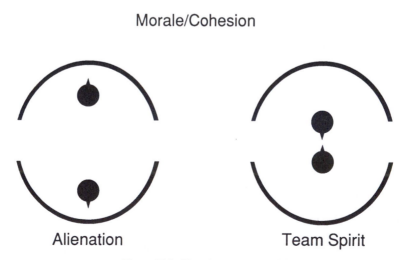

Morale/Cohesion

Alienation   Team Spirit

Figure 12-3. Alienation vs. team spirit.

Structure/Differentiation

If the structural arrangements, including hierarchy, job descriptions, and so on, that prevail among people are faulty and yet dictate who interacts with whom, when, and for what purpose, another impediment to effective results may be present. Many times work relationships are structured to avoid conflict, keeping people or departments separate and apart. The underlying assumption is that lack of contact equals lack of conflict, but it may also equal lack of cooperation and coordination. It can mean the difference between success and failure in the face of tough competition. Another possibility is that effort is redundant; job responsibilities are unclear; they overlap. The hope is that someone takes the initiative to see that the important work gets done. However, if this doesn't happen, because responsibility lies with no one person, no one is to blame. Nevertheless, we as a team have failed. Alternatively, when structure represents a sound arrangement for how best to achieve the work of the organization in a productive and effective way, this maximizes the potential for full use of resources. "Overlapping" and "interdependent" structural arrangements are illustrated in Figure 12-4.

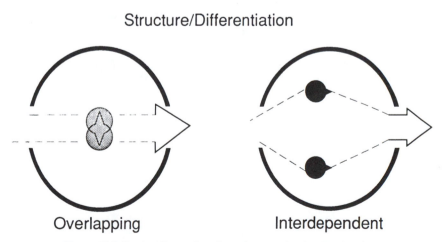

Structure/Differentiation

Overlapping   Interdependent

Figure 12-4. Overlapping vs. interdependent structural arrangements.

Goals/Objectives

If the goals and objectives that dictate how effort is to be channeled are unclear or unacceptable to those who must interact, it follows that the resources organization members have to contribute are unlikely to produce good results. People need to *own* the goals they are responsible for implementing. This requires participation and involvement in the process of goal setting. In this way there is created shared understanding of the rationale for what we are seeking to accomplish. Effective management recognizes the importance of letting people know *why* as well as what, who, when, and how. When personal goals and objectives are divergent from organizational goals, this creates tension and conflict that drains energy from what could be constructive effort. It diverts the resources and blocks their conversion into results. The effective leader seeks to align individual and organization goals and to establish shared objectives toward which all can strive, the result being that everyone stands to gain.

Sound versus unsound goals and objectives are shown in Figure 12-5.

Goals/Objectives

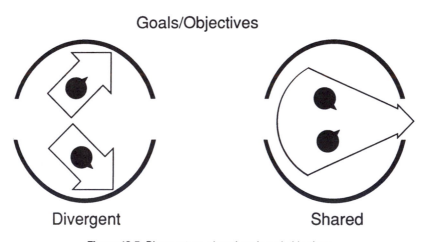

Divergent   Shared

Figure 12-5. Divergent vs. shared goals and objectives.

Critique/Feedback

Feedback and critique may occur, or fail to occur, in the realm of R_2. Feedback and critique are the "natural" way for an organization to constantly study itself and thereby be in a position to induce changes as needed to rectify operating difficulties. However, more often than not, feedback and critique do not happen.

The absence is seen in teams that operate in a reaction/response fashion, moving from one crisis to another, without ever stopping to observe the process by which they are operating. Alternatively, critique may occur in the form of blame and criticism. Or, it may be used in a carrot and stick way—rewards when you're good and punishment when you're bad. None of these are effective ways of using critique to strengthen performance.

The option is a built-in team standard of ongoing critique to monitor a task as it heads toward completion. Critique occurs before we start an activity as we consider the possible consequences and likely barriers to success; it occurs at every point along the way to ensure that we are staying on track; and it occurs upon conclusion of an activity because here lies the great potential for learning. We don't need to repeat the mistakes of the past if we just stop and consider what we have done and how we might do that same task or a similar task better on a future occasion. This is an important step to engage in, both in our successes and our failures.

Two versions of critique, one unsound and the other sound, are illustrated in Figure 12-6.

Feedback/Critique

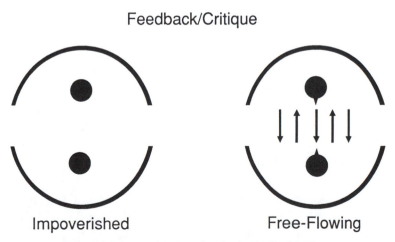

Impoverished   Free-Flowing

Figure 12-6. Impoverished vs. free-flowing feedback/critique.

When these six dimensions are carried out in the R_2 arena in an unsound manner, R_1 resources have difficulty getting past R_2. In contrast to this, when the six dimensions are being managed in the soundest way, resources flow into R_3 results. This is maximizing available resources through sound teamwork dynamics to create productive and effective outcomes.

These six dimensions—power/authority; norms/standards; morale/cohesion; structure/differentiation; goals/objectives; and critique/feedback—constitute the six key aspects of teamwork that impact how effectively we use our resources and convert them to real results. When each of these dimensions is being approached in a sound manner, resources can be fully mobilized and converted into something greater than could be accomplished by each of us working on an individual basis. Instead of $1+1+1=3$, we can get $1+1+1 =$ something more than 3; we may be able to achieve a result of 5 or 6 or 7 or more. This is the very purpose of "organization," to allow us to do more by working together than we could do working alone. If that were not so, there would be no reason for us to "organize" for the sake of joint effort. Organizations allow us to pool our resources and, optimally, in a way that expands each of our individual capabilities into something greater. It is the job of leadership to successfully manage this process in a way that leads to soundest results. To reiterate, what kind of leadership a manager exercises is a function of how he or she puts the three R's together. The outcomes achieved depend on the effectiveness of the approach used.

Changing "Team Culture"

An organization can maximize its members' contributions by employing critique on a continuing basis. This in turn can lead to relationships among members characterized by trust and respect, the end results of sound behavior. Productivity, creativity, personal satisfaction, and health are best served when principles of 9,9 interaction are employed.

When the six dimensions of teamwork are examined for Al's team, it's apparent that Al's team has not got it all together. Though its individual members appear capable of outstanding achievement, poor teamwork prevents them from mobilizing their resources for the kind of peak performance that can lead to total accomplishment. Viewed against this model of human interaction, the contrast with how Al's team operates in actual practice is dramatic. It is clearly evident that human resources are being needlessly sacrificed.

The problem of introducing change can be illustrated in the following manner. Al and his team are "hooked." They have come to accept what might be called a 10:00 o'clock way of thinking about how to harness people into productive activity. This represents their current team culture. At the center is a "Do your own thing" mentality, a "live and let live" approach that seems acceptable to all (with the exception of Ben, and perhaps Ed), provided the team's current behavior is not challenged by some outside source.

To mobilize resources more fully, they need to acquire a new team culture. Call this a 2:00 o'clock way of thinking and acting, one that links people to productive outcomes and creates circumstances approaching the formulations contained within a 9,9 approach to leadership.

How does a team—or an organization—change its culture? Several basic approaches are currently being employed. Only one, however, is relatively certain to produce the kinds of changes that are essential if human motivation is to be fully released.

Bring in a Team Consultant

One way is to hire a consultant, a kind of coach who can help the team see the errors of its ways. How often has it been said, "He (or she) can't see the forest for the trees!" This is often true within an organization; it may take an outsider to provide an objective perspective. The consultant may work with the top person or with the team as a whole or with each individual member; a combination of these approaches is often desirable.

On the surface this approach may look better than proves to be the case in practice. More often the results are disappointing. In many instances the consultant becomes a political football and people start playing games; tempers flare if there is the slightest hint of favoritism or bias, and the latter is difficult to prevent as someone must by necessity, initiate the contact.

The more significant factor, though, is the creation of what we call "consultant dependency." The fact of the matter is that the more insightful and helpful the consultant is to the team, the more dependent they become on this person. In this role of expert or authority figure, the consultant becomes a substitute boss and, when the time comes for the consultant to leave, the team flounders, unable to function on its own. The skills of good management have not been transferred and, without a model to imitate, the team reverts back to old ways.

Send the Boss to School

A second approach is to teach the top person, let's say Al, the skills of leadership necessary for unlocking the resources of other team members.

Here's the scenario. Al goes to school and learns a new way to do things; he comes back and tries out what he has learned. For example, he approaches Liz, Gil, and Dan in the hall one day and says, "I'd like your input on something. We have the opportunity to bid on a new project. It would be a new area of endeavor for us. What do you think we should do?" Ten seconds pass, and no answer. Twenty seconds; then thirty. Finally, Gil says something about referring the matter to a task force with the charge that "they" study the problem in more detail. Al, who was trying to act in a new way by seeking team member input and getting their thinking to test against his own, feels exasperated. How can he hope to act in a new way if they won't play by the same rules? Al may try again, but it's likely that he will receive the same cool reception. After all, he's the one who is acting in a "strange new way." Before long, he conforms, and the result is that nothing has changed.

Why does this approach generally result in failure? The answer is simple. While Al may have gained new insight via direct experience in a laboratory learning environment, other team members have not had this opportunity and these are not skills that can be edicted by a boss. Al's learning may have been reinforced by comprehensive theory, such as that presented in this book. By doing this, Al has gained "freedom of choice," in other words, the ability to see different management styles in a comparative fashion and then to select the soundest approach. In our experience, over 99% of managers choose a statement characterizing the 9,9 Grid style as the soundest way of working with and through people in the accomplishment of organization tasks. This is strong evidence in support of its inherent soundness.

The problem is that Al (or Ben for that matter) cannot replicate his seminar experience and his new basis of insight for other team members. Al may be convinced that there is a better way to manage, but unfortunately that same thinking isn't automatically transferred to his subordinates. What is more likely to happen is that the boss they once saw as fairly predictable is now acting in an entirely unpredictable way. They don't know whether to be suspicious or worried for his health.

Therefore, Al might try to act in a "2:00 way" for a while with the remainder of his team continuing along the lines of a "10:00" way of thinking. The result of this continued "culture clash" eventually leads Al to say, "While I know that the 2:00 way is a better way to manage, it simply doesn't work in practice." Soon Al reverts to the 10:00 way of thinking and the status quo is once again firmly entrenched. Another effort to change fails.

Send the Whole Team to School One by One

The next angle is to say, "Al seems to have gotten something out of this learning. Maybe we need to get everyone on the same wavelength. There just might be some merit in the idea of us all going to school." This is a sound move, and this is the tack Ben takes. Now all team members can operate from a common set of assumptions. Only one problem remains and that is, "How do you stop team action long enough to allow change to occur, especially when people lack previous experience in doing so?" Team members return with new ideas about how to operate but soon they are caught up in daily activities that demand their attention. "Fade out" is the common result. Although team members may have acquired new skills, they have no practice using these with one another.

Take critique, for example. Liz may have learned this skill in an outside seminar or even in a program run by her own company. But she has no experience using critique with Al, or Gil, or any of the other team members. She may feel threatened for the stakes are considerably higher back on the job. Others may mistake her good intentions as having an axe to grind or in some other way wanting to take advantage of the opportunity to square past debts. The missing step that needs to be introduced is team building.

School Plus Team Building

The most successful approach is for all members to experience freedom of choice, one by one, and then to bring 9,9 into use by employing the systematic approach of Grid Team Building.

Team building is a three- or four-day on-the-job activity to apply what has been learned in school. We say Grid Team Building to emphasize the deep and dramatic impact on team culture that is required for real change to occur. Some approaches to team building overlook the important process issues that lie in the realm of R_2. In Grid Team Building team members examine in depth what it is that each member does that impedes greater productivity of the team, as well as what strengths each member possesses that can further be built upon. This is done in an atmosphere of mutual trust and respect in which each member aids the others to contribute his or her full resources, not merely in an additive way, but in an interdependent meshing of effort that leads to synergistic results.

Team building consists of activities that help the team exercise and evaluate every facet of its functioning. But how is this undertaken so that participants know what it is that is important to examine, and then how is it carried through to success?

Grid is key. Any activity can be analyzed from a Grid point of view. The seven alternatives provided constitute a comprehensive overview of the available options for conducting any undertaking.

The members of the team pick an option that characterizes how any significant activity is being performed. When the team convenes, these perceptions are compared, examples in support of each alternative are provided, and then agreement is reached as to the single option that is the most accurate assessment for the character of teamwork. Done in this way, the members of the team retain responsibility for diagnosing their own situation and they share and teach one another as they discuss, illustrate, and agree on the most objective self-assessment.

The second major step is to evaluate the options in order to identify the best way to perform the activity. Once again, as individuals, they have each chosen what they believe to be the soundest way for the team to operate with regard to the significant activity being diagnosed. They convene, compare perceptions, provide examples of consequences of operating in one way versus another way, and finally agree on what would characterize the soundest way to operate in regard to this activity.

Steps that follow are concerned with how to change from the actual to the optimal model. A gap has been created and team members now work together to establish concrete actions that lie within their area of responsibility and that they can take to move toward the soundest way of operation. These are documented in specific detail and put in a time frame of deadlines for success, progress checks, and replanning.

This is a structured model for the induction of change that provides participants (1) a framework within which to see, think, and diagnose; (2) a basis for selecting a model for the future; (3) action steps for implementation; and (4) a timeframe for assessing progress and success.

Listen as Ben's team "works" this model into their thinking about the manner in which they are controlled by their traditions, precedents, and past practices rather than by what is needed for successful accomplishment.

□ □ □

The team had just returned from a lunch break. There is a lot of enthusiasm and anticipation. Dan takes the initiative to refocus the group, quickly summarizing the last activity before they move into the next task.

"Okay," Dan began. "We selected the third alternative as representing how we have been operating. We agreed that the statement 'Cost consciousness is characterized by a fairly good balance between the necessity for cost control and meeting the desires of members, with occasional imbalances tolerated' expresses how we do things. Do we still agree on that?"

Members looked from one to another, nodding. Ed spoke for the group, "Yes, but I think we're beyond that right now. Under Al, cost consciousness consisted more of team members being continually reminded of cost considerations with members thanked for compliance, but I think we've moved beyond that stage."

"Definitely," said Liz, "but we need to keep on moving toward the ideal. Please read what we selected again, Dan."

"Okay," Dan responded. "For the ideal statement, that is, the one that should characterize our approach to cost consciousness, we selected item F: 'Team members know how their actions affect costs and thus are motivated to minimize expenditures.'"

All team members nodded agreement with this choice.

Ben said, "The next element has to do with team norms and standards. Frank, why don't you read it out loud for us?"

"Sure," answered Frank. "Traditions, precedents, and past practices . . . That's the stem and from now on I'm just going to call it T, P, and PP, for short. Now the first alternative reads, 'T, P, and PP are evaluated in the light of requirements for excellence and, when necessary, are modified or replaced through thoughtful discussions.'"

"That sounds pretty good," said Gil.

"Let's hear them all before we decide," said Liz. "Keep going, Frank."

"Wait a minute," said Dan. "Wouldn't it be easier if we wrote them up on a flip chart where we could see them altogether and compare them?"

"That's a good idea," said Ben. "I think it would be helpful for our discussion. Do you want to volunteer, Frank?"

"Sure," Frank said good-heartedly. "I'm already up and running."

Frank moved up to the flip chart and listed all the alternatives as follows.

Traditions, precedents, and past practices

A. Are evaluated in the light of requirements for excellence and, when necessary, are modified or replaced through thoughtful discussions.
B. Provide guidelines for what is enough to get by.
C. Are established and supported by those in authority; new ways of doing things are suspect until proven beyond reasonable doubt they will succeed.
D. Promote good relationships among people, sometimes even at the expense of profit and production.

E.   Are recognized as representing "tried and true" standard operating procedures that keep things on an even keel.

F.   Are pragmatic and based on common sense; it is up to each individual to interpret them according to the specific situation.

G.   Promote results; practices not oriented toward production are not tolerated.

"That second one—'enough to get by'—is 1,1," said Gil. "I know that by heart!"

"We're looking for the ideal statement, right?" asked Ed. Before anyone could answer he firmly stated, "There's no doubt in my mind. That's statement C."

"I don't think so, sport," said Liz. "It has a distinct 9,1 flavor to me."

"You're putting the cart before the horse," said Frank. "We're still on actual."

Ed wasn't ready to give up. "Just a minute. Liz, read that last item. That's 9,1. Don't you agree?"

"You're right," Liz conceded. "But I still don't think C is the ideal. Actually, I guess it's 9+9. That's paternalism, isn't it?"

Ed still looked perplexed but Ben interceded.

"I'd agree with you," said Ben. "But we're getting off the task. Let's determine the actual for this team before we decide where we would like to be. Let me ask it as a question, 'In actual fact, what are the norms and standards, that is, the traditions, precedents, and past practices, that guide our current team action?'"

"Well," said Liz, "we do let ourselves be guided—too much, I think—by the tried and true. We feel safe with what has worked in the past and tend to shy away from anything new or novel, even if it offers a good opportunity. We're too conservative."

They were silent for a moment and then Gil spoke up. "We're complacent. Remember the bid we almost lost?" Everyone's eyes grew big and they nodded their heads.

"We don't pursue excellence as a norm," said Frank. "'Good enough!' is our motto."

"I think we measure ourselves by last year, that is, we try to do a little bit better," said Ben, "but we never stop and look at what we could really be achieving if we put our minds to it."

"I think you're right," said Ed. "We are committed to optimizing the status quo but we never look beyond that."

"The fifth alternative characterizes how we have operated up to this point," said Liz. "It's not bad. We stay afloat. But, you know, if you really stop and think about it, we could be doing so much better."

Everybody agreed.

"Okay," said Frank, "if that's the actual, what's the ideal?"

"That first alternative," blurted out Gil. "From what Liz just said, it follows that we should be measuring ourselves against standards of excellence, not against past achievement or even present performance."

"I agree," said Liz. "And that last part about 'thoughtful discussions,' well, that's just a fancy way to say ongoing critique! And that is a skill we really need to develop."

"Right," said Ed. "You've even sold me on that one."

"Does everyone agree that that's the ideal?" Liz looked around.

"I guess so, Liz," said Ben. "That's a valid standard for future performance as far as I'm concerned. I would really like to see us operate according to criteria of excellence in the future."

Ed ventured to tie this agreement down by getting to specifics. "Beyond these general statements, what would have to change for us to be able to say, 'We're driven by excellence?'"

"We'd have to develop an attitude of inquiry," said Liz. "Like on that successful bid we got, or should I call it the 'near miss'? We'd have to be on the lookout, constantly probing and checking and cross-checking."

"I agree," said Gil. "And along with inquiry goes advocacy. We'd all have to be responsible for advocating our point of view so that the best thinking got out on the table. Furthermore, if I ever fall back into my 1,1 corner, I'd expect you to pull me out or charge me rent!"

Everyone laughed because the changes that had taken place in Gil had been none less than dramatic.

"I have another," said Ed. He paused a moment before proceeding. "It goes hand in hand with thoroughness. I think we've had a norm of superficiality rather than an attitude of deep digging."

"Can you give us an example?" asked Ben.

"I can," said Liz. "And this is going to be like 'True Confessions' but I want to come clean." Everyone waited to hear what Liz might have to say.

Liz continued. "Ed, remember that report you gave to Al for his feedback?" Ed acknowledged the particular incident. "And Al was busy so he passed it along to me?"

"Yes, I remember," said Ed. "I'll have to say that I was a little bit irritated with Al for passing it to you, but, then, you were the one who caught that glaring error, so . . ."

"Only by sheer coincidence, Ed," said Liz.

"What do you mean?" asked Ed. "You questioned the numbers and when I reran them through the computer, you were absolutely right."

"No, Ed," confessed Liz. "I only put a question mark there because I had no idea what the calculation was all about. That was a note to myself so I could check it out with someone who might provide an explanation. I would have erased it but then I forgot about it altogether."

"Then why did you take credit for it?" Ed looked somewhat perturbed.

"I only took what you handed me on a silver platter," said Liz. "I was too embarrassed to tell the truth. It seemed easier to let it slide by."

"I think we all appreciate your honesty," said Ben. "That's a good example, though, of our typically shallow approach."

"I know I could be a lot more thorough," said Gil. "If I just sat down and reviewed the material before coming to a meeting, I'd have a lot more ideas about how to solve problems and how to take advantage of the opportunities that we've so often let slide by."

"I think one of the main things," said Dan, "is that we develop better communication between us. Then we're more likely to have shared values about how we go about doing things."

"It's more than that," said Liz. "We could communicate until we're blue in the face and still live by outmoded traditions, precedents, and past practices. I see two major areas of potential improvement that would enable us to say that we're driven by excellence. The first is a willingness to give and to receive constructive critique and feedback. In the last few months there's not one of us in this room who hasn't acknowledged a deficiency in this area."

"Basically it's been absent," said Frank.

"I certainly agree with you," said Ben. "What's the second one, Liz?"

"I'm sure you know but I'll say it. It's our avoidance of conflict," said Liz. "We each have our own little way to avoid a confrontation but it all spells the same thing. Conflicts never get solved."

"Never may be too strong, Liz," said Dan. "But I think you're right. I'm not very fond of conflict myself and I'm not that wild about critique and feedback. But I realize that I lean just a bit in the 1,9 direction and I'm committed to becoming more 9,9, with the help and support of you and my subordinates as well. I don't know about this change stuff. I asked my subordinates for help and they sure are being helpful. They've given me some feedback that's tough to swallow but, on the other hand, I believe I can say that for the first time in my management career I have the respect of my people."

Everyone smiled because change had begun in each and every one of them. The team was pleased with their effort thus far. Having concluded this element, they moved on to look at some of the other norms/standards that had guided team action in the past as well as what might guide it in the future. Some of these included communication, team decision making, planning, initiative, and performance standards.

□ □ □

As the team went through the different elements of team culture, they discovered that they had been operating in a fairly safe 5,5 way in the past. They unanimously agreed on the 9,9 alternatives to each element as the ideal model that they should strive toward in future team interaction. Studying the past and comparing it with a future goal is only one part of the exercise. It helps the team to see that change is needed, but by itself it doesn't identify much that is specific and concrete. That is the reason for agreeing on particulars that give the team a comprehensive and operational view of what would characterize a truly excellent situation.

So the next activity involved having the team determine specific steps for how to move from a 5,5 stance toward a model of 9,9 excellence. For example, they provided personal feedback to each member. Taking on Gil, they told him, "Gil, you're going to have to get off your tail and really commit yourself to a total push in the future. You've come out of your shell but we're asking you to do more. You're still in the habit of sitting back in your office. We want you out where the action is." Gil agreed that this was true. He asked the team for help to identify action steps that would aid him to become more involved. This was done with each of the team members in turn, including Ben.

The question was raised, "How can we ensure that we stay committed to these agreements we have reached?" This was discussed and then it was proposed that they set a time to convene in three months to critique their progress. Someone added that by that time they might also see even more ways they would be able to improve team performance based on experience up to that point. This met with unanimous agreement and Gil took responsibility for setting up the details and reminding everyone of the date when it arose.

Cockpit Behavior—A Real-Life Case Study of Change

Team building has been used in many areas of human interaction for both industrial and non-industrial application on a worldwide basis. An example of this approach is the one successfully employed by United Airlines in its efforts to strengthen cockpit teamwork to promote air safety. The concern for production in this case is a concern for corporate bottomline in terms of maintaining flight schedules, preventing loss of planes, or hulls, and enhancing the reputation of the airline in the eyes of the public and government regulatory agencies. The concern for people is apparent in the desire to prevent loss of lives for both passengers and crew members and to create a working environment where people feel involved and fulfilled by what they are doing.

The traditional culture of the cockpit is one of strict authority/ obedience. The tendency is for the captain to centralize authority while excluding input from the first and second officers, falling back on a compliance-based style of leadership that dictates what others are to do without question. The description that follows is taken from real life and serves to illustrate the problem. An air crash is described that could potentially have been avoided had fuller use of resources in the cockpit been examined and used in the decision-making process:

It looked as though all systems were go for United Airlines Flight 173, carrying 8 crew members and 181 passengers on board, to make its descent into the Portland airport. Visibility and weather conditions were good; air traffic was not a problem; the flight was on schedule. Indeed, there was no reason to believe that all aboard the fated flight would not soon be home with their families or departing for their next destination.

As the landing gear was lowered for touch-down, one of the three indicators failed to light, signaling that the gear had not locked in place. The captain quickly pulled out of the landing formation and proceeded to put the plane in a racetrack pattern while he and the first officer sought to determine where the malfunction lay. It could be the gear itself or it might just be a faulty light switch.

During this time, the second officer was keeping the crew apprised of the diminishing fuel situation, but the captain's focus remained centered on the equipment factor, almost to the exclusion of the potential fuel dilemma. At one point, the captain requested that the second officer calculate fuel for another fifteen minutes, and the second officer replied, "Not enough." No further action was taken as attention was turned back to the equipment malfunction.

Approximately one hour after the initial landing attempt, all four engines suddenly ceased to operate and the plane dropped like a lead weight. As fortune would have it, the plane snagged on some electrical wires, which lessened the impact of the crash. Nonetheless, ten people on the aircraft died—eight passengers, a flight attendant, and, ironically, the second officer. In the aftermath, it was concluded that less than ten gallons of gas remained within the plane's tanks.

Had the captain acknowledged the fuel shortage dilemma and instructed the second officer to calculate the remaining time and options available, the situation might have been rectified. The tragedy was not a function of lack of time, but rather one of poor use of time. As a team, they might have discussed the implications of potential problems and determined actions to be taken, making sound decisions based on the information they did know, delegating responsibility to each member to seek answers to what they didn't know, and setting in place a deadline for when some specified action must occur to avoid crisis.

This learning is significant, clearly bringing into view a new formulation of the teamwork problem: "How can cockpit leadership be experienced to bring forth collaborative use of resources in the interest of safe flying?" This is the confrontation approach to conflict resolution with the captain becoming accessible to the potential contributions of colleagues in an atmosphere reinforced by norms of openness and candor. Although there can be no doubt that the captain is in charge and maintains responsibility for reaching the ultimate decision, one key to increased safety lies in keeping the crisis situation open to interaction as long as possible or necessary rather than shutting it down. It is critical for the captain (or any leader—executive, manager, or supervisor) to keep information flowing back and forth instead of issuing arbitrary commands to "do this" or "do that."

Although insufficient time is often used to justify the centralization of authority—whether in the cockpit or in the boardroom—it is, in fact, only a rare case where time is actually too limited to tap into other resources. Whether one minute or thirty, there usually exists sufficient time to permit input that could make a vital difference.

Before undertaking this program to resolve the teamwork problem, United Airlines had already begun to institute changes in technical procedures and crew selection. The new objective they sought to accomplish was the development of a multifaceted, all-encompassing change strategy, one that would lead to improved problem solving and also would create an atmosphere of openness within the cockpit that could lead to more efficient and safe operation.

The first step in the program was to provide crew members with an operational understanding of behavioral dynamics. The Managerial Grid was used as the framework to bring about understanding and to provide a common "language" in the succeeding application phases of the program. The Grid provided a basis for examining each of the seven leadership styles within the cockpit, allowing those pilots who participated in the training experiences to draw their own conclusions about the effectiveness of the various leadership approaches.

In the initial experiments, first and second officers were excluded from the training on the premise that it might embarrass captains who were seeking to practice new leadership skills. The idea was that if captains could learn how to solicit input from other crew members (in contrast to the traditionally 9,1-oriented way in which they tended to exercise authority) that this would solve the teamwork dilemma. In other words, they determined to use the "Send the Boss to School" approach. The problem with doing this is much as we have previously described. The captains went to school and became convinced that 9,9 was indeed a better approach for operating a cockpit. They received critique and feedback from their own peers indicating that while their strong leadership sometimes got the job done, the quality of the decision made often suffered. In other words, they had missed sounder solutions because crew members had been given little opportunity to provide necessary data. Even in cases where input of a problem-solving nature had been offered, it had not been "heard." By participating in this training, captain after captain became aware of how conventional behavior had prevented them from tapping available resources before deciding which course of action to implement.

Like Al, many of the captains returned to the line with a fundamental commitment to change, convinced that a 2:00 or 9,9 way of conducting the cockpit was the sounder approach. They sought to implement dynamic leadership according to the conventional ideas for bringing about improvement, that is, they "intuitively" selected modeling as the way to promote the desired behavior. In effect, they said, "The way to get better cockpit performance is for me to act differently, to open the situation up, and to let crew members experience the benefits of greater participation in cockpit problem diagnosis." What happened when captains had a new view of how to exercise power and authority and the importance of openness and candor norm, but first and second officers still did not? Like Al's team, crew members continued to operate according to the 10:00 norm (waiting for the captain to take charge), while, as perceived by them, the captain was acting in a contradictory and incomprehensible way.

For example, during a flight, the following scenario might occur. Some condition not covered by standard operating procedure arises, and the captain turns to the other crew members and openly solicits their input: "We seem to have a problem. What do you think we should do?" The other two crew members, traditionally dependent upon the captain for direction, especially in situations of crisis, are shocked. Their immediate thought is, "Why is he asking our opinion? He's the leader. He's supposed to have all the answers. If *he* doesn't know what to do, we're in trouble!" While the captain expects a spirited and enthusiastic response, crew members continue to act in the traditional manner, unaware of alternative and perhaps sounder approaches to problem solving.

After a while, many of these captains concluded that the 2:00 way of mobilizing resources was sound on paper and even produced better results in experiments, but that it was simply impractical for use in real-life flying. The result was that they shifted their reliance back to centralized captain authority.

A significant factor is revealed in these experiments. If all team members do not understand the importance of open interchange, their expectations are shaken. That is, if a boss seeks to create an atmosphere of openness and candor and turns to subordinates for input, this may be interpreted as uncertainty, weakness, or indecisiveness, thus increasing confusion and chaos. The key point is that whenever a norm or standard of conduct is shared, the problem of change ceases to be an individual matter. It becomes a group or organizational issue. Ideally, all norms-carriers must be involved in changing the norms by which they have previously interacted with one another.

The thinking that emerged was that participants needed the opportunity to reach a consensus on what was being learned, thereby establishing shared norms. Such episodes demonstrated that it was critical for all crew members to engage in the dilemma-solving training so as to create a common way of thinking about how best to mobilize resources. This elevated the change effort to the third level: Send everybody to school one by one. This was a sound step but more was needed. This training intervention in and of itself failed to bring about an immediate and effective turnaround in anything so deep as cockpit culture, particularly with shifting membership in teams, as is true in the airline industry. Thus, team building to deepen Grid understandings as they affect cockpit safety practices was seen as the logical extension to the change effort.

This step in the process is undertaken in the simulators used for training pilots in 727's, 747's, etc. During the simulated flight, the instrument presentations and circumstances that the crews encounter create "difficulties" that test crew effectiveness under nonroutine circumstances. Crew members are aware that a video camera has been mounted in the back of the cockpit, and they can view the videotape later as first-hand evidence of their effectiveness in dealing with the situation. The simulator instructor records the critical incidents to be focused on in critique. These points are made known when crew members receive the videotape for personal review.

Crews then assemble, usually as three-person groups, each responsible for conducting its own critique. The tape is played, with particular attention placed on critical incidents that reveal issues of teamwork effectiveness. Crews play the tape, discuss it, rewind it, and play it again—sometimes repeatedly until a consensus is reached among the group as to what happened. They also seek to determine the soundest handling of the circumstance as it took place. A standard reaction observed in crew after crew is that seeing themselves and their interactions under simulator conditions approximates the "real thing." Therefore, it offers validating evidence as to the importance of effective teamwork, along with skill in implementing it.

In this way, crews were given the opportunity to apply what they had learned from their initial training intervention to an "on-the-job" setting by solving dilemmas in actual flight simulators. The testing and reinforcement of leadership principles under near-flight conditions were sufficient to strengthen the shared readiness to implement a 2:00 (open cockpit) culture. Yearly reinforcement of these principles under flight simulator conditions is still underway and expected to continue well into the future.

The Grid training is required for all United Airlines pilots and is currently in use by thousands of flying personnel from domestic and international carriers as well as many from corporate aviation and the military. Most of these follow up with recurrent training of the kind described here where crews work through incidents or scenarios in a flight simulator and then critique how well they use the available resources.

The organization development principle that is clearly identified in this example is that all who participate in carrying out an activity must necessarily share similar values and therefore contribute behavior consistent with those values in order for effective performance to result. Otherwise, when one member of a working party embraces certain values that are unrecognized by others with whom he or she must cooperate, one of several things is bound to happen. The person whose values are contradictory either chooses to leave the situation or else slowly but surely comes to accept the values embraced by the others, given that the others refuse to reverse their points of view. When a person has learned something of a value-relevant nature in a training or development environment, this new value or concept, if ignored or contradicted by others in the workplace, is abandoned in the interest of moving forward. The unfortunate consequence is that old values that may be obsolete and even counterproductive are retained.

The Discovery of "Teamwork Plus"

Before we leave the concept of teamwork to explore the still deeper issues involved in organization change, that is, what can happen on a systemwide basis in a whole organization, we need to examine what teamwork really means from a 9,9 perspective.

Teamwork has come to be widely appreciated within business and industry. What the term really means, however, and how people behave with regard to accomplishing goals in interaction with one another is an important question that remains to be clarified.

The most frequent use of the word teamwork is in the circumstance where each person in a social setting has a job to do that bears some connection to the other jobs that are collected into the group. When each person contributes his or her own effort a good result is expected. Under these conditions jobs are often well structured and defined. The connections between them have been made in advance with the expectation that all will run smoothly. The whole is equal to the sum of its parts because, when each contributes the piece for which he or she is accountable, the end result adds up to 100%.

This concept of teamwork has led to important developments in the field of job analysis, as well as to the profession of job analyst. The idea is that any complex work can be subdivided, differentiated, segregated into its component parts, and then recombined in such a way as to ensure effective coordination. It is a rational model for how work can be broken into its elements and put together again in a reasonable way that permits all the parts to fit.

But there is another meaning. It is contained within the idea of interdependent teamwork. Interdependent teamwork is beyond the additive concept outlined above. It occurs when each person contributes that part for which he or she is responsible but goes further and maintains a constant monitoring and surveillance of how the whole is emerging. Under the interdependent concept, if a problem of performance is being experienced by a team member, it not only is the responsibility of that individual to solve it but, equally, it is the responsibility of the person who is observing the whole to take whatever actions are necessary either to help the person who is having the difficulty or to bring the difficulty being encountered to the attention of others who are in a position to exercise initiative.

Because the first meaning, i.e., additive teamwork, is so widely accepted as the "official meaning," the interdependent concept of teamwork might be called "teamwork plus." It is more than the mechanical fitting of the parts together to produce the overall end result. It acknowledges the existence of a human element which is not subject to literal definition but goes beyond mere responsibility for one's own actions. Some examples of how important this distinction is suggest what is needed to gain the unique advantages that are available to any team from effective interdependence.

Consider the surgical amphitheater. A number of medical specialists surround an operating table. The surgeon in charge leads the effort. He or she does so in the context of also having a direct technical contribution to make. Much attention is focused by the surgeon in charge on that part of the operation for which he or she is uniquely responsible. In addition, there are many ancillary personnel who support the total effort. The anesthesiologist is concerned with the patient's ability to tolerate the surgery and to ensure that the pain is not so great as to be unbearable. Other specialists, nurses, and other medical personnel contribute their own expertise. These sometimes reach far beyond the operating room itself, into the medical laboratory where tests are carried out with feedback critical to decisions as to how the operation should proceed being provided in a timely way.

This is an optimal example of teamwork. Each of the job activities entailed in the operation is specific. Each member is a specialist and knows, in competency terms, what is expected. The underlying premise is that when each has done his or her assignment based on specialist knowledge, the overall result should be favorable.

In spite of the many efforts that go into such a complex and challenging activity, often all does not go well. Numerous explanations are offered but three seem pertinent. One is that each of the various participants concentrates on his or her own speciality and loses sight of the whole. The phrase for this is, "No one was looking after the patient." In some technically legitimate sense, this is what can happen when the concept of teamwork being implemented is additive in character.

The second difficulty encountered is that "things fall through the crack." These are activities that need to be undertaken, but they are literally not within the job specifications of any participant. This can happen when a novel problem occurs and there is insufficient precedent to indicate within whose job responsibilities the initiative for dealing with the problem lies. In an ever changing world of tools, technology, and competency variations, the "crack" problem is an inevitable one.

The additive concept is based on the premise that these crack problems do not exist. The underlying thesis is that teamwork can be regarded as a closed system. All the variables and influences expected to be at work have already been identified and accounted for and, therefore, there are no "cracks." Yet we know that human activity is an open system and that what happens under any set of circumstances cannot be fully determined in advance.

A third difficulty arises from the indirect aspect of additive teamwork. People do not interact with one another, yet neither has the desirable solution. However, together, they can find it. This is $1+1=3$; not the $1+1=2$ concept inherent in additive teamwork.

Interdependent teamwork offers a solution to the three limitations that arise from additive teamwork.

When individuals are responsible not only for executing the activities assigned them but also maintaining a constant concern for the end result, accomplishment is not by the individuals exclusively or additively but by the team working interdependently. Then everyone engaged in the activity is responsible for the "whole" and everyone is alert for problems that otherwise get lost in the shuffle. This means each person has accepted the challenge of looking over the next person's shoulder to see that what's going on "in the neighborhood" is what should be occurring in the interest of the overall outcome or achievement. However, looking over the other person's shoulder has come to be anything but widely accepted, and the counterreactions are, "Mind your own business," or

"People who live in glass houses should not throw stones." There are social and work norms, in other words, that operate to severely limit the use of interdependent teamwork no matter how desirable it otherwise might be.

How do we get beyond additive teamwork to "Teamwork Plus"? The advantages of interdependent teamwork are clear and yet the difficulties encountered in achieving them are equally massive. The development problem becomes one of how teamwork situations can be dealt with so as to shift them from the additive concept to the interdependent basis.

Team building as described in this chapter is one means for doing so. For the sake of illustration, let's examine this from the perspective of several of the key dimensions of teamwork.

For example, one is concerned with how the boss exercises power and authority. If a boss's power and authority are applied against the concept of additive teamwork, then it is inevitable that the basis of cooperation is additive in character. If the boss embraces the interdependent concept, the conditions are set which may enable "teamwork plus" to be realized. Power and authority, in other words, are critical regarding which concept of teamwork is implemented.

A second idea in teamwork is with regard to the tasks themselves and who is to implement each of the multiple tasks needed to accomplish the whole. This is the idea of structure and differentiation. It is that area to which job analysts have contributed much. Now a new need has arisen that is beyond the job analyst's conventional role. While the job analyst may contribute to structure and differentiation, his or her contribution is unlikely to move a team to "teamwork plus." Team members themselves may be in the best position to see how structure and differentiation are impeding or helping coordination as they directly experience it. They are the ones who must introduce the necessary changes for bringing interdependence about. Grid Team Building enables them to do this.

The third area of team building for shifting from additive to interdependent teamwork deals with norms and standards. If the norm that prevails is "Mind your own business," people relate to one another premised on that norm. If on the other hand, the operating norm in the team is "Brother's keeper," then each person feels the responsibility for not only doing his or her own task in the fullest possible way but for ensuring that others all make their task contributions in such a manner as to result in synergistic achievement; the whole being more than the sum of its parts. The "brother's keeper" norm also increases the likelihood that problems are no longer overlooked because rather than "no one" being responsible, all have a vested interest in achieving success.

Critique and feedback are the essential activities for learning from any experience. Without critique and feedback it is evident that teamwork remains additive in character. This goes hand in hand with maintaining an atmosphere of openness and candor, based on the new norm that feedback and critique is offered in the sense of mutual helpfulness.

When viewed in a deeper way, trust and respect are probably the human emotions of key significance to interdependent teamwork. If the members of a team have trust in one another, they appreciate that a challenge from a colleague is in the interest of team achievement and has no stamp of personal aggrandizement, viciousness, or vindictiveness about it. It is motivated by mutuality and helpfulness. Trust and respect are the essential ingredients for other team members being able to accept help, with understanding of the reason for its being given rather than the result of a "busybody" or "troublemaker" or someone who has to be a "Mr. Know-it-all."

Team building premised on the interdependent model can be the single greatest insurance that human resources are more fully utilized. This in turn promotes creativity and innovation from the human interactions produced by teamness.

Summary

Team building provides a second step in the direction of positive change. Al's group as presented throughout this book clearly demonstrates how a team can fall into unproductive habits that reduce the use of R_1 resources to a low level, with the price paid in failure to get high level R_3 teamwork results. This is so even where the individual members of the team are talented and capable of contributing significantly above their current performance. It can be a matter of whether it's additive or interdependent effort. Without developing a team through a formal team building approach to form an effective unit for collaboration and problem solving, these talents continue to be wasted.

Earlier we said that team building is only the first step toward real change. Real change within an organization begins at the top and that is the issue we turn to next.

Chapter 13

Organization Development: Bringing About Change in a Big Way!

The team took Ben up on his suggestion to participate in learning the Grid. Following this they undertook team building. Ben's team continued the effort down through each of their own departments. R_3 results went up, up, up. This didn't escape the attention of headquarters.

Two years have now elapsed. Ben has been invited by the chief executive officer, Tony Ramos, to meet with him and key members of his staff to explore the implications of this development work and to see what it might mean if that kind of effort were to be embraced by the organization as a whole. Harriet Turner and Joe Thompson joined these discussions.

□ □ □

"We've been dabbling in the organization development business for several years now," Harriet began, "and I've worked closely with Ben on the efforts within his division. He's begun to get some real payout."

"Our efforts have undoubtedly been good," said Ben. "You can measure them by our results. But it's not OD exactly. It's Division Organization Development. OD begins at the corporate top." He looked at Tony.

"Well, I've been quite interested myself in what you've been up to," stated Tony. "That's why I cleared today for this meeting. Harriet has painted in a lot of the broad details but I'd like to get a first-hand version from you on what's been going on."

"It's my pleasure," replied Ben. "A lot has happened in the last two years. Let me start by filling in the chronology. I've been with Celarmco seven years now. Prior to that I worked for our main competitor across town. Part of my induction here was to go to a Grid. I found it an exhilarating experience, just what I needed to get a good start. It didn't involve a lot of step-by-step mechanics; rather it cut through surface problems in a way that helped me see fundamental impediments to human effectiveness in mobilizing resources—and it really made me focus on my own leadership in that regard. I think you would find it to be a very useful first step to go to a Grid."

Tony laughed. "I think I'm in a two-to-one situation. I know Harriet feels the same as you do. In fact, she's been pushing for some time to get me into a chief exec seminar. I've listened and been impressed with what I heard, but I always seem to have other commitments that press for attention. I call it lack of time but at a deeper level I think my reservation is that I'm simply not convinced the expenditure of time and effort is justified."

"I understand," said Ben. "But I'd add that I know a couple of top execs at your level who started with similar attitudes. After reexamining their own commitments, they finally participated in a Grid seminar. Neither has any regrets about this step. In fact one told me he had a half-million-dollar training budget and this was the first time he had ever spent a nickel on himself. In any event, when Al moved up to the Global Businesses Committee and I was asked to take over, I immediately saw it as a wonderful opportunity to experiment with the possibility of implementing a change effort within our division. It seemed an ideal situation for undertaking a project to mobilize human effectiveness in a way quite different from classical approaches to management."

"That's the experience," said Tony, "that I'd like to understand in more detail. You see, your results have made me look up and pay attention. Something is going on that is working that wasn't going on before. Either you've got us all fooled or else deep and widespread change is taking place. So tell me. What exactly have you done in your division? What's this Grid magic all about?"

"First of all," began Ben, "I haven't done it alone. I have made full use of Harriet's knowledge and background about organization development. She and I deliberated how to proceed at each major choice point. The result of this effort has been that our decisions have been grounded in fundamental values rather than convenience or what might have seemed pragmatic at the time. When I took over from Al, I formulated the dilemma to my team and encouraged people to get into Grids. Just that first step moved us forward in terms of how we operated."

"You all began to communicate," interjected Harriet, "and team members started 'hearing' what the others were saying."

"Exactly," said Ben. "From there we decided to get more people involved. The reactions varied but were generally positive. People at lower levels were tired of the status quo. In some ways they were more aware of the problems than we had been. They sensed that change was in the air. We did encounter some problems, though, and they had to do with tempo. We got into a situation of the 'haves' and 'have nots.' So we picked up the pace, using diagonal slice, to get more people involved."

"Diagonal what?" asked Tony.

"We had started on a horizontal slice basis," explained Harriet. "Doing Grid level by level in the hierarchy. Diagonal slice as the basis for seminar composition cuts down through the levels of hierarchy, not in a vertical way, but taking people level by level diagonally so as not to include any boss-subordinate pairings."

"What's the problem with having a boss and subordinate to-gether?" asked Tony. "I would think that I could learn a lot from my direct reports."

"Obviously," said Harriet, "and you get that opportunity in Team Building, Phase 2. But first you need to develop the skills of openness and candor, and the Grid Seminar is designed to help people do that by providing them a laboratory experience in which they can practice and develop these skills by learning to use critique and feedback. Therefore, a boss and subordinate may be present in the same seminar but they do not engage in learning in the same study team."

"I understand," said Tony. "That's great insight. Go on."

"The main conclusion at this point," continued Ben, "was very positive. People who attended liked it. They recognized that the Grid is based on sound values that offer every individual a range for seeing how personal effectiveness might be increased."

"And productivity began to soar," Tony interrupted enthusiastically.

"Not exactly," said Ben. "Although the reactions were favorable and people had embraced the learning, not much real change was produced. The actual work teams continued to operate in pretty much the same way. This was true in our own team as well. You could say that we were a bit more tough-minded. We put our individual resources together in a more effective way. At least $1+1+1+1+1$ equaled 5 and not 4 or 3 or 2. But I wanted us to achieve something more. I wanted us to shoot for 10 or 15."

"Was that a realistic objective?" Tony asked dubiously.

"Yes!" Ben answered emphatically. "As you can see by our results today."

"Ben and I discussed this matter in depth," said Harriet. "Although team building seemed like the logical next step, I suggested he enroll in an Organization Development Seminar."

"Tell me about that," said Tony.

"An OD Seminar is a strategic and logistical study of how to make a business more effective rather than a personalized study of personal leadership effectiveness," Harriet explained. "That enabled Ben to see the bigger change picture."

"To sum up operationally our progress at this point," Ben continued, "we had taken the first step of immersing ourselves in Grid concepts and values but we had not taken the second. That is, applying these concepts and values for diagnosing our effectiveness as a real-life team. Once it was seen from this perspective, we all committed a three-day block of time when the operation of the division could be delegated and we were able to break away and concentrate on learning and sharing more about ourselves as a team."

"I can see the value, based on my reading of Chapter 11 last night," said Tony, reflecting. "When I first took over ten years ago, the situation was tight. People had been subjected to years to close control by my predecessor. I tried to loosen that up a bit and to give people more leeway to move on to the problems they should have been dealing with. I think it helped but then we plateaued. More recently, the way I've come to see it is that we're like a bunch of islands. Each has its own center of energy and its own momentum, moving forward like gyroscopes but not in a common direction."

"And occasionally two of them hit," added Harriet, "head to head."

"Right," said Joe. "Collide might be a better way to express it."

"That sounds like intergroup conflict to me," stated Ben.

"It couldn't be anything else," remarked Tony. "But what's the solution?"

"Well, for a start," said Ben, "let me describe the big picture as I learned it in the OD Seminar. That might give a clue."

□ □ □

How do you go about shifting from current practices of leadership rooted in the organization's history and culture to stronger and more effective practices based on principles of sound human effectiveness? To speak about organization change is well and good, but the fact is that it is much more difficult to bring about than individual change. You don't need permission from anyone in order to undertake the latter, but the former requires a high degree of cooperation from others, and it can't be had by decree. The incentive, of course, is that the payout is much greater. True organization development is a systemwide approach to change aimed at improving the "whole" organization. Individual development helps individuals; that's about as far as it goes. Team development may facilitate better team interaction contingent on a team being able to operate in a sound and effective manner within the context of the larger organization culture. Organization development helps organizations; it is the big change we are looking for.

The first question to consider in undertaking an OD effort is "Who's in charge?" If you are in charge, your ability to effect change is far different than if you are not in charge. That was Ben's dilemma before he took over leadership of the division. Even then, he had to exercise within the constraints of the larger organizational system. Ben had enough autonomy to initiate the beginning of OD within his division but only the CEO of the organization could launch a full-scale OD effort. We want to explore how to go about the introduction of organization change under both these situations because there are steps that can be undertaken in either case.

Are You the Person in Charge?

There is a straightforward answer to this question. If you are the top person, you are in charge. This means that there is no one in a position above you from whom you have to get approval or authorization for the actions you take. Others may guide or counsel you, but you shoulder ultimate responsibility for the decisions. If you are the chief executive officer, you may be responsible to a board of directors and be required to go to them for permission to take certain actions. Nevertheless, it is still up to you to determine how to use organization resources in the most profitable manner. If you decide to take the steps necessary to bring sound principles of behavior into everyday use, you can do this under your own authority.

An important distinction needs to be made between the top person and the person in charge because they are not necessarily one and the same. For example, what if you are head of a subsidiary or the manager of a plant, district, or region? Under these conditions, you may or may not be the person in charge, even though your job description says you are the responsible person. One key test is whether you have line authority for expending funds. If you don't, you probably are not the person in charge. There are exceptions, of course. You may need to report to a higher up what you intend to do and to receive a perfunctory review and a nod of the head to proceed. For all practical purposes, you are in charge. Take Ben as a case in point. When he assumed leadership of Al's team, he developed plans to proceed with a development effort within his division. These plans were checked out with Harriet, but essentially he had the autonomy to implement his decisions in this area as he saw fit, granted the requirement to design division change with the limits imposed by the larger context.

If you do not have the authority to approve organizational change, you are not the person in charge. Introducing change is a different problem in this situation. You may still be able to wield a lot of influence in that your ideas can stimulate a keen interest among others. Therefore, even though it may not be within your authority to initiate development action, you may see the importance of sound development.

Let's assume that neither you nor your boss is the person in charge. What then? In this situation you have no direct linkage to the person in charge. Several possibilities still exist to get your ideas heard and circulated to places where such authority exists. Word of mouth is a significant approach to get others interested in development. Or you may distribute literature or pass this book along to get them thinking about theory-based change. You might choose to attend a Grid Seminar to evaluate that option for yourself. This can put you in a position to recommend it to others if you find it a worthy endeavor. If your boss starts thinking along the same lines as you, he or she may serve as the foundation for interest higher up in the organization. All of these are ways to get the message to the person in charge.

In the last chapter we looked at team building, which deals with one unit of the organization. Organization development means seeing the organization itself as the unit of change. While individuals may change on a one-by-one basis, it is highly unlikely that the sum of these individual efforts is meaningful in an organizational context. Grid Organization Development is development that focuses on lifting the level of an entire organization to a higher plane of achievement. It is a fully integrated approach that can result in rethinking how to optimize the operation of an entire system. But, before we proceed, let's examine the options.

We return to the story. Ben is describing in his own words how he put a Grid OD program into place.

□ □ □

"I can really see the value of a theory-based approach like the Grid," said Tony. "You said earlier that you went to a Grid Seminar when you came with this company. So you knew about the Grid all these years. When you took over Al's team, how did you actually go about implementing an OD project? You'll need to spell it out because this is relatively unfamiliar territory for me."

Ben laughed. "Okay, no problem. Before describing how we did it, let me raise several considerations for introducing this kind of an effort that are critical factors in its success. This issue is particularly significant for you as head of the organization."

"You've got my attention," Tony replied enthusiastically. "Please proceed."

"First, let me inquire," asked Ben, "how much do you know about the Grid?"

"Oh, I know the Grid itself," explained Tony. "The seven styles and the principles of 9,9 management."

"Okay. That's a good beginning." Ben cleared his throat and went on. "Obviously, it's important to develop awareness about the importance of an OD effort among people in the organization. But you can't order their commitment and involvement. Issuing a mandate that 'This is what we're going to do' just won't cut it. It violates the very principles of 9,9 that you're seeking to instill."

"Can't I just assume that they'll see the value?" asked Tony. "I don't mean to be naive but won't they know a good thing when they see it?"

"I don't think that's the point," said Ben. "They may or they may not. The point is that it's contrary to the very thing you're trying to achieve. It's you saying, 'Here, take this medicine because it's good for you.'"

"Or, 'do as I say, not as I do,'" added Harriet.

"I see what you mean," remarked Tony.

"A sounder approach is to introduce exploratory steps that permit people to become oriented to the possibilities. Then they can test the implications of Grid OD without being obliged to swallow it hook, line, and sinker. Done in a planned way like this lets people develop their own commitment through a series of self-convincing experiences. Orientation without obligation creates the opportunity to test the temperature before plunging in and produces awareness of possibilities from which a conviction-based decision can then be made."

"Bravo!" exclaimed Tony. "I've definitely got the point. What are these exploratory steps?"

"Some of them include the following, basically in this sequence," replied Ben. "First, of course, there is background reading. People can begin to educate themselves about behavioral science and how it can be used to strengthen organization effectiveness."

"Like reading the Grid book?" Tony asked.

"Exactly," responded Ben. "Next I did some seeding."

"You're going to have to explain that one to me," said Tony, looking curious.

"That means exposing others to a Grid Seminar. As you know, I had already been, so for me, it meant encouraging the members in my team to go. But for you, as head of the organization and possible initiator of an organization-wide project, it means something a little different. It means getting several key organization members, including yourself, involved in Grid Seminars in order to develop deeper insight and convictions into this change methodology. This puts you in position to make a sound decision on the commitment to do more. Additionally, some of these people whom you get to go can serve as instructors for a pilot program. That's an in-house test-tube trial of what would be involved were the organization to engage in Grid learning. And, once again, probably the best way to do that is diagonal slice so you get maximum spread up and down the ranks and you don't end up with a situation of haves and have nots."

"Basically that's how we did it in Ben's division," Harriet explained. "After his team members had gone, they were committed to the Grid and wanted their own people to be involved. Liz volunteered to go to an Instructor Preparation program. She and Ben ran the first pilot."

"Isn't that a staff function?" inquired Tony. "Why you two?"

"It's important that responsibility for development activity be vested in the line," replied Ben. "We use staff support as well but leadership of the effort stays with line management."

"If you do that," responded Tony, "aren't you asking a line manager to give up his or her job?"

"Not at all," said Ben. "It's best done on a rotational basis. That is, I may qualify as an instructor and then take responsibility for leadership of several activities. During the course of these activities, I train you to take my place. I pass the responsibility on to you, and you do the same with another. Not only does this relieve any one manager of the burden of full responsibility, but it spreads the learning among different members of the line. There's a wealth of information to be had by listening to people, and these seminars provide the opportunity for that. People come together and on the final day they address operational problems and create specific proposals for their resolution. It's an incredible experience and you'll just have to witness it for yourself."

"Now you mentioned a Grid OD Seminar as well, did you not?" Tony asked.

"Yes," replied Ben, "that provides the big picture. It describes both conceptually and procedurally the six phases of Grid OD, as I will do for you in just a moment."

"Alright," said Tony. "You said your team members had an enthusiastic response to the Grid. What happened next?"

Ben continued. "Well, I had always harbored some reservations about the quality of our teamwork. While the Grid enabled us to communicate more effectively, we still weren't there. We didn't have 'teamwork plus.'"

"So they began to explore Grid Team Building," said Harriet. "Ben will tell you more about that in a moment. It's Phase 2 of the Grid OD approach."

"Right," said Ben. "Before I go into that, though, I want to mention that another key step we took was to appoint an OD Steering Committee for the purpose of considering strategies and tactics for long-term OD."

"Who's on that?" asked Tony.

"It's a diagonal slice with heavy top-level line involvement. For instance, I'm a member. Ed as well. Do you know Ed?"

"Oh, yes," responded Tony. "He's a tough nut. I'm amazed you got him into this."

"He's very committed," Ben smiled. "One of the best advocates. He also keeps me in line."

"Well," said Tony, "you've kept me in suspense long enough. Why don't you outline the six-phase approach?"

Ben looked up thoughtfully. "I think I'll use the flip chart. Do you mind?"

"No, by all means," said Tony and sat back expectantly.

The Six-Phase Approach

Ben proceeded to outline the process for the CEO, basically stating that once a decision had been made to move forward, the first activity to undertake is Grid Seminars, Phase 1.

"In the initial phase of OD, everyone in the organization is involved in learning the Grid and using it to evaluate their personal styles of managing. This is made possible by attending the five-day in-house seminar, preferably conducted off site."

"How many people are we talking about?" asked Tony.

"In one program?" Ben looked questioningly. When Tony nodded, Ben proceeded. "Anywhere from 12 to 24, 36, or 48. It depends on how many people an organization can free up at any one time for a five-day period. People work in teams of six to eight members so it's figured on that basis. The basic idea is for each Grid team to replicate to the degree possible the composition of the organization itself. This basis of grouping makes possible exchange of perspective not only among persons from different functions but among those from different levels as well."

"Can lower level members participate effectively with persons from higher levels?" asked Tony.

Ben responded, "Although the implication is that lower level members, because they are more likely to be persons with practical experience only, may not be able to learn as fast as persons with college backgrounds or advanced degrees, this is not the case. Lower level persons often have a depth of practical human experience as rich as any. When those with background and practical experience, who have risen from the ranks, have opportunities to study and learn with college-educated managers, they gain a better understanding of each other's thinking—how different people go about analyzing problems, formulating alternatives, weighing advantages and disadvantages, and deciding on a given course of action. For a person from the ranks, this in itself can be a useful educational experience. It's an eye-opener for the technically qualified, too."

"I see what you mean," Tony agreed. "What you've described would work for us. Just out of curiosity, though, how does a smaller company go about this? There's got to be a limit to how many people you pull off the job at any one time."

"A smaller company might choose to send its personnel to public programs on a pair basis or one after one, and then proceed with the rest of development in-house," Harriet said. "All the phases that follow deal with actual on-the-job work activities and usually take place on-site."

"There are some ground rules but there are no hard and fast answers regarding how many should participate in any one seminar," said Ben. "Achieving speed and getting many through must be balanced against ensuring that organization performance does not falter because too many people are absent from work at any one time. Most companies find that under the diagonal slice concept about 10% of the organization can be away from the job without undesirable effects on organization performance. Furthermore, the diagonal slice approach ensures that no work unit is seriously depleted."

Ben continued, "Maximum impact is possible when everyone participates. This includes all those who are responsible for managing others, though some companies extend participation to include technical, hourly, and other salaried personnel. There are some specialized Grid designs for the sales force, professional and technical people, secretaries, hourly workers, supervisory personnel, administrators, and even corporate pilots. Additionally, it's possible to get a tailor-made design specific to an organization's situation."

"Nonsupervisory personnel are often included," Harriet added, "particularly in high tech, knowledge-oriented organizations like ours. This means that those who engage together in study teams are upper-level management, professionals, as well as hourly personnel. This is desirable because participants gain insight into cleavages between management and operating levels. Participants have often pointed to this as one of the important contributors to strengthening organization integration."

"There is one limitation in the diagonal slice approach that must be considered," said Ben. "It has to do with the number of levels represented rather than the method itself. When levels are too far apart within the hierarchy—vice-president and front-line supervisor in a large company, for example—participants may find it difficult to talk back and forth in an easy and understanding way. Their scope is just too different. While the diagonal slice method is highly desirable, a sounder approach might be to limit the number of levels in any one team to three or four."

"What is the minimum formal education a person needs to benefit from a Grid Seminar?" asked Tony.

"Formal education is less important than the ability to comprehend concepts. Anyone with sixth-grade-level reading comprehension usually has the learning skills essential for benefitting from a Grid Seminar," responded Ben.

"What about those who are nearing retirement?" asked Tony. "Should they be included in the development effort?"

"A person nearing retirement may not see value in further involvement with the organization within the time remaining," replied Ben. "On the other hand, many managers near retirement find gratifying personal reward in the learning itself and in the opportunity to study and be with others. More than that, though, why waste a person's last several years with the company when they can make a more valuable contribution? Just look at my own team. There was one member who only made the minimum contribution but now he's come to life. He's one of my best people today."

"You must be talking about Gil Phillips. Is that right?" asked Tony.

"Why, yes," responded Ben.

"Gil is making history," Tony said with enthusiasm. "He's become a celebrated case study in Celarmco. The whole company is talking about the change that has taken place in him. All positive, I might add."

"Yes," replied Ben. "Gil is really something. He has some magnificent undertakings underway in his department. My belief is that managers preparing to retire should certainly be invited to participate."

Harriet said, "Ben, why don't you outline the specific objectives of Grid learning for Tony?"

"That's a good idea," replied Ben. "Here, let me write them on the flip chart."

Ben outlined the objectives as follows:

☐ Increase self-understanding by
  • learning the Grid as a framework of thought, analysis, and comparison,
  • gaining insight into how others describe one's own Grid style,
  • increasing personal objectivity in self-critique of work behavior,
  • reexamining managerial values, and
  • developing a common language for communicating about behavior.

☐ Experience problem-solving effectiveness in teams by
  • experimenting with and revising ways to increase effectiveness,
  • studying the use of critique,
  • developing standards for openness and candor, and
  • examining the need for active listening.

☐ Learn about managing interface conflict by
  • studying barriers between teams,
  • examining conflict within teams and the origins of distrust and suspicion of other teams, and
  • exploring ways of reducing or eliminating such conflicts between groups.

☐ Comprehend organization implications by
  • understanding impact of work culture on behavior and
  • gaining appreciation of Grid OD and how it can be used.

"That's a lot," exclaimed Tony. "It sounds like hard work."

"It is," assured Ben, "but it's only worth as much as the effort a person is willing to put into it."

"The program requires about 20 or 30 hours of prework or self-directed study," explained Harriet. "This involves reading the book and answering some questions about what they've read. Participants come prepared with a foundation of theory to build on. If they fail to do this prework in advance, they are basically operating in the dark."

"Does that ever happen?" asked Tony.

"Sometimes," laughed Ben. "Obviously, we strongly encourage people to do the prework and we even provide rationale. We let them know that it forms the basis of the very first activity of the seminar. Still some people, one or two maybe, show up without having cracked the book."

"Do you send them home?" asked Tony.

"I guess we could," answered Ben. "But basically we leave it up to them. You'd be surprised how much peer pressure they get from other team members. What I usually find happens is that they stay up most of that first night finishing what they easily could have accomplished before their arrival. They come in tired, but prepared, the next morning."

"You said it's a five-day program," said Tony. "Is that right?"

"Yes," responded Ben. "It usually starts on a Sunday evening and ends on Friday. During the week, participants are actively involved in learning teams that solve projects and study how they did and what to do to improve. A high point of seminar learning is when participants receive critique of their leadership effectiveness from other members of the team. Another is when they critique the dominant style of our organization culture. A third involves outlining steps for increasing the effectiveness of the whole organization."

"As I said when we first started," remarked Tony, "what caught my eye is the results you are achieving. Has there been any effort to assess actual impact?"

"Yes," answered Harriet, "both in quantitative and qualitative terms. It might be useful to put these on a flip chart as well." Harriet rose and wrote the following on flip chart pages that were posted in order on the wall. She turned and said, "These are some recent results from an organization that has been involved in Grid OD for the last five years." The following is what she wrote on the flip chart for Tony and the others to see.

☐ Changes in promotion practices following Grid OD favor merit over seniority.
  • those promoted are three years younger on the average.
  • time of service to promotion is reduced 2.8 years.
  • promotion rate to higher positions in same company but outside plant is up 31%.

☐ Behavior changes are toward sounder relationships.
  • 62% better communication between bosses and subordinates
  • 61 % improvement in working with other groups
  • 55% better relationships with colleagues
  • 48% more leveling in one study, 21.8% in another
  • 22% improvement in goal setting
  • 20% more openness to influence
  • 14% increase in delegation

Harriet paused and remarked, "These kinds of changes all are in the direction of a 9,9 orientation. They suggest that significant changes occur through Grid Seminar participation. Now let me outline some of the qualitative reports, and I'll just do that verbally and quote some typical comments I've heard.

"For example, one production manager in Ben's division, a 'tough nut' like Ed, I must say, reported that the Grid Seminar was a real eye-opening experience for him. He claimed that it provided, and I'll quote him, 'Much greater insight into my managerial style and has shown a number of ways in which to improve my effectiveness.' He went on to say, 'It gave me new perspective for seeing my own performance in more objective terms. It forced me to take a critical look at myself and also, through practical Grid experience in a team setting, showed me how some of my beliefs can actually be detrimental to the company.'

"One of Liz's people said, 'Now I see a means of improving in a total way rather than a piecemeal way.' I think that's important. It's a whole new ball game when you're operating according to a sound theory base rather than just shooting in the dark. That's the main distinction between theory-based OD and the other kinds of OD that Ben described earlier.

"A significant feature of learning is critique. Participants claim that it is central to valid problem solving. For example, one participant wrote," Harriet said, looking down at her notebook, " 'It was the best personal learning experience I ever had, particularly since we learned through experience with continuous feedback and the positive reinforcement of feedback from other individuals on our team.' "

"Others began to realize that openness is basic to sound relationships. One reported, 'The frankness and openness created by the Seminar experience is a significant factor in enabling useful discussions to be carried out in depth with team members.' Additionally, the value of teamwork in achieving better outcomes was clear when several individuals made statements such as, 'I saw synergistic action and understand now that when a group works well together, its end product is superior to the sum of the products of the same group members working individually, or a watered-down compromise.' "

As Harriet sat down, Tony reflected on what she had said. "That's very powerful," he finally remarked.

"The really powerful aspect of Grid learning," Ben said, "is when you put it to work on the job. I want to run you through the rest of the phases to give you an idea of how Grid OD proceeds. But perhaps we should break for lunch first? What do you think?"

"Good idea," said Tony. "But we can keep talking, right?" They headed towards the dining room. Tony had carefully placed himself between Harriet and Ben and continued to direct questions at one or the both of them, eager to learn more about this approach to change.

□ □ □

Upon returning, Ben picked up the conversation of the six-phase approach to Grid OD where he had left off. The following is a synopsis of what Ben and Harriet outlined for Tony and the executive group:

Phase 1A Projects

After people experience basic Grid training, culture-wide issues can be brought more clearly in view through Phase 1A projects. This is where bottom-line results from the training investment made thus far begin to appear.

By this time many or most organization members have been in a learning seminar and have found the opportunity to work as self-regulating team members to be a new and rewarding experience. Now the potential exists for family teams to engage in the same kind of learning regarding the actual culture prevailing in that team, that is, Phase 2 Team Building. However, this must be delayed until all members of the family team have attended the basic seminar. Thus an enthusiasm for effort to improve work has been created, but the chance for concrete application has not yet come about.

We can, however, focus on and subject to change one kind of work problem even at this early point in the game. The problems we are talking about are those that belong to no one in particular and yet in another sense they belong to all. These are not problems that are lodged within any one team. Rather, they evolve from the corporate culture itself. They derive from norms that govern ways in which people interact with one another as they perform work tasks. They are, for example, problems that arise by virtue of not wanting to look bad when compared to one's peers. In other words, it may be known that a certain action is right, but a supervisor may choose instead to ignore the problem on the basis that his or her colleagues are also reluctant to take action. Historically these problems have not been subject to resolution by the exercise of power and authority. Rather, they tend to persist in spite of efforts to solve them. This leads to the notion that a different character of intervention may be needed.

Quality might be thought of as such an overriding problem. Safety is another. Both are normative problems that presume the existence of a shared practice by which people act, almost on second-nature. When organization members have acquired understanding of the Grid way of operating, this learning can be brought to bear on changing these kinds of organization-wide norms to overcome complacency and to achieve greater levels of effectiveness. However, this requires the employment of special designs for grappling with normative issues that are present beneath the problem itself.

The goal of a 1A project is to bring responsibility to bear on those who can solve a given problem. It focuses on the rationalizations that exist for not solving the problem and brings new insight into the true causes to develop commitment to its resolution. It is the application to a real-life problem all the tools learned in a basic Grid.

Phase 2 Team Building

Chapter 12 has pointed out the value of teamwork for increasing organization effectiveness. Phase 2 Team Building comes after Grid Seminar participation. Its purpose is to diagnose specific barriers to sound teamwork and identify opportunities for improvement within actual work teams of boss and subordinates.

The goals of team building are:

- [ ] Replace outmoded traditions, precedents, and past practices with a sound team culture.
- [ ] Increase personal objectivity in on-the-job behavior.
- [ ] Use critique for learning and for improving operational results.
- [ ] Set standards of excellence.
- [ ] Establish objectives for team and individual achievement.

Issues of problem solving and decision making are central, such as when 1/0, 1/1/1, and 1/all teamwork are needed. However, many more facets of teamwork are explored in depth. These include each team member's reactions to the contributions of others, assumptions about what constitutes effective teamwork, identification of particular problems existing within the team that are barriers to effectiveness coupled with specific plans to remedy them. Setting team objectives for future achievement is the final assembled activity. Later follow-up in three or four months is a useful additional step.

Team building can begin when all members of any management team have completed a Grid Seminar and are ready to apply Grid concepts to their own team culture. It is initiated by the person in charge and those who report to him or her and it moves downward. Each manager then meets with subordinates to repeat the activity as a team, studying their barriers to effectiveness and planning ways to overcome them.

Grid team building typically is a three-day activity usually implemented on the job during working hours. The activities can be segmented into parts and conducted over a longer period if this is necessary or desirable.

Impact. The following quotation indicates that team building can have a major impact on team effectiveness—

> "Phase 1 is like getting a check; Phase 2 is when you cash it . . . The period of Phase 2's implementation in the automotive division coincided with a 300% increase in divisional profits—a significantly better profit improvement than that of the rest of the domestic organization—even though we concede that market conditions, expanded plant capacity, the state of the economy, etc. may have contributed to the improvement in profits. Top management believed that Phase 2 and the striking turnaround in the division were more than a coincidence, that Phase 2 made a substantial contribution to the performance, even though it was impossible to measure precisely."

Taken together, Phase 1 and 2 unlock communication barriers—

> "In the past, when we would set budgets, I would calculate what each department would get . . . Then they would yell and complain, 'Why did you give me this?' I would say, 'This is the way it is. I'm the boss.' Now, since we went to Grid last year, that's over. Perhaps we've got to reduce our margin in meat. We know we've got to make it up somewhere else. The group comes to a decision. This year it

took us an hour and a half to set our budget. Before the Grid, we were in there for eight solid hours pounding the table. But now we're committed to excellence. We're working towards a common goal."

One marketing manager put it this way—

"I never realized our department could really work as a team. Phase 1 of the Grid was great, but it really took Phase 2 to bring it all out. Sure, I was apprehensive at first. Everyone was. But when it came right down to it, we were able to work together, solve the problems, and really open up and communicate with each other. It wasn't what you would call an easy experience, but it was certainly worthwhile."

Phase 3 Interface Development

The third step is to achieve better problem solving at interfaces between groups through a closer integration among those that have working interrelationships. The need for Phase 3 development activities comes about when a department or unit or division concentrates on its own assigned responsibilities, without considering the effect on total company performance or its relations with other units. People may act and react in the interests of their department and neglect the interests of the entire organization. This is viewed from inside the department as selflessly serving the corporation, but such preoccupation may mean less attention is paid to other departments than is needed to produce cooperation and coordination. The second department may ask, "Why are they dragging their feet? Why are they unable to provide the service we need, which is the only reason for their existence in the first place? They are deliberately ignoring our requirements."

The importance of an integrated approach to development is made evident when the extent to which the industrial world is segmented into artificial divisions is recognized. Some of the common splits are between manufacturing and marketing, personnel and operations, central engineering and the plants, operations and maintenance, etc. Each of these separations is intended to facilitate better use of personnel and the assignment of specialists who have competence to deal with the problems in the segmented components. However, there is a need to integrate with the other side of the split, and yet no particular understanding of issues that have been "put" on the other side of the split can be presumed. As a result, a heavy expense is paid in misunderstandings, distrust, suspicion with resultant lack of coordination, empire building, and so on.

The situation is particularly evident when the problem is examined on a splits-within-a-split basis. Often, for example, different people in personnel are involved in designing performance appraisal as though it were separated and isolated from promotion and reward policy. Both of these may be treated in a separate manner from selection and all of these may only indirectly be connected to training and development. Furthermore, the specialists in each of these domains may at best be casually or mechanically connected with the line personnel, who in many respects should carry ultimate responsibility not only for implementing but also designing the subsystems under which they exercise leadership.

If the artificiality of this multiplicity of splits were understood, those who make these decisions would know that performance appraisal and training are so intimately interconnected that they cannot truly be separated and compartmentalized, that the reward system and operational performance are so closely connected as to be interdependent. All these separations produce subsystems that at the worst may effectively contradict one another and even under the best of conditions may not provide the needed coordination.

An integrated approach makes it possible to redesign subsystems so that a coherent basis of organization is available for strengthening overall performance, and this is one purpose of interface development as the central activity of Phase 3.

Interface attitudes of frustration can quickly turn into feelings of mutual hostility, rooted in mistrust and suspicion. These are easily provoked and, once formed, become win-lose power struggles. When this happens, needed cooperation is sacrificed, information is withheld, requests are perceived as unreasonable demands, etc. When members are asked what their problems are, they tend to answer, "poor communication." However, the underlying problems of distrust and suspicion at the interface must be resolved before fundamental changes in effectiveness of communication can be brought about.

The goals of interface development are:

☐ Use a systematic framework for analyzing barriers to interface cooperation and coordination.
☐ Apply problem-solving and decision-making skills for
  • Depolarizing antagonisms.
  • Confronting relationships based on surface harmony or neutrality that hide problem-solving difficulties.
  • Resisting compromise when differences cannot be solved in this manner.
☐ Utilize confrontation to identify focal issues needing resolution.
☐ Plan steps for achieving improved cooperation and coordination between units with scheduled follow-up.

Phase 3 is engaged in only by those groups where actual barriers to effective cooperation and coordination exist. It is not a universal phase in which all groups automatically take part. Locally, interface development usually is undertaken after Phase 2 Grid Team Building has been completed, but some interface problems may be so acute that earlier attention is warranted.

Impact. How Phase 3 resolves union-management chronic difficulties is described in the following:

"The union-management Phase 3 allowed us to systematically analyze the relationship. We were able to agree upon an ideal model for each of the key elements of interface and to outline action steps for moving towards this ideal. Some of the areas covered include overtime, job performance, grievances, seniority, job ownership, the union agreement, work fluctuations, job evaluation, communications, compensation, the pension plan, and objectives.

"Overall, the Phase 3 activities served to develop trust and respect between union and management participants and provided an excellent forum for the candid discussion of problems. Many traditions were broken down and a new culture has emerged. There are two particularly striking features to this new atmosphere. The greatest improvement has come in the area of listening and trying to understand the other side's viewpoint. Secondly, this and the very nature of the Phase 3 design (management presenting how it sees itself and how it sees the union on various elements, and the union presenting how it sees itself and management) have tended to make both sides more objective. As a consequence, many of the flare-ups that occurred in the early stages are no longer happening.

"That is not to say that both sides agree on everything by any means. However, where disagreement arises, it is approached rationally and there is a basic trust between the two groups that each is committed to finding a sound and acceptable solution."

In reviewing recent Phase 3's it is interesting to note that many are concerned with the interface between the supplier and user and even more striking to see most involve computers, computer technology, and software linages. Recent examples include:

☐ An interface between the claims division of a major health insurance company and the supplier of its computerized claims software. A key executive was quoted as saying, "Things are 300% better."
☐ A multinational food and tobacco company saw Grid Phase 3 as a way of confronting difficulties between its computer applications division and its research and development activities many of which are powered by computer technology.
☐ Antagonisms between regional offices and central computer services were so bad that people were hardly speaking. After three days of Grid Phase 3 activities members of both groups report a new era of cooperation.

The content subjects for Grid Phase 3 vary widely, but organizations see effective coordination and collaboration at the points of interface as crucial to success. In today's business environment, positive user interface with suppliers is essential to productivity, particularly in the face of expectations of speed and accuracy created by computer applications.

The first three phases of OD deal with strengthening behavior to allow members to become more effective. The last three phases can then be undertaken with greater likelihood of success. These last phases are concerned with the *fundamental business logic* on which the firm is based by testing its soundness and strengthening it wherever needed. This step is prior to *planning*, because planning can be no better than the assumptions on which it is based.

Phases 1 through 3 make important contributions to corporate excellence, but none are sufficient for reaching the degree of excellence potentially available to corporations based on the systematic development of the business logic. The key to exploiting organizational potentials is in the organization having a business model of what it wishes to become in comparison with what it currently is or historically has been.

Designing an Ideal Strategic Organization Model: Phase 4

The top team of a corporation is situated to carry out such a fundamental approach by examining and rejecting whatever in its current business logic is outmoded and unprofitable and by formulating a replacement model. The model is based on the organization's defining its future business activity to be geared to the needs of society for products and services; to the corporation's need for profitability; to the employees' needs for security and satisfaction with work based upon involvement, participation, and commitment; and to the stockholders' needs for a meaningful return on invested funds.

The goals of Phase 4 are:

- [ ] Specify minimum an optimum corporate financial objectives.
- [ ] Describe the nature and character of business activities to be pursued in the future.
- [ ] Define the scope, character, and depth of market to be penetrated.
- [ ] Create a structure for organizing and integrating business operations.
- [ ] Identify development requirements for maintaining thrust and avoiding drag.
- [ ] Delineate policies to guide future business decision making.

The top team studies, diagnoses, and designs an ideal corporate model for what the organization should become in a step-by-step examination of business logic. The study is an intellectual investigation of the most basic concepts of business logic currently available. These are drawn from the writings of managers who pioneered in the development of a systematic discipline of business logic.

Using concepts of "pure" business logic with which the team is in agreement, the second step is for the top team to specify the operational blueprint for the redesign of the corporation. Phase 4 is completed when this strategic corporate model has been evaluated and agreed to by the next layer up and approved by the board of Directors.

Impact. The kinds of changes brought about through Phase 4 are described as follows:

> "Other important outcomes of the OD effort that must be evaluated are in the area of strategy. There is a widespread conviction that the strategic insights that occurred during Phase 4 have been been beneficial and have served to start the corporation moving in the right direction.
>
> "The Phase 4 team at . . . first reached agreement on details of what actually exists in the present organization. That is, the team developed a clear picture of . . . management, with no rationalizations, excuses or apologies; they developed simple, concise statements that picture the actual model today. Then, using the same format, they developed statements as to how a hypothetical, ideal . . . would operate. This ideal model served to focus attention on needed changes in policy.
>
> "All participants committed themselves to action based on statements of concepts and principles that were agreed upon. In support of these concepts and principles, policies were drafted that are to serve as the specific basis to guide management action."

Implementing Development: Phase 5

Phase 5 is designed to implement the model developed in Phase 4. It is unnecessary to tear down the whole company and start from scratch to build a new company to meet the requirements of the model. What is done is more like remodeling a building according to a blueprint of what it is to become. Architects and engineers study the existing structure to identify what is already strong, sound, and consistent with the blueprint and should be retained, what is antiquated and inappropriate and must be replaced, and what is usable but needs modification or strengthening to bring it into line with the blueprint. Phase 4 develops the blueprint; Phase 5 identifies and implements what must be done concretely to shift from the old to the new.

The goals of Phase 5 are:

☐ Examine existing activities to identify gaps between how it is now being operated and the way it is expected to operate according to the ideal strategic model.

☐ Specify which activities are sound, which can be changed and retained, which are unsound and need to be replaced or abandoned, and what new or additional activities are needed to meet the requirements of the ideal model.

☐ Design specific actions necessary to change to the ideal model.

☐ Continue to run the business while simultaneously changing it toward the ideal model.

A series of steps provides the basis for changing the organization from what it is to what it should become. They begin with analyzing and subdividing the company into its components. A component is a smallest grouping of interrelated activities that are tied together because they all are essential in producing a recognizable source of earnings and an identifiable cost or expense, with as little dependence on sources within the company but outside itself as possible.

Another step is to compute the investment related to these activities tied up in plant and equipment, and personnel. Once these steps have been taken, it becomes possible to evaluate whether the business activity identified by that component meets or can be changed to meet the specifications of the model. Test questions such as the following are answered with regard to each identified component. Is the return currently realized on this investment consistent with the strategic model? If not, are there controllable expenses or pricing factors that could be altered to bring it within specified return on investment standards? Is this area of business activity consistent with market areas identified within the strategic model as areas for sound future growth? These questions are typical of the many employed to decide whether each segregated activity should be expanded, shortened, changed, or eliminated in pursuing corporate development.

Implementing Phase 5 often contributes a quantum leap in productivity because of the depth of change involved. The results shown in Figure 13-1 demonstrate the character of improvement possible. It illustrates the profitability of two autonomous subsidiaries operating nationwide on opposite sides of the United States-Canada border. Subsidiary A engaged in Grid Organization Development. Subsidiary B did not. They are owned by the same parent, located in a third country. They engage in similar businesses and face the same character of competition in comparable markets.

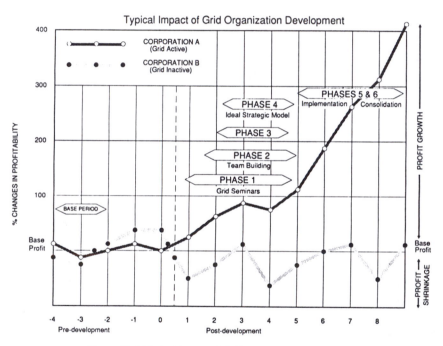

Figure 13-1. Typical impact of Grid organization development.

The starting comparisons show that for five years prior to the introduction of Grid development, the control subsidiary, B, appeared to be obtaining somewhat better economic performance, but the results were well within the range of chance fluctuations. Then, after introduction of Grid Organization Development, Subsidiary A experienced a continuous and rising curve of profitability during the next nine years. By the end of the study, profitability in the Grid company was 400% greater than in Subsidiary B, which had not engaged in Grid Organization Development. Subsidiary B had just managed to hold its own over the fourteen-year period.

The following remarks by the president of Subsidiary A at a time when his company had been engaged in Grid OD for six years offers his evaluation of the change:

"There is no doubt that OD has had a significant and positive effect on profits . . . A major objective of the Grid was to change behavior and values within the organization in the direction of showing a high concern for both task accomplishment and human motivation, and then to sustain these changes and institutionalize them . . . There has undoubtedly been a substantial transformation in this area, with positive effects accruing through improved communication, the use of critique, profit or cost consciousness, some aspects of planning, the handling of conflict, meaningful participation in a group, and commitment among key managers . . . there is one other most important benefit that has accrued from the OD program and that is a substantial improvement in the working relationships between management and union officials."

"Much of the work involving the union can be considered as a breakthrough in the application of OD principles and there is little doubt as to its success."

Impact. An organization member who was directly involved in his company's implementation project summarized his reactions.

"Once we could specify how we needed to change to meet the Ideal Strategic Model, we were in the management-by-objectives business in a way that wasn't limited by blind acceptance of the status quo. Some of the specific things we learned included:

1. How to approach the business in a scientific way to analyze and evaluate variables selectively.
2. Taking corporate perspective as opposed to previous functional or departmental view.
3. Looking at existing business more critically, growing more and more displeased with current efforts.
4. Gaining a new perspective on the role of planning in effective management.

5. Focusing on results expected by using return on assets as the basis for business decisions in comparison with conventional profit and loss and share of market thinking.
6. Grasping the deeper implications of effective teamwork for increasing the soundness of any implementation plan.
7. Developing more basic insight into the dynamics of change."

Consolidation: Phase 6

Phase 6 is used to stabilize and consolidate progress achieved during Phases 1-5 before recycling into another period of change. The goals of Phase 6 are:

☐ Critique the change effort to ensure that activities that have been implemented are being continued as planned.
☐ Identify weaknesses that could not have been anticipated throughout the implementation and take corrective action to rectify them.
☐ Monitor changes in the business environment (competition, price of raw materials, wage differentials, and so on) that may indicate that fundamental shifts in the model are necessary.

Three features of business life suggest the importance of a consolidating phase in organization development. Managing change is the opposite of managing the tried and true. People tend to repeat the tried and true, but they may lose interest, convictions, or courage about something novel and unpredictable, and reduced effort in making the novel work as it was intended may cause it to fail. A second reason to consolidate progress is that by continuing the study of what is new, additional improvement opportunities may be identified that add to organizational thrust. A third is that significant alterations in the outer environment may occur to cause changes specified in the model and implemented in Phase 5 to be more or less favorable than had been anticipated. The monitoring activities of Phase 6 provide a basis for specifying needs for additional change.

Phase 6 strategies and instruments enable an organization to assess its current strengths and to consolidate its gains.

The significant aspect of Phase 6 is that the consolidation effort must be managed rather than left to its own momentum.

Impact. The following is a quote which relates the importance of Phase 6 activities.

"It's important to keep in mind that the Grid is not a fad that is 'in' for a few years and then phases 'out.' The program is designed so that the last step is never-ending. The company will always be monitoring what is being done, judging how far that is from the ideal, and taking the necessary steps to reach the ideal."

We now return to one last look at Ben and his push to bring about corporate excellence within Celarmco.

The Challenge

Tony had a look of satisfaction on his face. "This has been a challenging and invigorating day for me. We have really gotten down to the basics. Ben, you've led us in a discussion that we've engaged in many times before—but with a new twist. It's the same old problem of how to increase organization effectiveness but you have offered a brand new solution that seems to stand above the rest. That's because it incorporates what many other approaches leave out, that is, the dynamic processes of interaction so essential to getting work done. In fact, you can't leave out the dynamics and hope to accomplish organization purpose. I don't know where we were coming from in the past trying to implement all these piecemeal solutions."

"It's not that the piecemeal solutions don't or won't work," said Ben. "But they fail in the absence of a sound, integrated, and organization-wide approach to change. Grid OD integrates these dynamic processes with the rational aspects of the business. That's what puts it in front of the rest."

Harriet added, "Before, we thought we could solve the problem by rearranging structure, changing a reporting relationship or cutting a layer out of the hierarchy. Convert to matrix. Go back to line. Then go to structureless. What a zoo!"

"Structure is important," said Ben, "but it's only a symptom of the larger issue. Ideally, organization change begins at the top because that's where organization culture gains its initial shape. Culture derives from many influences, some unplanned and unintended, and some deliberate and calculated. Top executive leadership style is critical to this process because to a larger extent it dictates what people below think."

Ben continued, "Grid OD is designed to permit an organization to reformulate its culture in deliberate and systematic terms that can rectify limitations from the past and add strength to areas heretofore not given sufficient attention."

Harriet picked up at this point and added, "The first step is to develop sound behavioral dynamics in the components of the organization that must work together to accomplish corporate goals and objectives. The primary consideration here is how conflict is dealt with—by individuals, by teams, and by groups that interface. That's a key purpose of Grid OD designs—learning how to deal with conflict in a constructive manner—because that's probably the major impediment to successful organization function today. We can attribute it to communication, planning, and on and on, but when you dig down to the underlying causes, how we handle conflict is key. Only when these interpersonal, team, and interface relationships have been put on a sound footing can the organization turn its focus to the business side of the business and strategize how to move the corporation towards excellence."

"It makes a lot of sense," said Tony. "You have placed overriding concentration on process rather than on form, and the strategies that have been described have powerful implications for a new corporate direction. A direction that I fully intend to give further attention to."

"I'm really pleased to hear that," Ben said warmly. "Because you are the person in a position to bring about great things for this organization."

"I hope I'm up to the task," laughed Tony, "but I feel good that you and Harriet are behind me. Ben, I want to thank you both for your courage and determination to bring the division to a higher level of achievement and quality performance as well as to your success in having carried this feat out. And, furthermore, Harriet, I now understand more fully what you've been doing. This is the kind of staff leadership that corporate can and should provide."

Ben and Harriet both acknowledged Tony's remarks. Tony continued, "Would it be possible, Harriet, for us to get together in the morning—just for a few minutes. I'd like to check into the schedule for upcoming executive seminars and see if I can fit myself in. I'm anxious to keep the momentum going!"

□ □ □

Summary

Grid Organization Development is a six-phase model for bringing real change to bear on organizations through a fully integrated approach. From a behavioral point of view Grid OD sets in place a common framework for understanding the dynamics of interaction that take place in meshing the efforts of people with required organization purpose. This is accomplished by focusing attention on the interpersonal relationships, team relationships, and interface relationships. We are talking R_2 because sounder interaction in that domain spells better R_3 results. Once this is in place, Grid OD turns to the business side of the business and enables organization members to design and implement a system of corporate logic that is supportive of operational results, whatever the criterion used to measure success in that endeavor might be—profit, quality, etc.

Chapter 14

Implications and New Directions for the Future

Human effectiveness is the key to successful organization productivity and vitality. An attitude of collaboration towards those within the organization and a spirit of competitiveness towards those with whom one competes is what keeps companies on the forefront of their respective industries. Much of what makes human effectiveness truly effective lies in how an organization manages its most important resource—people.

In the conduct of business, particularly on the American scene, the strategies of thinking and the techniques of analysis, measurement, control, and development presently employed are resulting in a significant underutilization of people. The financial and material resources that they manage tell the negative side of the story. If human resources are not put to good use, we lose whatever advantage we may have had in terms of other resources possessed. Without sound human interaction, the "raw" resources cannot be deployed in an effective manner. Although we can only speculate, we might guess that the average American company is only achieving one-third to one-half of its potential. This is a serious underutilization of human resources and hence of financial, material, and technical resources as well.

We started an exploration of change by asking the question, "Can an individual change?" A certain amount of successful change may be accomplished by an individual in terms of exercising initiative to increase his or her own effectiveness. This is significant in and of itself and can be reinforced when organization values emphasize self-change as an important factor in personal career development as well as strengthened organization effectiveness. But self-change is limited by those negative influences that act on an individual from the environment in which one works but which are beyond one's control. These are the context influences which become accessible to change through Organization Development, discussed in more detail in the previous chapter.

As companies have sought to address the issue of underutilization of human resources, three basic approaches to change have been relied upon in order to accomplish this end. They include technique-centered OD, process-centered OD, and theory-based OD. The sketches below convey the underlying assumptions about change on which each of the approaches is based.

Technique-centered OD, as its name implies, means reliance on technique to induce change. This can include such things as job enrichment, flexi-time scheduling, quality circles, and survey research. A mechanical approach to management by objectives where boss and subordinates discuss goals and then subordinates are held accountable for achieving them falls into the same category. All are technique-centered because they involve introducing managers to different ways of managing on a piecemeal or segmented basis. Little or no effort is expended to enable managers to investigate their own management styles and to learn to distinguish sound and unsound principles as the basis for using these techniques.

A 9,1-oriented manager like Ed is likely to embrace the mechanics of management-by-objectives in a wholehearted way, not because he sees it as a way of aiding subordinates to strengthen their contributions, but because it permits him to strengthen control over subordinates by forcing agreement with goals and then holding them accountable for reaching them. A manager like Dan (1,9) may grab hold of this same technique and then invite subordinates to set their own objectives at whatever level of excellence or output they may be prepared to accept. He doesn't help them think through which goals are important for accomplishment. This is perceived as an intrusion that could lead to resistance—and rejection.

Comparable distortions can be seen when a manager's basic orientation is 1,1, 5,5, paternalistic, or opportunistic. The point is that any technique-centered approach to change tends to be distorted in the direction of the Grid style of the person implementing the technique. When implemented in a piecemeal or segmented way, this is even more true. As a result, many potentially sound ways of strengthening operational effectiveness are weakened by the manner in which they are brought into being. Technique-centered OD has been found to be unsatisfactory time and time again but, being unaware of the impact of Grid style on the utilization of an otherwise neutral technique, managers persist in repeating the approach.

Another approach to increasing the effectiveness of behavior in organizations is process-centered OD which involves managers studying their own behavior. Basically, this is a sound approach, however, the manner in which the learning occurs often causes it to be weak and for the most part ineffective.

Generally it involves group learning where members study the behavior of each individual and provide feedback on how to be more effective. Sometimes it is called sensitivity or T-group training, role playing, or even psychodrama. Whatever it's called, it relies on an outside facilitator, or catalyst, who aids in group learning. It can be summed up in the following way. The initial reaction is that it is a useful procedure that aids a group in solving its problems. However, later on members often find that they are unable to make significant use of the learning back on the job without the presence of a facilitator. It's the same problem as behavior modeling. While the model is present, everything's okay. When the model departs, people revert to old behaviors. Transfer of learning has not taken place. In our view it is premised on a faulty assumption, that is, it draws a line between behavior and performance on the assumption that personal insight is sufficient to promote strengthened practices at the operational level, better long-range planning, financial analysis, etc. but it fails to take the next step to produce a fully integrated approach.

A third option, theory-centered OD, is based on a different set of premises regarding how human effectiveness may be acquired. The fundamental notion is that people are behaving about as well as they know how; therefore, it is essential that people first learn more about what constitutes effective behavior. When this learning is coupled with direct experience, particularly in terms of one's own exercise of initiative, inquiry, advocacy, and so on, then a person can relate with others in ways that are sound according to the model or to stop conventional ways of behaving that are now recognized as unsound.

The Grid is a major approach to organization development in which the change strategies are premised upon learning to think more systematically about how to behave effectively, and then to gain personal insight into concrete actions that enhance one's own effectiveness. This approach avoids the mechanical presentation of technique without insight into the human assumptions underlying technique. It also avoids problems of experiencing interaction processes in a subjective way in the absence of an objective framework for evaluating it.

When change is viewed in this manner, it becomes self-evident that the culture of one's own company is also made up of operational habits, many of which have come into use in an unthinking or unsystematic way. These continue to be employed not because they are necessarily sound but because they typify the way things have been done in the past. Thus, the Grid approach rests upon (1) aiding all managers of an organization to learn Grid theories first in personal terms that clarify to each the current ways in which he or she is trying to achieve production with and through people, and (2) helping them learn the skills necessary for applying sound principles of behavior to solving the major problems of organization.

This book has provided a comparative theory of human effectiveness along with numerous illustrations of how people deal with one another in ways that can enhance or reduce organization productivity. A model has been described that permits the evaluation of interaction between people as they seek to get the resources they possess as individuals into measurable results.

Chapters 1 and 2 introduced a framework for understanding the underlying problems of human effectiveness. Chapters 3 through 8 portray six examples of less than effective approaches to working with and through others in the effort to achieve results. Chapters 9 and 10 offer the preferred Grid solution which provides the maximum likelihood of restoring competitive advantage. The fundamentals for restoring human effectiveness to organization are defined in the final three chapters. Chapters 11 through 13 reveal three major points of leverage for bringing about change from less to more effective human resource utilization.

While individual and team change are important factors to be considered, they can be severely constrained as self-initiating change agents by the organization's culture. We might call this cultural drag which promotes conformity and complacency, thus blocking initiative and stifling innovation. Organization development is key to strengthening human systems of individual behavior, team action, and intergroup relations which thereby enables managers to penetrate barriers to effectiveness on the business side of the business. Then it becomes possible to generate the thrust so vital to the achievement and maintenance of corporate excellence.

Grid Organization Development is a systematic program through which a company can instill human motivations and emotions of involvement and commitment on an organization-wide basis. An almost endless supply of human energy is available to be tapped when an organization is operating by standards of excellence. Energy is unleashed and funneled into finding and creative and effective solutions to problems of production, quality, and sales, many of which may have plagued a company for years. In dynamic organizations that have attained this height of effectiveness, ordinary men and women are freed to act in extraordinary ways so that they come to know how to motivate and manage the problem-solving effort.

Faced with these dilemmas of leadership, can the conditions that demand Grid solutions gain the attention and effort they merit in order to restore competitiveness to our business enterprises? This is a question that is to be answered as we move into a new decade and a new century of effort to mobilize human resources toward organization productivity. Providing a strong foundation of theory-based principles to replace the makeshift and pragmatic approaches currently being employed is one solution to the dilemma. Grid OD is a fully integrated approach to corporate achievement because it provides the basis for bringing all aspects of the business into one manageable, coherent whole. A positive outcome to the leadership dilemma as we see it lies in the Grid solution to change—planned, deliberate action for putting into place a corporate culture based on standards of excellence.

The potential for doing this, achieving real and enduring change, today more than ever before, lies in Grid and Grid Organization Development. This is change by design, and it offers a deliberate and systematic approach to moving our organizations into the future. From this perspective, one of the last barriers to excellence— the human factor—can be incorporated into sound principles of participation, involvement, and commitment to valid organization goals and objectives as the company and its individual members strive for competitive advantage.

References and Suggested Reading

1. Blake, Robert R., & Mouton, Jane S. *Executive Achievement: Making It at the Top.* New York: McGraw-Hill Book Company, 1986.
2. Blake, Robert R., & Mouton, Jane S. *The Managerial Grid III: The Key to Leadership Excellence* 3rd Ed. Houston: Gulf Publishing Company, 1985.
3. Blake, Robert R., & Mouton, Jane S. *The New Grid For Supervisory Effectiveness.* Austin, Texas: Scientific Methods, Inc., 1979.
4. Blake, Robert R., & Mouton, Jane S. *GridWorks: An Approach that Increases Employee Participation and Promotes Esprit de Corps.* Austin, Texas: Scientific Methods, Inc., 1987.
5. Blake, Robert R., & Mouton, Jane S. [Scientific Methods, Inc.] and Command/Leadership/Resource Management Steering Committee and Working Groups [United Airlines]. *Grid Cockpit Resource Management.* Denver, Colorado; Austin, Texas: Cockpit Resource Management, 1982.
6. Prather, Stephen E., Blake, Robert R., & Mouton, Jane S. *Medical Risk Management.* Oradell, New Jersey: Medical Economics Books, 1990.
7. Blake, Robert R., Mouton, Jane S., & Tapper, Mildred. *Grid Approaches for Managerial Leadership in Nursing.* St. Louis: C. V. Mosby, 1981.
8. Blake, Robert R., & Mouton, Jane S. *The Grid for Sales Excellence* 2nd Ed. New York: McGraw-Hill, 1980.
9. Blake, Robert R., Mouton, Jane S., May, James, & May, Wanell. *The Real Estate Sales Grid: Dealing Effectively with the Human Side of Selling Real Estate.* Englewood Cliffs, New Jersey: Prentice-Hall, Inc., 1980.

10. Blake, Robert R., Mouton, Jane S., & Williams, Martha S. *The Academic Administrator Grid*. San Francisco: Jossey-Bass Inc., Publishers, 1981.

11. Blake, Robert R., & Mouton, Jane S. *Grid Approaches to Managing Stress*. Springfield, Illinois: Charles C. Thomas, 1980.

12. Blake, Robert R., Mouton, Jane S., & McCanse, Anne Adams. *Change by Design*. Reading, Mass: Addison-Wesley Publishing Company, 1989.

13. Blake, Robert R., & Mouton, Jane S. *Grid Approaches to Managing Stress*. *op.cit.*

14. Blake, Robert R., & Mouton, Jane S. *The New Managerial Grid* 2nd Ed. Houston: Gulf Publishing Company, 1978.

15. Blake, Robert R., Mouton, Jane S., & McCanse, Anne Adams. *Change by Design*. *op.cit.*

16. van de Vliert, Evert & Kabanoff, Boris. "Toward Theory-Based Measures of Conflict Management," *Working Papers Series*, The University of New South Wales, Australian Graduate School of Management, Working Paper 88-024, November 1988. See also, van de Vliert, Evert, Paul S. Kirkbride, and Sara F.Y. Tang, "The Pattern of Conflict Styles Across Organizations," paper submitted for presentation at the Second Bi-Annual Conference of the International Association for Conflict Management, University of Georgia, Athens, Georgia, June 11-14, 1989.

17. Blake, Robert R., & Mouton, Jane S. "Theory and Research for Developing a Science of Leadership," *Journal of Applied Behavioral Science*, 18(3), 1982.

18. Keinan, Giora. "Decision Making Under Stress: Scanning of Alternatives Under Controllable and Uncontrollable Threats." *Journal of Personality & Social Psychology*, 1987, 52(3), 639-644; and Holmes, T. H., and Rahe, R. H.: "The Social Readjustment Rating Scale." *J Psychosom Res*, 11:213-218, 1967. Copyright © 1976 by Thomas H. Holmes, M.D. Reproduced by permission.

19. These concepts on A, B, C are derived from the original formulation by Alfred Korzybski in Korzybski, A. & Kendig, M. *General Semantics*, Lakeville, Connecticutt: The International Non-Aristotelian Library Publishing Co., 1942.

Index

Notes